To ~~[redacted]~~ and his be? who are our very good friends

Mali~~

June 1997

Reconstructed Lives

Reconstructed Lives

Women and Iran's Islamic Revolution

HALEH ESFANDIARI

The Woodrow Wilson Center Press
Washington, D.C.

The Johns Hopkins University Press
Baltimore and London

Editorial offices:
The Woodrow Wilson Center Press
370 L'Enfant Promenade, S.W., Suite 704
Washington, D.C. 20024-2518
Telephone 202-287-3000, ext. 218

Order from:
The Johns Hopkins University Press
2715 N. Charles Street
Baltimore, Maryland 21218
Telephone 1-800-537-5487

2 4 6 8 9 7 5 3 1

Library of Congress Cataloging-in-Publication Data

Isfandiyārī, Hālāh.
    Reconstructed lives : women and Iran's Islamic revolution / Haleh
Esfandiari.
        p. cm.
    Includes bibliographical references and index.
    ISBN 0-8018-5618-3 (cloth : alk. paper).—ISBN 0-8018-5619-1
(pbk. : alk. paper)
    1. Muslim women—Iran—Social conditions.   2. Muslim women—
Iran—Civil rights.   3. Iran—History—Revolution, 1979–   4. Iran—
Social conditions—1979–   5. Iran—Politics and government—1979–
I. Title.
HQ1735.2.I75   1997
305.48'6971055—dc21   97-3080
                                                                                                              CIP

For Shaul,
and for Haleh and her generation of Iranian women,
who must carry the torch

CONTENTS

ACKNOWLEDGMENTS

THIS BOOK WOULD not have been possible without the friends, colleagues, and institutions whose support it is my pleasant duty to acknowledge. A generous grant from the John D. and Catherine T. MacArthur Foundation and a fellowship from the Woodrow Wilson International Center for Scholars permitted me the time to travel to Iran, conduct interviews, and research and write this book.

I would like to thank professors Bernard Lewis, Charles Issawi, and Jack Censer for their encouragement and support; Sam Wells, Robert Litwak, and Ann Sheffield for the hospitality they extended to me at the Woodrow Wilson Center, and Bahman Amini for the efficient research assistants he provided to me during my stay there. My childhood friend, Fereydoun, generously placed at my disposal his time and his laptop computer and listened with endless patience to the stories of my travails and triumphs. My mother allowed me to type away on my computer night after night, without ever complaining that I was not spending my "free time" with her and my father. Safieh, Guity, and Haleh read and wisely commented on the manuscript. Goli suggested the painting by Shideh Tami that graces the cover of my book. Many friends in Iran arranged introductions to women I did not know and made available their homes and places of work for interviews. Marc Plattner invited me in the spring of 1995 to be one of the first three visiting scholars at the Forum for Democratic Studies in Washington, D.C.

Joe Brinley, the director of the Woodrow Wilson Center Press, and his able colleagues Carol Walker, Robert A. Poarch, and Ann Hofstra Grogg provided invaluable editorial input.

I would have not dared to embark on this project without the encouragement of Shaul nor finished it without his support.

Finally, I am grateful to the many women in Iran who over a period of four years talked to me about their experiences and told me their stories. I am deeply indebted to them.

INTRODUCTION

I LEFT IRAN in the winter of 1978, when the country was on the brink of a revolution, its very social fabric being torn apart by the struggle between the old order and the new, between the monarchy and its enemies. I returned for the first time fourteen years later, in the summer of 1992. I found a country and society that seemed at once familiar and yet profoundly transformed by a decade and more of revolutionary upheaval. Many of the faces and friends, the streets and sights, the rhythms of life in the cities, seemed the same—as I had known them during a lifetime in Iran. Yet Iran was unfamiliar as well, as if a master craftsman had split apart the tiny tiles of an intricate Iranian mosaic and laid them down again in a new, complex set of patterns.

The Islamic revolution had a marked and transforming impact on all areas of Iranian life. But for women, its consequences were especially profound—legally, socially, professionally, psychologically, both in the home and in society. This is hardly surprising. From its earliest days, the new regime regarded a successful resolution of the "women's question" a major yardstick for measuring the achievement and legitimacy of the Islamic Republic itself. The state set out deliberately and consciously to reconstruct and redefine the place of women under the law and in the public and the private spheres.

I wanted to write a book about the experience of being a woman under the Islamic Republic. During several trips to Iran over four years from 1992 to 1996, I interviewed at length and in depth a selected group of professional and working women. I wanted to know what the coming of the Islamic Republic has meant to them in their personal and professional lives. I was curious to learn how they coped with a changed and, for women, a largely hostile environment. I asked women to tell me how the revolution has influenced their relationships with their husbands, children, family, and friends. I asked them to describe their encounters with the new revolutionary authorities. I also asked them about their relationships with other women—their mothers, friends, women in the workplace. In large part because of the state's policy toward women, women's rights have become a critical and widely discussed issue in the Islamic Republic, and I wanted to understand how women in Iran feel today about this issue. I wanted to know if women's sensibilities were changing in any way.

I focused on professional and working women for a number of reasons. The impact of the revolution has been greatest on women who have already made, or are making, the transition from home into the workplace, from village, small town, and traditional backgrounds into the secondary schools and universities, and who are aware of or awakening to the idea that, as women, they can study, work, pursue a career, secure economic independence, and make choices. Nor are the numbers of professional, working, and educated women any longer small. As was the case before the revolution, almost half of all university students are women. Millions of women work—in factories and as secretaries, clerks, nurses, and teachers but also as lawyers, doctors, civil servants, administrators, and businesswomen.

Moreover, working, professional women have become the model for an entire generation of younger women. If in Iran today, young women insist on going to secondary school and university and compete with men in the professions and civil service, if they aspire to write, paint, or direct plays, and if they fight to retain freedom of dress and choice in deciding their own future and interest themselves in women's issues, it is because an older generation of women paved the way and set an example. Besides, again and again, it turns out that mothers, though supposedly traditional, wish for their daughters education, employment, and economic independence. One of the striking discoveries of the interviews I conducted is the extent to which women's sensibilities are changing across the social spectrum.

Some of the women I interviewed were born and raised in Tehran, some grew up and went to school in the provinces, and came to Tehran to attend university or to work. Life in the provinces was generally more restricted and conservative than in the capital. Even before the revolution, the integration of women into the work force and mixed society in the provinces lagged behind Tehran. For provincial women, the transition from provincial to capital-city life was therefore dramatic. This explains why many of the women I talked to made it a point to mention their provincial backgrounds.

In Iran there is a tendency to distinguish between those who received their education at home and abroad, and, if abroad, between those educated in Europe and in the United States. The different educational experience is believed to make for differences in attitudes and outlook. Not surprisingly, my interviewees think it important to specify their educational background.

For my interviews, I selected four or five women from a number of fields and professions—lawyers, doctors, university professors, publishers, editors and journalists, writers and translators, secretaries and businesswomen. Some had had professional careers before the revolution. Others are daughters of the revolution, whose professional lives coincided with the beginning of the revolution and whose careers have advanced under revolutionary auspices. The women I interviewed for the most part ranged in age from forty to sixty, so the youngest were in their early twenties or late teens when the revolution occurred. Although I structured the interviews informally, I asked each of my interlocutors the same set of questions. The questions themselves were drawn up in part on the basis of discussions with informants who helped me identify the most significant issues for women since the revolution. The chapters are organized thematically.

To preserve their anonymity, I have given my interviewees fictitious names. Otherwise, I have preserved their own words and let them speak for themselves. Not every woman I interviewed appears in the book. I also spoke to a number of much younger women and girls; their views are reflected in many of my own comments here, in Chapter 1, in the introductions to subsequent chapters, and in the conclusion. Brief biographies of the women I interviewed follow the introduction. As a guide to the reader, I have also provided a glossary of Persian words that appear in the text.

Women from all classes were active participants in the events leading to the overthrow of the monarchy in 1979. They joined the revolutionary movement for a variety of reasons—religious and secular, economic and political, conservative, moderate, and radical. But the vast majority of women expected the revolution to lead to an expansion, not a contraction, of their rights and opportunities. They did not expect that the gains they had made in the previous five decades would be put on hold or reversed. They did not anticipate men would once again secure the right to divorce their wives on demand or that women would need the permission of their spouses to work. They did not imagine they would find themselves unwelcome at their places of work, that a new penal code would impose special punishments on women, or that they would lose the right to choose what they wore. They did not foresee that a society segregated on the basis of sex was in the making.

But women very soon discovered that the Islamic regime had its own women's agenda and that this agenda was not in keeping with the promises that had been made to them. The state arrogated to itself the right to determine what jobs women could hold, what subjects they could study, how they should dress and behave in public, and how they should relate to men. Imagining women primarily as mothers, spouses, and homemakers, the state attempted to set procreation policy. It discouraged birth control and instructed women to bear more children. It frowned on female sexual abstinence in spousal relations and even declared such abstinence sufficient grounds for divorce.

The Islamic government suspended and rescinded most of the laws pertaining to women's rights, especially in the domain of personal and family law, enacted under the former regime. Women were encouraged and pressured to leave government jobs, and they were purged from decision-making positions. Segregation of the sexes was imposed in many spheres of life. Women were and are still barred from a number of educational fields. Islamic dress was enforced, and women have been punished by flogging for violating the dress code. A woman out with a man in a car on the street or in a restaurant could be stopped by the revolutionary committees or the "morals police" and asked to show proof she was in the company of a husband, father, or brother. Once arrested, single young girls were sometimes held in jail, humiliated, and, informants allege, bodily examined to ensure that they were still virgins. For all the talk of the sanctity of a woman's body, women found themselves stared at and minutely examined by total strangers. Men determined whether a woman was in conformity with the Islamic dress code. "You suddenly were told that, as a woman, your body is 'sin-provoking,' " one interlocutor told me. To this day women are harassed in numerous ways on the streets and in public places.

Women also experienced the presence of the state in the privacy of their homes. Members of the revolutionary committees felt free to enter and search homes. Families could not entertain, listen to music, or watch a film without worrying that an unfriendly neighbor or revolutionary guard would summon the authorities. A woman could not be alone at home with a man who was not a husband, brother, or father. She would think twice before opening the door of her house with her hair showing.

Remarkably, the government's policy did not succeed. The reasons are many and complex and are rooted in part in the profound changes already under way under the former regime: the considerable integration of women into many spheres of life and the work force; the extensive educational opportunities that had opened up for girls and women; and the subtle but widespread permeation of new ideas regarding the status, role, and rights of women that had occurred even among traditional and working-class women and among some revisionist Islamic thinkers. After the revolution economic necessity was a contributing factor. Many women had to work, and the state needed the skills women could bring to the work force. Iran's clerics also proved sensitive to international opinion.

The eight year Iran-Iraq war (1980–88) also had a galvanizing influence. It drew women into the workforce, as the government needed women nurses, doctors, and as back up for the war effort. Blackouts, rationing, and air raids drew women together. In addition, the war caused enormous physical destruction and deprivation, cost tens of thousands of lives, and left deep psychological scars. There is hardly a woman I talked to who did not speak of the trauma of the war, which steeled the determination of women not to be imposed upon.

The failure of the government's policy is also rooted in the massive mobilization and politicization of women—even those from traditional classes—during the revolution. The clerics contributed unwittingly but decisively to the injection of women into the public sphere. As the revolutionary movement gained momentum in 1978, Ayatollah Khomeini and his clerical lieutenants urged women to take part in the mass anti-Shah demonstrations they organized in Tehran and other major cities. Women from the lower classes turned out in tens of thousands. Clad in black *chadors,* the traditional full-length veil, and marching in well-organized phalanxes, they joined in shouting the standard slogans against the Shah and in support of Khomeini and the establishment of an Islamic Republic. Later, women in great numbers answered Khomeini's call to vote in national referenda in favor of the establishment of an Islamic Republic and for the new constitution.

In the early months after the fall of the monarchy, women joined tens of thousands of men for the huge Friday prayer ceremonies-cum-political rallies held on the grounds of Tehran University. For a few heady months, women, along with men, occupied the public, political arena. Predictably, it proved difficult, after the revolution, to persuade women retreat to their houses and to leave the public space exclusively to the men. Having mobilized the women for political purposes, the clerics found that women were equipped to use political instruments for their own purposes.

Postrevolutionary developments reinforced this process. Women had marched, demonstrated, shouted slogans, and voted. After the revolution, large numbers joined the work force. During the Iran-Iraq War, working-class and middle-class women stood in long lines to collect rations, and here they exchanged views and articulated common complaints and anxieties.

Women who before the revolution had not concerned themselves with women's issues and took for granted benefits stemming from labor legislation—the Family Protection Law, day-care centers, and the like—became active defenders of women's rights once these benefits were threatened. Women across the social spectrum were made vulnerable by reversions in divorce law; and it was women from traditional classes who protested most loudly the suspension of the Family Protection Law. Mothers from traditional classes may have piously observed religious rituals and Islamic dress, but they did not want to see their daughters denied a chance for higher education or excluded from more desirable employment. Women from all classes resented segregated buses. In two wage-earner families, women saw less and less rationale for a society that privileged males. Ironically, then, the revolution turned passive women into activists.

The Islamic Republic's women's agenda notwithstanding, women after the revolution simply refused to revert to the traditional role of housewife and mother that the regime tried to force on them. They devised strategies with which to cope, to resist, to defeat, or to neutralize the impact of the new, "revolutionary" measures directed at women. They met every government measure by a stronger countermeasure of their own. They made their presence felt by remaining in the work force in large numbers. Against all odds, they remained in the professions.

Women engaged more actively than before in literature and the arts. A substantial number of women writers, painters, sculptors, filmmakers, and dramatists have emerged since 1979, and these women address in their art and their writings the problems and difficulties that women face under the new dispensation. Women devised strategies for avoiding segregation of the sexes. Young women found ways to conform and yet challenge Islamic dress—showing a puff of hair—called a *kakol*—under their scarves, using lipstick and nail polish despite the "morals police." In myriad ways, they have reclaimed the public space.

In the end, the regime has been forced tacitly to acknowledge that it cannot exclude women from public life and the public sphere and that its ability to dictate how women will behave in the private sphere is strictly limited. It has been forced to reconsider and sometimes drastically to reshape its policy toward women.

For the women, none of this was easy. For many of the women I interviewed, the struggle of the years since the revolution has required profound psychological adjustments, rearrangements of home life, and a reconceptualizing of their role in the family, at work, and in society.

Almost all the women I interviewed said they had felt profoundly the humiliations visited on them by the regime's policies and actions regarding women. But they also told me they gained a new sense of themselves as women by refusing to be intimidated or cowed by the authorities, by being forced to wage a daily struggle over the right to work, by learning to develop subtle strategies for resisting the dress code, by having to fight in courts for rights of divorce.

For many women from professional, middle-class families, there was a further problem. Husbands who had been active in government and the private sector under the old regime often found themselves purged or retired, their businesses confiscated, and their working opportunities removed. But the depression into which many of these men sank, my interviewees told me, was a luxury they and other women could not afford. For the family to survive, women had to leave home and go to work, stay in jobs they already held, or find new professions and new work. In a reversal of traditional roles, in upper-middle-class families men sat at home while large numbers of women overnight became the sole breadwinners. None of the women I interviewed regretted this role reversal. On the contrary, they felt liberated by no longer being dependent on their husbands or the man in the family. Women, I found, also feel far freer to talk about their bodies.

Women did not organize; they could not have done so under existing political conditions. But, ironically, the revolution appears to have given women a keener sense of their rights, created among them a sense of community, and turned them into an informal constituency or pressure group. Interestingly enough, this pressure group includes women and young girls from traditional families who subscribed to the Islamic agenda and who rose in the civil service and in government-sponsored cultural, educational, and other organizations as a result of the revolution and as part of the Islamic movement. Such women, too, refuse a traditional role, and they are less vulnerable to accusations that they are Westernized, members of the "corrupt" upper class, or infected by the "American sickness." They are interested more in the substance than the symbols of feminism.

Yet the conversion of traditional women to a feminist agenda, their growing conviction that they have rights—to work, to careers, to opinions, to choice of career, lifestyle, and even husband, to a sense of self—suggests that the distinction between traditional and modernized women, between feminists and nonfeminists, cannot be sharply drawn. The blurring of these distinctions can tell us a great deal about what is happening to women's sensibilities in Iran. These are some of the reasons why the regime has had to retreat on many aspects of the women's question and why it desires to appear progressive on women's issues even while it continues to insist on a strict Islamic and restrictive policy toward women.

The condition and status of women under the Islamic Republic are therefore complex and full of contradictions, far more complex than the conventional and stereotypical account would have us believe. Women are oppressed and confined in many ways. Yet, at the same time, they are very much in the public sphere and part of a civil society that is reemerging and stands apart from and against the state. Women are arrested and flogged for improper dress; at the same time, they work and hold government office, they vote and sit in parliament. The regime denounces the monarchy's policy on women (the first woman to hold cabinet office under the old regime was executed by the revolutionaries); but it has adopted (after initially violently rejecting) many of the former regime's policies toward women. The president of the Islamic Republic now has an adviser on women's affairs, and there are offices for women's affairs in every major government organization. The regime tried to impose a more puritanical social code on society. Yet among some members of the younger generation, even from traditional backgrounds, greater sexual permissiveness seems to prevail. Upper-middle-class or Westernized women, as might be expected, resist the Islamic Republic's policies; but, more surprisingly, they are joined by women from traditional and provincial backgrounds and from religious homes.

This story, I believe, is best understood and told through the experience and lives of individual women set against its larger social background. The stories of careers rebuilt, lives reorganized, are striking. Here are some examples from among the women I interviewed: several women who quit successful public careers to start small businesses: food stores, catering, buying and selling rare books, publishing houses, art galleries, importing goods from abroad; a university librarian who became a seamstress on her way to opening a bookstore that is today also one of the centers of intellectual gatherings in Tehran; a woman university professor who refused to quit teaching even though she was shamefully insulted because a bit of hair showed from under her head cover; a woman judge, an ardent revolutionary, who was among the first to be purged at the Ministry of Justice because women could no longer serve as judges; a woman who submitted to seventy lashes rather than sign a false declaration she had dressed like a "prostitute"; a medical doctor who, dismissed from her hospital post because of the way she dressed, was reinstated when her patients demonstrated in her favor outside the hospital; a woman who grew up in a religious family, observed the veil all her life, rose up through the revolutionary ranks, but after the revolution took to wearing only a head scarf as a mark of her liberation and who today is the editor of the most vocal feminist magazine in Iran.

These lives, and many others, based on weeks of interviews, make up my book. Although there have been some published accounts of government policy toward women under the Islamic Republic, there has been no book focusing on the intersection of the state and the individual and examining in detail, through individual biography, what it has meant—in all its complexity—to be a women under the Islamic Republic.

The title of the book, *Reconstructed Lives,* was suggested to me by a phrase used by Masoumeh, one of the women I interviewed, who described her experience after the revolution as akin to "reconstructing my life."

BRIEF BIOGRAPHIES

Afsar: European-educated former university professor, now working for a private company. Afsar enjoys painting but has not gone near an easel in many years. She is tall, in her mid-fifties, with a light olive complexion, a woman of few words and an air of world weariness. She is divorced and lives in a house in downtown Tehran, where I interviewed her.

Amineh: French-educated researcher, translator, and writer in her fifties. Amineh is thin, tall, and has dark hair. She comes from a family with a religious background. As a young girl in Tehran and then as a student in Paris, she took part in political activities against the former regime. Her husband died a few years after the revolution. She talks at a rapid clip, so that it is difficult to keep up with her. I interviewed her in her house in the suburbs of Tehran, which is filled with paintings by contemporary Persian artists.

Atefeh: A European-educated woman. Atefeh has has been running the same business for the last thirty years. Her parents were divorced when she was quite young, and she grew up with her father. Her husband died before the revolution, and she raised her children on her own. Atefeh is a tall brunette with piercing eyes and a smile that can, at times, be warm and at other times chilling. Despite her soft-spokenness, there is a hardness in her, perhaps as a result of the difficulties she has had to endure. I interviewed her at her office in downtown Tehran on a hot summer afternoon.

Ayesheh: Educated in England, a woman in her mid-forties. Ayesheh grew up in the north of Iran. Her family, she recalls, observed all the religious rituals. She is petite, brunette, and speaks very rapidly, as though she is running against time. Ayesheh is married with children. Having worked for a government organization before the revolution, she has now joined the private sector. I interviewed her in her apartment in downtown Tehran.

Darya: Iranian-educated lawyer who worked for an organization affiliated with the government before the revolution. Darya is well versed in Islamic law and women's legal rights. She is in her fifties, tall, slender, elegant, and soft-spoken. She is married and lives in a house in a residential area at the foothills of Tehran. I interviewed Darya at her house.

Elaheh: University professor who finished her B.A. in Iran and went to Germany on a government scholarship for her Ph.D. Elaheh is in her early forties. She is single and recently moved into an apartment. She speaks very softly. There is a sadness in her looks and a voice that is haunting. I interviewed her at the office of a mutual friend. I felt a sense of desperation in her, as if she is trying to escape a whirlpool that is gradually sucking her in.

Farideh: Iranian-educated former civil servant, now working with a private company. Farideh was born into a merchant family in Tehran. She is in her late forties, with a light complexion and light hair. She is single and lives alone in an apartment in the suburbs of Tehran. I detected in her a sense of dedication to serve her people. She is a humorous person. I interviewed her first at a restaurant and subsequently at her house, overlooking the hills of north Tehran.

Fatemeh: European-educated woman, in her late forties, remarried with children. Fatemeh runs the family business, which has been operating for at least forty years. She is of average height and has dark hair and brown eyes. She is known among her friends as the most generous and kind person they know. Although soft-spoken and a good listener, in her daily work Fatemeh is tough and skillful in dealing with her customers and workers and with revolutionary authorities. I interviewed her in the family home in a residential suburb of north Tehran, overlooking the mountains.

Gowhar: Iranian-educated lawyer in her forties. A woman of average height with black eyes and dark hair, she is very precise when she speaks, and her sentences are extremely formal, as if in a written text. In her presence, I sensed a haste to get on with the next assignment. She is married and has children. I interviewed Gowhar at her law office. She hardly moved from behind her desk and maintained an atmosphere of formality throughout our meeting. Her office is on a side street in one of Tehran's new districts.

Jila: European-educated engineer in her fifties. Jila was raised in the north of Iran; her northern accent is still discernible, especially when she is angry. She is married, has no children, and runs her own business. Jila has black piercing eyes. She is a woman with a great deal of common sense. She speaks her mind freely and shows her anger and displeasure openly. I interviewed Jila in her apartment in Tehran.

Ladan: Educator and translator educated in Iran and Europe. Ladan is in her late forties, and she is a feminist. She worked for a government organization before the revolution and now works from home. She is petite and has a light complexion and light brown hair. Ladan is very intelligent and objective, with a sharp analytical mind. She is an avid reader and a person who reaches out to help people from all walks of life. She lives in the suburbs of Tehran with her husband. I interviewed her at her house, in a room full of books and memorabilia.

Lida: Iranian-educated physician in her late thirties, who got her first job after the revolution. Lida owes her career to the revolution and the avenues it opened to her. She has a very successful private practice and is the head of a government hospital. She is married and has one son. I interviewed Lida at her office in the hospital she runs; she sat at one end of a long conference table and sat me at the other end.

Lili: A woman with a high school degree who is holding two jobs—as a medical technician and as a secretary. Lili runs the second office with an iron hand, intimidating all callers. She is in her mid-thirties, tall, with black hair and dark eyes. She is a serious and hardworking woman who has set specific goals for herself. Lili is married with children and lives in an apartment in Tehran. Often, she comes across as difficult to get along with. I interviewed her at her office in downtown Tehran after office hours.

Manijeh: Iranian-educated woman in her early thirties. Manijeh grew up in the south of Iran. Her father was a civil servant and an educator. The family had religious inclinations. She is single and lives with her family. She works with a private organization and enjoys writing on women's issues. She is tall, with the light olive complexion common among Iranians. Manijeh is articulate, well-spoken, self-confident, down to earth, and capable— for me the prototype of the young educated Iranian woman who grew up under the revolution. I interviewed her in her office, in one of Tehran's established neighborhoods.

Mari: English-educated university professor. Mari is married, with brown hair and brown eyes. She was sent as a teenager to study in England. She is outgoing and witty and has a warm laugh. A workaholic and a prolific writer, she enjoys academic gatherings both in Iran and abroad. I interviewed her in her office, amid many phone calls and with students and colleagues dropping in to ask her for guidance or just to chat.

Masoumeh: Iranian- and European-educated businesswoman, writer, translator, and ardent feminist. Masoumeh just turned fifty. Her parents were divorced, and she was raised by her stepmother, with whom she did not get along. She is tall with gray hair and brown eyes. She is articulate and enjoys literary discussions and likes to share the latest reading with all who are interested. Influential in literary circles, she is described as one who can make a young writer's or artist's reputation. Masoumeh is married and lives in an apartment in the suburbs of Tehran surrounded by Persian objects old and new. I interviewed her at various restaurants over lunches that lasted as long as three hours and as short as half an hour, and at her house where she was constantly interrupted by phone calls.

Monir: Iranian-educated lawyer who worked in her profession before the revolution and continues to do so. Monir, in her late forties, was raised in the south of Iran. She is tall with an olive complexion. She is married and has children. She is an expert on women's rights under Islamic law. I interviewed her in her office in downtown Tehran.

Nahid: Swiss-educated woman in her late fifties. Nahid was a civil servant before the revolution and now runs her own business. She is petite with a fair complexion. She is soft-spoken and very rational when discussing any topic. Nahid is married, has grandchildren, and lives with her second husband in Tehran. I interviewed her in her Tehran apartment, where large numbers of books were scattered in every room.

Nargess: An Iranian-educated lawyer who worked for the government before the revolution and now has her own private law office. Nargess grew up in the provinces. She is a tall woman in her late forties, with brown hair and dark eyes. Her husband is a civil servant, and they live with their children in the northern suburbs of Tehran. Her mood swings between wanting to give up her practice out of sheer frustration and wanting to continue to work for the sake of the income and to prove that women can be as well versed in the law and legal procedure as men. I interviewed Nargess in her office in the suburbs of Tehran.

Nasrin: Iranian-educated journalist and writer. Nasrin is a married woman in her mid-thirties. She is of average height, with a light olive complexion. In our encounters she always wore the *maghnae*, so I do not know the color of her hair. Nasrin credits the revolution with her success and her current position. She is a feminist par exellence. I interviewed her in her office, sitting on steps to the balcony to avoid interruptions.

Nayyer: Iranian-educated feminist in her late forties. Nayyer was raised in a middle-class family, and she and all her siblings went to university. She worked for the government and today works for a private company and runs her own business on the side. She is tall and has dark brown hair and dark brown eyes. She is married and has children. Nayyer is an invaluable source of information on women's rights in Iran. I interviewed her both at work and at her apartment in Tehran.

Nazanin: European-educated woman in her fifties. A writer and translator, Nazanin was raised in the capital, where she attended an international school. She is single and lives with her mother. She is tall, has black hair, and is always immaculately dressed. She has strong opinions and does not suffer fools easily. I interviewed her at her home in a residential area in the suburbs of Tehran.

Neda: University professor educated in Iran and Europe, now with many publications. Neda is a striking, tall woman in her early sixties. She holds herself very straight and speaks beautiful, lyrical Persian. Her husband died some time ago, and she lives alone in Tehran. I interviewed her at the office of a friend.

Partow: Iranian-educated woman with a high school education. Partow, in her late thirties, is separated from her husband and lives with her three children in an apartment. She holds two jobs and gives herself a lot of credit for making the transition from housewife to working woman. I interviewed her at the hospital where she works as a technician.

Pouran: American-educated writer and university professor. Pouran returned to Iran after the revolution and started teaching immediately. In her late thirties, she is tall, with short hair and dark eyes. She becomes very emotional when talking about the condition of women in Iran. There is an unusual passion in her voice when she lectures to her classes. She lives in a residential suburb with her second husband and her children. I interviewed her in her apartment. We talked through the distractions of the telephone ringing and her children calling. Her restlessness affects her surroundings.

Ramesh: A woman in her mid-thirties, married with children. Ramesh worked as a secretary for a brief period between her two marriages. She recently obtained her university degree in Tehran. She is very attractive, tall, slender, with brown hair and brown eyes. She is a strong-willed woman who knows what she wants from life. I interviewed her in her house in the suburbs of Tehran, which is filled with nineteenth-century Qajar-period artifacts.

Shokouh: European-educated physician. Shokouh is married and in her fifties. Petite with light brown hair and a fair complexion, she was born in Tehran and went to Europe for her higher education. A vivacious feminist, she has a mind of her own and is known to be the best in her field of medicine. Shokouh is also an astute businesswoman. The interview was conducted in her spacious house in Tehran. She prides herself of having an interesting collection of primitive paintings on glass.

Soudabeh: Iranian-educated physician in her early fifties. Soudabeh was raised and went to school and university in Tehran. She is of average height, has brown hair and brown eyes, and prefers to wear glasses. She lives in Tehran with her husband, who is also a physician. I interviewed her at her home. She considers herself a successful professional woman but is proud of being a homemaker and mother. There is a serenity and calmness in her behavior and speech rarely found in women in Iran these days.

Sousan: English-educated businesswoman in her early forties. Before the revolution Sousan taught at the university. She is of average height. She is single and lives in a house in the middle of an old garden. I interviewed her at her house in the northern suburbs of Tehran and at a restaurant not far from her house.

Touran: American-educated feminist who returned to Iran after the revolution. Touran is in her mid-thirties, tall, with brown hair and dark eyes. She is married and has children. She does research from her home and collects contemporary Persian art. Normally calm, she grows animated and voices strong opinions when discussing women's issues. I interviewed Touran in her apartment in one of the newly developed districts of Tehran.

Zahra: Iranian-educated artist, film director, and businesswoman. Zahra grew up in the provinces and came to Tehran to go to university. She is in her early thirties and is married. Zahra is articulate and has a good sense of humor, even when discussing difficult situations she has endured. She credits the revolution for making it possible for women like her to pursue careers. I interviewed Zahra in her apartment.

Zohreh: Iranian-educated writer, businesswoman, and publisher. Zohreh is a tall, impressive woman in her early sixties. She has a commanding tone when she speaks, and one can't help but notice her strong presence. Her husband died a few years ago, and she runs her private business by herself. I interviewed her in an office she used to share with a lawyer.

One

Historical Background

THE COLLAPSE OF THE PAHLAVI MONARCHY and the triumph of the Islamic Republic in Iran in February 1979 resulted in near anarchic conditions. The leader of the revolution, Ayatollah Khomeini, had named Mehdi Bazargan as prime minister. Bazargan headed a cabinet of ministers and, on paper, was in charge of the government apparatus. But power lay in the hands of revolutionary committees and popular forces in the streets, and the authority of the Bazargan's government was contested by competing centers vying for ultimate control of the revolution. Iran, the prime minister said, was like "a city with a hundred sheriffs." As Bazargan struggled to establish order and control, the last group he imagined would oppose the government was Iranian women.

However, when Ayatollah Khomeini, the leader of the revolution and the country's leading religious authority, announced on March 8 that women working in government offices would be required to observe the *hejab,* or Islamic dress (ironically, the announcement coincided with the celebration of International Women's Day), thousands of middle-class and working women gathered in front of the prime minister's office to protest. The protests, later staged in front of various government offices, continued for three days. A bewildered Bazargan sent his deputy, Abbas Amir Entezam, to assure the women that the *hejab* would be voluntary and not obligatory for civil servants. But Bazargan was to be proven wrong. The *hejab,* it turned out, would be imposed not only for women in the civil service but on all women, in the workplace and in all public spaces. And although the women showed rare courage—few at the time dared voice disagreement with a ruling issued by Khomeini himself—it quickly became clear that no opposition to the dress order would be tolerated.

Already on that day in March, as news of the women's protest rally spread, club-wielding vigilantes and thugs attacked the protesters and beat

them. Women in *chadors* were mobilized to jeer at the protesters and to call
them "prostitutes," "European dolls," and "puppets." The next day, newspapers carrying the story referred to the protesters as spoiled middle-class
"dolls" with "monarchist tendencies." Thus was the battle joined against
women who dared voice concern about the direction of the Islamic Republic's policy toward women. Although few realized it at the time, this early
skirmish was but the opening shot of the postrevolutionary struggle over the
women's question.

The leaders of the Islamic Republic from the beginning were intensely
concerned, even obsessed, with the need to control women and to define in
the broadest sense women's role in society. This obsession on the part of
Iran's new leaders, and the resistance women put up to being controlled and
defined by the state, ensured that the women's question would remain at the
very center of revolutionary politics.

A Nineteenth-Century Awakening

Women opposed the imposition of the Islamic dress code in part because
they viewed it as symbolic of an incipient threat to rights they had achieved
in other spheres in previous decades. This thirst for education, employment,
legal protections, economic security, and participation in the social and
political life of the country that women were to display with such intensity
after the revolution did not occur in a vacuum. It followed from many
decades of struggle by women in a society inhospitable to such aspirations.

An awareness of the need to improve the conditions under which women
lived can be traced to the late nineteenth century, when those conditions
were decidedly adverse. The conventional wisdom is that women were sov-
ereign in their homes and free to run their households as they wished. The
power and influence wielded by some wives of Qajar rulers in the nineteenth century and other women of royal households is adduced as evidence
of this contention. But the idea of women as absent in the public sphere yet
enjoying a large and important role in the private sphere is largely a myth.
The average Iranian woman in town and village was not a royal princess,
and even among the very small elite of wealthy, upper-class families, the
women who played significant roles were few.

The vast majority of Iranian women led narrow, restricted, powerless
lives. Nineteenth-century European travelers to Iran commented unfavor-
ably on the plight of Iranian women, on the absence of women on the
streets and their seclusion and isolation at home. There was, of course, a

"women's world" of childbearing, child rearing, housekeeping, and social and religious ritual. But women were most often key members of households largely in the sense that, in all but the wealthiest families, they carried the burden of housework. In the villages, and among the nomadic tribes, they were burdened with heavy, backbreaking physical labor as well. A woman was at the mercy of the man with whom she lived. He was the breadwinner, and he dispersed the money as he liked. He had the right to take a second, third, or fourth wife and as many "temporary" wives as he wanted. He divorced his wife at his own pleasure. The custody of the children was his. If a woman appeared on the streets, for example to attend some religious gathering, she was expected to keep her head down, go about her business meekly, and hurry back to the four walls of a house that was more like a prison than a paradise.

In the last decades of the nineteenth century, contact with the West, foreign interference in Iran's affairs, and a sense that Iran had fallen behind the European powers in economic, military, and technological strength and even in terms of the desirable forms of social and political organization led some Iranian officials and intellectuals to espouse reform. These reformers were concerned primarily with drawing on Western models to strengthen Iran militarily and economically and to improve the efficiency and limit the arbitrary nature of government. However, some reformers also espoused the idea of improving the condition of women; they stressed the need to extend education and to establish schools for girls as well as boys.

In 1905–6, discontent with misgovernment and official corruption resulted in a widespread demand, led by the merchant classes, members of the clergy, and a new strata of educated Iranians, for a curb on royal autocracy, a system of laws, and a voice for the people in government decisions. These aspirations were eventually articulated in a demand for a constitution that the ruler, Mozaffar-ad-Din Shah Qajar (r.1896–1906), granted in August 1906.

The new constitution recognized the equality of all Iranians before the law. But the electoral law barred women from voting or being elected to parliament, and, despite the aspirations of educated women and some reformers, the constitutional era heralded no change in the legal status of women. Nevertheless, the constitutional movement witnessed a flurry of activities by women. They organized women's groups and pushed for expanded rights. In the struggle between the constitutionalists and the monarchy that followed the grant of the constitution, women's groups organized in defense of the constitution. When the new parliament was debating a humiliating Russian ultimatum and as Russian troops were pouring into the country in 1911, women marched on parliament with pistols hidden under their *chadors* to urge the deputies to hold firm. Although clerical and conservative opinion successfully opposed women's suffrage and similar measures, women wrote letters to magazines and to parliamentary deputies protesting their exclusion from the political process. Liberal newspapers and magazines continued to argue the desirability of giving women access to education, the vote, and participation in public life. They published articles (or translated articles from European magazines) on the condition of women in Europe and touching on women's education and health, marriage, divorce, and child rearing. Literate women were in this way exposed to new ideas.

In the period following the Constitutional Revolution, both in Tehran and in provincial cities like Isfahan and Mashad, women founded schools for girls, organized discussion groups and societies for women, and published newspapers and magazines of their own—all with little support from men or the government. The pioneers of this early women's movement were largely middle class. They had been educated at home and had grown up in enlightened circles. Somehow they found the courage to break with tradition and to espouse the strange and new idea of women's rights.

The founding of schools took place in the face of opposition from the clerical establishment. The clergy raised no objection to girls' receiving religious instruction or private tutorials at home, but they preached against girls', even if completely covered, venturing outside their homes only to attend school. The clerics also opposed a curriculum they could not control. But harassment, persecution, and threats of banishment did not deter the pioneers of the women's movement. A headmistress of that period recalls that every day thugs in the city of Tabriz would tear down the sign at the city's girls' school; the next day the sign would go up again. Hooligans would follow girls leaving the school and verbally abuse them; the girls would hit them on the head with their books.

The early girls' schools were established at private initiative. The government, careful not to antagonize the clergy or conservative elements in society, lagged far behind. (The American Presbyterian Mission girls' school, established in Urumieh as early as 1838, was attended only by girls belonging to the religious minorities, not Muslim girls.) But the government established the first school for girls in 1918–19. The government also established teachers' training colleges, one for men and one for women, in 1919. Teaching was considered a respectable profession for women. Needless to say, all the teachers at the women's college were men.

Despite governmental caution, the number of girls' schools developed rapidly. By 1925, when Reza Shah, the founder of the Pahlavi dynasty, came to the throne, a number of women had finished elementary and some part of secondary school and were pushing for wider access to education and for broader rights for women.

The Reza Shah Era

Reza Shah Pahlavi (r.1925–41), an autocrat and a centralizer, tried to modernize Iran on the model of Ataturk in neighboring Turkey. Women were among the beneficiaries of his reformist policies. The number of primary schools and secondary schools for girls grew rapidly during his reign, as did the training of women teachers. When Tehran University opened in 1936, twelve women were admitted alongside an overwhelming number of men. These women did not wear the veil, and they took part in classes alongside men. But they sat on separate benches, and the librarian tried to designate a special area for women in the library, separated by a curtain. There was no social mixing between men and women. The male professors were clearly discomfited by women in their classes, and for many years the university had only one woman on its academic staff. Under Reza Shah, a school for midwifery was also established. Until then illiterate, untrained midwives handled deliveries, not infrequently resulting in the death of the mother and the child.

The boldest step taken by Reza Shah was the abolition of the veil in 1936—a measure that went far beyond anything attempted in other Islamic states. In Afghanistan women of the royal family and in Turkey and Egypt women of the upper classes had begun to appear in public unveiled and in European dress. But the mass of women still observed the Islamic dress code, and in no Islamic country, not even Turkey, where Ataturk secularized the laws and disestablished religion, was the veil officially set aside.

The abolition of the veil in Iran took the majority of the population by surprise, but it was not entirely unanticipated. Women's magazines and women's organizations had discussed the desirability of discarding the veil for many years. In an effort to promote national unity, in 1928 Reza Shah had banned tribal and local dress worn by Iran's many communities and had imposed a uniform dress code, consisting of a European-style jacket and trousers and a peaked cap, which came to be known as the Pahlavi hat. Reza Shah and his lieutenants also concluded that the education of women and their integration into the work force and into active society required the abolition of the veil. By the early 1930s, some upper-class women began to wear European dress in the privacy of their homes; in Tehran, some women abandoned the black *chador* in public in favor of dark or even lighter colored ones.

The government actively promoted these trends. It encouraged senior civil servants and military officers to appear with their wives unveiled in public. It discouraged schoolgirls and teachers from wearing the veil. The uniform of the Girl Scouts, an organization promoted by the government, was based on the European model and made no provision for a veil. The government sent women speakers to girls' schools to explain the benefits of European dress. These speakers were sometimes turned away, even where the principal was a woman, and could return only under official protection.

Nevertheless, when Reza Shah appeared at the Women's Teacher Training College in January 1936, accompanied by the queen and two of the princesses in European suits and hats, and went up the stairs of the building flanked by girls in scout uniforms, the country collectively gasped. In a speech at the school, he announced the official abolition of the veil. It was a dramatic moment in the history of the women's movement.

While many women, especially of the younger generation, welcomed the new measure, the banning of the veil was hard on large numbers of both men and women. For a man to allow his women to appear in public without the veil and to expose them to the gaze of other males was tantamount to letting them go into the street naked, to failing to protect their honor and chastity. Yet civil servants who did not appear with their unveiled wives in public were reprimanded, fined, and even dismissed. The new requirement also imposed an economic hardship.

The Ministry of Interior was inundated with letters from provincial government offices asking for financial assistance for civil servants whose women could not afford Western-style clothing. The clergy strongly opposed the measure and preached against it. Yet Reza Shah ordered the government to implement the law by force if necessary, and women who appeared veiled on the streets had their *chadors* or scarves torn away by policemen. A number of women chose not to leave the house at all rather than to appear in public in what they regarded as a form of undress. But to appease the authorities, most women were eventually forced to appear on the streets wearing an odd assortment of Western clothes.

The abolition of the veil opened the door to an expansion of employment opportunities for women. Women entered the nursing profession and took up secretarial work. They entered the civil service, primarily in clerical jobs. They were employed in textile, cigarette, and other factories. The education of women also accelerated. By 1936, a quarter of all primary school children and 19 percent of secondary school students were girls. The number of coeducational primary schools increased rapidly after the first one was established in 1935. These mixed schools improved educational opportunities for girls, especially in the provinces where schools were limited in number. The government sent about one hundred male students abroad for study each year, but no government scholarships for foreign study were available to women. However, girls were occasionally sent abroad for study by their parents. In 1939 scouting became compulsory for all students, girls as well as boys. Schoolgirls took part in team sports and gymnastics; and these uniformed girl students and representatives of the Girl Scouts and other girls and women's organizations became a common sight during public celebrations and similar occasions. Newspapers and magazines printed articles, and the state-run radio broadcast programs promoting the idea of the "new" Iranian women.

Encouraged by the government, women's organizations also proliferated. The titular heads of many of these organizations were the female members of the royal family, but the work was done by activist women. The majority of women's organizations were involved in charity work. Women visited hospitals and orphanages, did voluntary work with the mentally retarded, and raised funds by organizing garden parties and balls. This work gave middle-class women experience in running organizations, brought working-class women into contact with new ideas, and helped expand the constituency for women's causes. In 1932 the Oriental Women's Congress met in Tehran and was chaired by the crown prince's twin sister, Princess Ashraf. Women from several Middle Eastern countries and India participated. They recommended changes in family law, reform of Islamic law pertaining to women, adult literacy programs for women, and female suffrage.

Reza Shah was more cautious in altering the political and legal status of women. He did not attempt to enfranchise women, as did Ataturk in Turkey. Polygamy was not abolished (Reza Shah himself took three wives), and only modest changes were made in marriage laws. The age of marriage was raised. A man was required to notify his future (second) wife if he was already married. Marriage contracts, including temporary marriages, had to be registered in notary offices regulated by the Ministry of Justice. Women could stipulate the right of divorce in their marriage contracts (an Islamic right that was seldom exercised).

Mohammad Reza Shah and Voting Rights

In 1941, Reza Shah was forced to abdicate, and he was succeeded by his son. The first years of the reign of Mohammad Reza Shah (r.1941–79) witnessed relative freedom for political groups and the press and the proliferation of political parties across a broad spectrum from the extreme, nationalist right to the Tudeh, or communist, party on the left. Many of these political parties organized women's branches, and these politically active women called for an expansion in educational opportunities and an improvement in the social status of women, a change in family laws that discriminated against women, female suffrage, and an improvement in the working conditions for women. They ran literacy and vocational classes (sewing, knitting, and the like) to assist less-affluent women, criticized the "do-nothing" policy governments adopted on women's issues, lobbied members of parliament, addressed letters to the prime minister, and used the queen to petition the Shah regarding their demands.

However, the first two decades of Mohammad Reza Shah's reign brought no major changes in the status and condition of women. The ban on the veil was no longer enforced, and women wearing the *chador* once again appeared on the streets. The clergy, silenced by Reza Shah, found their voice again and began to play an important role in the politics of the country. In 1951, a member of the Muslim Brotherhood assassinated Prime Minister Ali Razmara. During the oil nationalization movement under Prime Minister Mohammad Mossadegh in 1951–53, a cleric, Ayatollah Abol-Qasem Kashani, was Speaker of the Majlis, or parliament, a symbol of the growing political power of the clergy.

Women were active in the political agitation for oil nationalization. But Mossadegh, a highly popular national leader, was focused on oil nationalization, not on social or women's issues. He appointed no women to senior government positions. A bill to give women the right to vote was not even debated in parliament.

After the overthrow of Mossadegh in 1953, the Shah consolidated his power and grew more assertive and increasingly intolerant of opposition. He also began to distance himself from the more traditional clerical community. In 1962, he threw his support behind a program of reforms that came to be known as his White Revolution. The most important measure in the program was land distribution, but the White Revolution also sent a Literacy Corps of young men of military age into villages to set up literacy classes, reformed electoral laws to give more representation to workers and farmers on election supervisory committees, and nationalized forest and pasture land. The White Revolution was put to a national referendum in January 1963, and this referendum led, almost fortuitously, to the enfranchisement of women.

For decades women's leaders had pressed for the right to vote. They wrote articles, petitioned the Shah and the government, and drew unfavorable comparisons of their lot with that of enfranchised women in neighboring Turkey. But their efforts were invariably rebuffed. The clerical community was almost universally opposed to granting women the right to vote, and clerical leaders published articles and spoke from the pulpit against it. They equated female suffrage with the collapse of public morality, and they made their views known to government officials. They argued that the handful of women seeking political rights for women and changes in family laws did not speak for the millions of ordinary, pious Iranian women.

The government attempted to grant women the right to vote in a roundabout way, at least in local elections. In October 1962 the government of Prime Minister Asadollah Alam promulgated a new Local Councils Law that was so worded as to permit women to vote in local council elections and non-Muslims both to vote and be elected to the local councils on the same footing as Muslims. Women welcomed the new law. But clerical leaders viewed it, correctly, as an attempt to extend the franchise to women and to erase distinctions between Muslims and non-Muslims, including Bahais,* in voting and standing for elective office. They vehemently opposed the law, wrote letters to the prime minister demanding he withdraw it, mobilized their followers, and prepared for mass protests. A then not well-known cleric, Ayatollah Khomeini, played a prominent role in these events. Confronted with this hostile clerical reaction, the prime minister announced two months later, in December, that he was suspending—in effect withdrawing—the Local Councils Law. The real losers were women, whose interests the government once again appeared willing to sacrifice to appease the clerical community.

When the referendum on the White Revolution was held in January, the government refused a request by women's leaders that women be allowed to vote in the referendum. However, on the very eve of the voting, a suggestion by Minister of Agriculture Hasan Arsanjani—that women set up their own

---

*The Bahai religion originated in a nineteenth-century movement that broke away from Islam. Bahais are regarded as apostates by the clerical community in Iran.

voting stations and poll women—provided an opening. Women leaders scrambled over the next twelve hours to set up polling stations and ballot boxes and to mobilize their followers. In some provincial towns women used ordinary wastepaper baskets as ballot boxes. The clerics were caught by surprise, and the women's vote—confined to the major towns and cities—passed off without incident.

The government refused to include the women's ballots in the official referendum returns. But newspapers carried pictures of women voting and published the results of the women's vote, which endorsed the referendum. The exercise laid the basis for more decisive action. A month later, in February 1963, the Shah announced that he was granting women the right to vote and the right to be elected to parliament. In terms of legislation, all that was subsequently required was for parliament to strike the word "women" from clauses in the laws specifying those barred from voting and standing for elective office.

In parliamentary elections held in September 1963, six women were for the first time elected to the Majlis. The Shah appointed two more women to the Senate. (The Senate was composed of sixty members, half elected and half appointed by the Shah.) These women deputies and senators shared a largely similar profile: middle-aged, traditional, and Islamic in terms of family background; teachers or school principals by profession; and each with a record of a lifetime of struggle, often under difficult and humiliating conditions, for the emancipation of women and the improvement of women's rights. All the women came to parliament persuaded that it was possible to enact legislation that would improve the status of women and yet adhere to Islamic law.

New Opportunities and the Family Protection Law

The participation of women in the 1963 referendum, the extension to women of the right to vote, and the election of women to parliament in 1963 set the stage for nearly two decades of expanding opportunities for women. In parliament, women acquired a platform for articulating women's issues. The Women's Organization of Iran worked effectively in a range of fields to expand women's rights. The government itself often took the initiative, particularly in the area of employment, with measures both substantive and symbolic. The number of women in the civil service expanded rapidly. For the first time, a woman, Farrokhru Parsa, was named to the cabinet as minister of education. Women were named deputy ministers in other ministries. Women's divisions were created in the Literacy Corps and the other service corps, and women were included in the police force, initially as traffic police.

A rapidly expanding economy created job opportunities in the private sector: in factory, clerical, and secretarial work; in a range of services; in the professions; in lower-level and middle-level management; and also in the arts—film, music, theater, the press, radio, and television. Many women started businesses of their own. The number of women in decision-making, top management, and executive positions remained limited. Nevertheless, the pace and breadth of change were striking.

The expansion of secondary and higher education at home and study abroad provided better-qualified graduates who could fill a range of new jobs. These women graduates, like their male counterparts, also generated pressure on the government to create employment opportunities. Young women, like young men, albeit in smaller numbers, flocked from villages to towns and from towns to large cities in search of employment and especially of educational opportunities. In the cities they were exposed to new influences—urban life, film, television, popular magazines, and political and religious ideas circulating on college and university campuses. These young women became part of a younger generation pushing for entry into employment and into social and eventually political life. This period of rapid change also generated deep social, economic, and political tensions, but these tensions did not become evident until the late 1970s.

One of the striking developments of the period was the enactment of the Family Protection Law (FPL) in 1967. For decades women had voiced their objections to existing family laws, which, based on interpretations of Islamic law, gave men the right to divorce on demand, the freedom to take several wives and enter into temporary marriages, the custody of children in case of divorce, the authority to prevent their wives from working or traveling abroad, and other privileges.

Once women were enfranchised, women activists turned their attention to the family laws. Women members of parliament, speaking for the "silent" women's community, stressed the inequity of the laws. Their concerns were echoed by other women activists. Together they generated a great deal of publicity for their cause both inside the country and abroad. For example, in 1965 Iran hosted in Tehran the conference of the United Nations Commission on the Status of Women. The conference not only adopted resolutions relating to women worldwide; it also focused international attention on the activities of Iranian women.

The Iranian government was mindful of the potential resistance of the clerical community to any changes in the legal status of women. But it also concluded that the economically dynamic society it wished to create and the progressive and reformist image it sought to project both at home and abroad required acquiescence to at least some of the demands of the leadership of the women's movement. In 1965, the Iranian Women's Lawyers Association had published a proposal for some major changes in family law. The following year, a group of women working with government officials drafted a proposal to amend the existing family laws and circulated it at a seminar organized by the ruling Iran Novin party. This draft provided the basis for legislation drawn up by the Ministry of Justice (eventually known as the Family Protection Law) to strengthen women's rights in child custody, divorce, and marriage. Care was taken to avoid conflict with Islamic law. With the draft law in his pocket, the justice minister, Javad Sadr, flew to the shrine city of An Najaf in Iraq and succeeded in securing an endorsement of the new law from Ayatollah Hakim, then the most eminent *marja'*, or source of emulation, in the Shia world.* Parliament enacted the FPL into law in March 1967.

The Family Protection Law established special Family Protection Courts to handle disputes regarding marriage, divorce, and child custody. Husbands required the permission of these courts to divorce their wives, thus ending the right men had enjoyed unilaterally to terminate a marriage. Women received the right to sue for divorce on a number of grounds, including incompatibility. A man needed the permission of his wife to take a second spouse, and the wife could demand a divorce if he insisted on marrying against her wishes. The marriage age was raised from thirteen to fifteen for girls. Awarding of child custody was left to the discretion of the courts rather than being automatically granted to the husband. Both the government and the leadership of the women's movements were careful to describe the new law as compatible with a reasonable, if new, interpretation of Islamic law.

The Family Protection Law worked sufficiently well for the leadership of the women's movement to seek its further expansion. Revisions in the law, approved in 1975, gave a wife the right (which the husband alone had

---

Marja': source of emulation. A term referring to the most learned of the Shia clergy in Iran to whom believers turn for guidance on matters of religious observance and daily conduct. There are usually no more than half a dozen *marja's* at any one time. The Shia is one of the two great branches of Islam and the branch to which the large majority of Iranians adhere.

enjoyed in the past) to prevent her spouse from entering into work that would bring dishonor on the family, assigned custody of children after the death of the father to the mother (according to Islamic law a male member of the deceased husband's family took precedence over the wife), and raised the age of marriage for girls to eighteen. For the first time, women could serve as judges, and women lawyers could plead before the courts, including the Family Protection Courts. (Women were barred from sitting as judges under Islamic law).

During this period of legal reform, a number of controversial laws were nevertheless left untouched, including the Passport Law, the infamous Article 179 of the criminal code, and the Inheritance Law. The Passport Law required a women to obtain the written, notarized permission of her husband to leave the country. Women found the law irksome. On several occasions professional women going abroad to attend conferences or on other business were stopped at the airport because they lacked written permission from their husbands. Article 179 of the criminal code prescribed no punishment whatsoever for a husband who found his wife in bed with another man and killed her. The law prescribed only eleven to sixty days in prison for a man who caught his sister or daughter in bed with a man other than her husband and put her to death. The law treated such killing as a so-called crime of passion and thus justified to restore family honor. The Inheritance Law, based strictly on Islamic law, was not revised either. Under Shia laws of inheritance, a daughter inherits half of what her brother inherits; and a widow inherits one-fourth of her husband's estate if he is childless and one-eighth if he has children.

The Women's Organization of Iran

Some of these developments reflected changes that were taking place in the leadership of the Iranian women's movement. The Women's Organization of Iran (WOI) was under the titular presidency of Princess Ashraf. But in the late 1960s, a new generation of younger feminists took over the leadership of the WOI. These women built on earlier efforts but had innovative ideas on women's rights, the role of women in society, and the means for achieving their aims. In the decade preceding the revolution they pushed for change and reform in many areas.

The ultimate goal of the WOI was women's total equality under the law. To this end, the organization continued to lobby members of the government and parliament. It worked strenuously to secure further legal reform.

It vastly expanded its network of branches and centers and the services it provided to women. It launched a program of public education—for both women and men. It sought to link the Iranian women's movement to the movement of women worldwide. The WOI also concluded that it must direct its efforts at the vast majority of Iranian women, bringing the "ordinary" Iranian woman into the women's movement and sensitizing her to women's issues. It reasoned that middle-class and upper-class women were well on their way to gaining access to education and jobs and integration into society. The mass of Iranian women, however, were unaware of these opportunities or less well equipped to take advantage of them. It was primarily at these women that the WOI directed its programs.

The WOI deliberately set up its branches and centers in the less-affluent neighborhoods of Tehran and provincial towns and cities, and it designed these offices to serve the needs of women who had little recourse to other sources of support. By 1978 the WOI had set up 400 branches and 118 centers across the nation, each run by a professional staff and assisted by a substantial number of volunteers. The centers ran vocational and literacy classes, gave women free legal advice, provided family planning counseling, and operated day-care centers for children. The vocational classes focused on both traditional and modern skills—sewing and knitting as well as typing and radio repair—and remained flexible, adapting the curriculum to the needs of the women who attended them. Legal counselors assisted women in divorce, child custody, and alimony cases. WOI family planning centers provided women with free family planning advice, devices, and medical consultations. Women visiting the centers and branches regularly used the day-care facilities.

The WOI provided women with illustrated booklets setting out newly gained legal rights in clear, simple language. It organized talks to explain the intricacies of the Family Protection Law. Its radio programs sought to encourage women to participate in improving their condition in society. By 1978, it was estimated that a million women a year were making use of WOI services.

The WOI leadership continued to lobby the cabinet, women members of parliament, and women in decision-making positions in the government or in the ruling party for major changes in legislation. The 1975 revision of the Family Protection Law was one product of these efforts. In addition, laws and regulations discriminating against women in employment were amended. New regulations gave working mothers up to seven months paid maternity leave and the option of working halftime up to the child's third year. Factories, offices, and other places of work above a certain size in both the private and public sectors were required to provide day-care facilities.

Over a period of two years, the WOI organized seven hundred seminars for women in the provinces, inviting grass-roots suggestions for ways of improving the status of women. The ideas generated by these seminars were incorporated in a report presented to the government in the spring of 1978 that came to be known as the National Plan of Action. The Plan of Action, which received cabinet endorsement, was designed to achieve, over a period of years, total equality for women under the law. As early as 1976, the secretary-general of the WOI, Mahnaz Afkhami, had been appointed as the country's first minister of state for women's affairs. Since she retained her position as secretary-general of the WOI, she was able to turn a cabinet post without portfolio into an unofficial ministry with necessary staff.

After the Islamic revolution, it became part of the conventional wisdom that the leadership of the WOI was too Westernized, had violated traditional taboos, and had been oblivious to the needs of ordinary, traditional, and religious Iranian women. Such criticism is off the mark. The vast majority of the users and beneficiaries of the services offered by WOI branches and centers—vocational training, legal counseling, birth control advice— were traditional, working class women. Educated upper-class and upper-middle-class women had other means of protecting their interests. The Family Protection Law and the Family Protection Courts benefited all women; but again, it was working-class women who most urgently needed legal protection in marriage, divorce, and child custody cases. The WOI's vocational training classes gave precisely those women who most needed it the opportunity to work and to secure a degree of economic independence. The vast expansion of education and employment of women in the two decades before the revolution was made possible by economic growth, government policy, and the efforts of the WOI. These developments created opportunities for women from all classes, including rural and working-class women, to a degree that would have been inconceivable in an earlier period.

The WOI kept abreast not only of feminist movements in the West but also developments regarding women's rights in other Islamic countries. Western ideas and concepts of feminism were studied, reshaped, and reworked for a traditional society like Iran. Each piece of legislation sponsored by the WOI was drawn up after long and detailed consultation with Islamic jurists, although inevitably such legislation reflected a modern definition of Islamic law. Moreover, respect for certain basic rights for women and a degree of equality under the law were not exclusively Western ideas.

Nor did the Family Protection Law, the Family Protection Courts, and regulations extending protection to women in the workplace seem to offend the sensibilities of women. The majority of women, and certainly a younger generation of women, appeared to embrace both the growing opportunities to work and study and the new rights and protections afforded under law.

On the eve of the revolution in 1979, Iranian women were serving as ministers in the cabinet, as deputy ministers, as directors-general and department heads in the ministries, and as ambassadors in the diplomatic service. Women sat as judges in the courts. They ran private businesses. They were engineers, lawyers, and doctors. Women worked in factories and on the land. They taught at all levels, from nursery school to university. Women served in the military and acted as traffic police. A common sight in the rural areas was a young woman in uniform doing her military service as a member of the Literacy Corps or the Health Corps. In 1978 almost 2 million Iranian women were in the labor force. There were more than 150,000 women in the civil service. More than 1,500 women held managerial positions. The number of women deputies in parliament had increased to 22; more than 330 women served on local councils. There were five women mayors as well. More than a million and one-half girls were in school. Thirty-three percent of all students in higher education were women.* On the eve of the revolution, the aspiration to education, independence, and economic betterment was no longer exclusive to a small group of women. It had become a widespread phenomenon, cutting across class and social background.

The Islamic Reformers

Even members of the clerical and religious community had to take cognizance of these developments. In 1962 virtually the whole clerical establishment, including Ayatollah Khomeini, had vehemently opposed granting women the right to vote. A decade later, clerical leaders like Morteza Mottahari and nonclerical Islamic thinkers like Ali Shariati were looking for ways to show that Islam was compatible with a decidedly modern view of a woman's role in society. Both Mottahari and Shariati argued in their writ-

---

*Statistics from Mahnaz Afkhami, "A Future in the Past: The Pre-Revolutionary Women's Movement," in *Sisterhood Is Global: An International Women's Movement Anthology*, ed. Robin Morgan (New York: Doubleday, 1984), 330–38.

ings, talks, and sermons that Islam does not stand in the way of women's education, work, and active participation in society. On the contrary, they asserted that Islam accords to women an honored and privileged place in the community. Shariati depicted the Prophet's daughter, Fatemeh, as the ideal woman: a model wife and mother, but also a companion to her husband, an active participant in the great religious and political struggles of the time, and an intrepid warrior for justice and truth. Both Shariati and Mottahari emphasized the qualities of modesty, piousness, and sobriety of their idealized Muslim woman (in contrast to the allegedly corrupt, frivolous, luxury-loving, over- or underdressed Western woman, whom they decried). Both preached an Islam that appeared compatible with women's rights, and both, particularly Shariati, attracted a large following among the young and educated, especially those from traditional families trying to reconcile tradition and modernity, Islam and the West.

There were differences between the two men. They were only thirteen years apart in age but a generation apart in upbringing and mentality. Shariati, the younger man, was a layman, Mottahari a cleric. Shariati had received a religious upbringing, but he was the product of a basically secular education, of state schools, Tehran University, and graduate training in Paris. Mottahari was comfortable in discourse with lay intellectuals and taught at Tehran University. But he was the product of the religious seminary and a classical clerical education.

Shariati did not advocate the separation of women and men in the workplace. Mottahari was uncomfortable with mixing between the sexes and advocated a separation of men and women at work. Shariati preferred the *hejab* but did not wish to impose it on women. A daughter did not have to observe the *hejab* even if her mother adhered to it, he said. Mottahari insisted on the *hejab,* although he argued the *hejab* did not prevent a women from actively participating in society. His own wife observed the *hejab* and was also a schoolteacher. Mottahari also saw no reason to ban the practice of temporary marriage, comparing it to the practice of keeping a mistress in the West.

Yet Mottahari, like Shariati, set out to reconcile Islam with what girls and women were demonstrably doing—going to school and university, working, pursuing careers, appearing in public. Significantly, Mottahari chose the women's magazine, *Zan-e Ruz* (Today's Woman), as the vehicle for a series of articles on women under Islamic law. *Zan-e Ruz* was the leading women's magazine in the country. It projected a modern image of the Iranian woman, devoting space to fashions, clothes, and cosmetics.

Each year it sponsored a "teen princess" contest whose winner it sent abroad to take part in an international "teen princess" competition. The magazine had been denounced by some clerics for propagating un-Islamic, Western values and for its supposedly corrupting influence on women. But Mottahari chose it as a forum in which to plead for the tolerant attitude of Islam toward women precisely because of its wide circulation and its popularity among younger, upwardly mobile, educated girls and women. In doing so, he and other Islamic reformers like Shariati were responding both to the reality of a changing role for women in Iran and the growing aspiration of young women from traditional backgrounds to follow in the footsteps of their middle-class counterparts and share in the benefits of these changes.

There was a strong conservative streak in the attitude toward women in both thinkers. Mottahari, as noted, favored the *hejab,* the separation of men and women in the workplace, and the permitting of polygamy. Behind Shariati's fulminations against the supposed artificiality and superficiality of the rouged and lipsticked Western woman, and the emphasis both he and Mottahari placed on female modesty and the woman's role as mother, wife, and homemaker, lay a discomfort with the idea of the career woman and male-female equality. But their conservatism was not immediately evident to their followers.

In addition, even as some Islamic thinkers sought to reconcile Islam and the woman's role in modern society, among other thinkers and within certain elements in Iranian society a backlash was developing against female emancipation. Modernity, economic development, and industrialization conferred material benefits but also caused dislocations. Rural and provincial migrants attracted to the large urban centers were discomfited by the proximity of men and women on the streets, in the shops, and in the workplace. Refrigerators were a welcome part of city life, but movie billboards and newsstand magazine covers depicting women in swimming suits or revealing dress were not. Traditional families may have wished to educate their daughters, but they frowned on the easy mixing of men and women on university campuses. Wives working in factories or in offices, as secretaries, teachers, or administrators, brought in extra income, but their entry into the work force also meant that they left the house every morning and mixed with strange men, that husbands were no longer the sole breadwinners, that women were competing for the same jobs as men, and that women were more independent and visible in society.

The Coming of the Revolution

Moreover, after a decade of steady economic growth, the sudden infusion of huge amounts of oil revenue after the 1973 oil price explosion caused severe economic dislocations in Iran. The country experienced rapid inflation, shortages, high rates of rural migration, a housing crunch and shantytown growth in urban centers, overcrowded schools, and an overburdened infrastructure. The salaried middle class and the working class felt squeezed even as huge fortunes were made by importers, developers, contractors, industrialists, and those with connections to the royal court.

The dislocations came to be associated in the minds of many with Westernization, and rapid change generated fears that, in his scramble to emulate the West, the Shah was threatening Iran's national and religious identity. Discontent against the way the country was being run reinforced discomfort among more traditional elements with the changing role of women in society.

The reversion to religiosity expressed itself in different ways. At Tehran's leading technical university, male students demanded Western music not be played in the cafeteria and called for separate cafeterias for men and women. There was a marked increase in mosque attendance among students. On university campuses, an increasing number of women appeared in scarves, either because they felt more comfortable with their heads covered or as a sign of protest against a government associated in the minds of its opponents with the West. In urban areas, a growing number of religious schools for girls catered to daughters of rural migrants or traditional families, and women attended religious gatherings led by women preachers.

At the same time, political repression meant there was no outlet for articulating grievances. Radio and television were in government hands, the press and professional associations were tightly controlled, a one-party political system was in place, and parliament had been reduced virtually to a rubber stamp. Political protest tended to be articulated increasingly in the mosque and from the pulpit and to be expressed in a religious idiom. When the opposition finally found its courage and its voice in 1977, it is true that demands for greater freedom of speech and political participation were initially advanced by secular groups and lay intellectuals. But the large-scale protests, demonstrations, and riots that followed in 1978, in which millions participated, were dominated by religious groups and clerical leaders and, increasingly, by demands not just for the overthrow of the monarchy but for the establishment of an Islamic republic. Once the monarchy was overthrown, Ayatollah Khomeini and his clerical lieutenants, calling for a political and social order founded on Islam, came to dominate the revolution itself.

Women and the Islamic Revolution

In the year or so of political turmoil preceding the overthrow of the monarchy, women, too, were caught up in the revolutionary fervor. Huge numbers from across the political and social spectrum took part in the mass demonstrations and protests of 1978—religious and secular women, the politically active and the apolitical, women from the political left and the political right, poor, middle-class, and wealthy women, housewives and working women, rural women and urbanites. Those who did not take part in the marches and protests came out in the streets anyway, to watch or to cheer. Women organized protest meetings, strikes, and strike committees and joined fellow civil servants in work stoppages.

Like the men who took part in the protests and eventually in the call for the overthrow of the monarchy, these women represented a range of political views. But there is little doubt that most expected that political change would result in an amplification of women's rights and equality for all citizens. Women could not imagine that revolution would lead to a reversal of rights they had gained in the previous decade.

Few women thought it significant that, to appease the religious community during the revolutionary turmoil in 1978, the Shah's government abolished the position of minister of state for women's affairs—as if tacitly conceding that its support for women's emancipation was misguided. Very few women noticed that in the declarations issued by clerical leaders or the main secular opposition group, the National Front, in the course of revolutionary pamphleteering, no reference was made to women even if women were assured that the revolution would promote their interests. At the same time, radical left-wing groups were silent on the women's question, taking refuge in the assertion that the liberation of the country took precedence over the future status of women. Nor were women alarmed that Ayatollah Khomeini, expelled from Iraq in October 1978 and temporarily headquartered in Paris, responded with generalities to questions regarding the position of women under a future Islamic government: women's rights, he said, would be fully respected within the framework of Islamic law.

Pictures from Paris showed women received by Ayatollah Khomeini wearing the scarf and the women of his household fully covered by the *chador.* But nothing significant was read into these images. Women who visited religious dignitaries traditionally observed the *hejab* as a mark of respect and wore the *chador* on pilgrimages, at religious gatherings, and when visiting a shrine. Such situations aside, it was assumed that women would be free to dress as they wished after the revolution. In the euphoria that followed the fall of the Shah in January 1979 and the victory of the revolution in February, women remained oblivious of the fact that not a single woman was included in the revolutionary council or in the cabinet of Mehdi Bazargan, the first prime minister of the Islamic Republic.

In the immediate aftermath of the revolution, it seemed as if nothing had changed for women. Most went on with their lives, continued to appear in public without the *hejab,* and continued to work. Those who had been politically active before the revolution found fertile ground for their activities. They organized women's groups, addressed gatherings, or joined one of the proliferating political movements. But women could not remain unaffected by the general revolutionary turmoil: the widespread purges and dismissals of civil servants, revolutionary trials and executions, confiscation of private property and state seizure of private enterprises, and closing of the universities.

Measures against Women

Before long, the revolutionary government implemented measures directly touching on women. Laws enacted under the previous regime, including the Family Protection Law, were suspended or abolished. The *hejab* was gradually made mandatory, and it was a sign of the times when Monireh Gorji, the only woman in the seventy-two-member constituent assembly that convened in August 1979 to draft the constitution of the Islamic Republic, appeared at the opening session wrapped in a black *chador*—dress that became the official attire of women holding high positions in the government and representing the Islamic Republic in an official capacity at home and abroad. Restrictions were imposed on the mixing of the sexes. Other measures restricted women's access to work and education. In the name of morality and the social order, a whole range of measures constricted the lives of women in myriad ways.

The new constitution, ratified in December 1979, devoted only four of 175 articles to women and these spoke only of woman's role within the context of the family and within the framework of Islamic law and principles. Women kept the right to vote, to be elected to parliament, and to hold cabinet positions. But the constitution barred women from becoming judges or being elected to the position of supreme leader, a prerogative reserved for the country's leading male clerics.

With the suspension of the Family Protection Law, the Family Protection Courts were dismantled, denying women virtually all recourse to the judiciary on matters touching on child custody and divorce. The suspension of the FPL once more permitted men to divorce their wives at will, engage in polygamy, automatically secure the custody of children, and, through divorce, repudiation, and similar measures, threaten the economic security of all women, regardless of class or social standing. Women could no longer file petitions before the courts for divorce on incompatibility or other grounds. The minimum age of marriage for girls was reduced to puberty, in keeping with Islamic law.

In time, authorities began to encourage *sigheh*, or temporary marriages, under which a man and a woman agree to contract a marriage for a specific time period. Under the laws governing the temporary marriage, the husband has no responsibility toward his temporary wife once the contract period is over. On one occasion, President Ali-Akbar Hashemi-Rafsanjani suggested that young people enter into temporary marriage in order to be free to associate with one another. He did not subsequently repeat this unusual suggestion, which was the source of amusement (and shock) among the public.

Women were harassed in other ways. In the aftermath of the revolution, revolutionary guards set up checkpoints on the streets and stopped cars to ensure that women were not in company of men not directly related to them (limited to fathers, husbands, and brothers). In the absence of proof of relationship, women were often fined or required to appear before a revolutionary court.

In several areas, segregation of the sexes was gradually imposed. A proposal to separate men and women in university classrooms was dropped as impractical, although men and women were required to sit in different sections of the class. Coeducation in primary and secondary schools was ended. On public buses, women had to occupy the back of the bus, while the men sat in front. Mixed bathing was forbidden, and women and men were segregated on the ski slopes. While strict segregation of men and women in the workplace proved impractical, any mixing between the sexes at work, on university campuses, and elsewhere was frowned upon and could result in job loss or punishment.

Islamic punishments of various kinds were revived and enacted into law. In 1981 parliament approved the Islamic Law of Retribution. Among other provisions, the law made adultery punishable by stoning for both women and men. A number of women were stoned to death on the basis of this law. Women were routinely sentenced to seventy lashes for showing hair beneath their *hejab* and for other infractions of Islamic dress.

The government decided to bar women from certain fields of study, such as agriculture, veterinary science, and some engineering fields. Girls were also gradually excluded from technical and business fields in high schools. Although these decisions were taken haphazardly, the net result in the decade following the revolution was to create an educational system that was not equally accessible to men and women. The government denied scholarships for study abroad to single women, requiring women to be married and accompanied by their husbands to qualify for foreign study under government-funded programs.

The execution of the former minister of education, Farrokhru Parsa, on charges of leading young girls into prostitution seemed an ominous indication of the regime's attitude toward career women. Parsa was an educator who had devoted a lifetime to the education of girls and the first woman in Iran to achieve cabinet office. The position of minister of state for women's affairs was not revived. Women in decision-making positions in the public sector were in many cases either purged or offered and sometimes forced to take early retirement. Conditions in government offices in any case made it very difficult for women to continue working. Many women professors quit the university rather than put up with harassment and the often unreasonable enforcement of the Islamic dress code.

Seemingly enlightened policies were often also aimed at encouraging women to drop out of the work force and back into the house. Parliament ratified the so-called Part-Time Work Law, which allowed women to work only half-time in order to devote themselves more fully to their husbands and children. Other legislation enabled women to retire after just fifteen years of employment. Day-care centers were closed down, making it more difficult for working women to continue to work. Women were also deliberately directed into such traditionally female areas as nursing and teaching. Women fared better in the private sector, where segregation of the sexes and the *hejab* were not enforced as strictly or women humiliated and working conditions made unpleasant with the same insistence as in government offices.

Women Fight Back

The government's attempt to dismantle most of the gains women had achieved over the preceding decades diminished the lives of women. But the government did not quite succeed.

Women fought for the restoration of legal protections. They refused to be excluded from the work force or to be denied educational opportunities. They resisted social segregation and the attempts by the state to dictate how they should dress. The new regime soon awoke to the realization that some policies of the old regime—family planning, for example—were dictated by economic necessity and common sense and that their abandonment could have catastrophic results. The new regime also learned that there was simply a limit to public tolerance for Islamic punishments, such as stoning and flogging of women. And there was the sheer weight of the women themselves: having experienced education and employment opportunities, legal protections, a degree of freedom in dress and life-style before the revolution, and having been politicized by the revolution, women in their overwhelming numbers, from both the modern and the traditional classes, simply refused to be cowed.

In virtually every field—family law, employment, the arts, presence in the public sphere and in public space, even in matters of dress—women forced the government to retreat. In time, where policy toward women was concerned, the Islamic Republic, ironically and despite itself, began to imitate the monarchy.

Women fought the suspension of the Family Protection Law by writing to the offices of well known clerics, including Ayatollahs Khomeini and Hosain Ali Montazeri and the then Speaker of the Majlis, Rafsanjani. They bombarded women members of parliament with letters. Women's magazines published articles on the plight of women in the absence of the Family Protection Law and the Family Protection Courts and filled their letter columns with letters on the same subjects. The government found it difficult to ignore these expressions of discontent with the drift of official policy because they came from women rooted in what the regime considered its own constituency. Monireh Gorji, who stood up in the constituent assembly to report on the grievances of women, was supposed to represent a model of Islamic womanhood. The editors of the women's magazines and journals, such as *Zanan* (Women) and *Zan-e Ruz*, who filled their columns with articles and letters on the plight of women in the absence of the Family Protection Law or employment opportunities, were the daughters of the revolution and had achieved their positions on the strength of their revolutionary and Islamic credentials. All this was further evidence that the legal protections and opportunities for education, employment, study abroad, and social mobility opened up under the former regime mattered to women from traditional, economically disadvantaged, and lower-middle-class backgrounds. Older women wanted protection under the law, a chance at some training and economic independence for themselves, and broader opportunities for their daughters. A housemaid I interviewed, though dressed in a *chador* herself, insisted on taking her daughter to English lessons. Younger, upwardly mobile, lower-middle-class girls, ardent supporters of the revolution, proved adept at turning the language of the Islamic reformers and the revolutionary clerics to their own advantage. If Islam accorded a high standing, rights, and equality to women, they asked, where was the payoff in civil service jobs, promotion, and advancement in revolutionary organizations, managerial positions, and the like?

On the Family Protection Law, the government gradually began to backtrack. It initially suspended the law as un-Islamic. Then, confronted by overwhelming opposition from women and evidence of the mounting problems unprotected women faced, it reintroduced major parts of the law. The government initially closed down the Family Protection Courts, but, since the need for these courts proved real enough, they were reintroduced in a new guise, as Special Courts, to deal with divorce and child custody cases.

Ironically, the new dispensation much resembles the much-maligned prerevolutionary one, even if enforcement is less vigorous. A man cannot unilaterally divorce his wife and must secure the court's permission to do so. Judges of these Special Courts decide child custody disputes. In 1994, the Majlis enacted a law giving a divorced woman the right to monetary compensation for the years she worked in her husband's home as mother and housewife.

In recent years the government itself has made available to marrying couples a printed, model marriage contract. It gives a divorced wife a right to half the property acquired during the marriage, provided she does not seek the divorce herself and is not at fault if the husband decides to divorce her. Another article of the contract consists of a power of attorney from the husband to the wife, permitting her to divorce herself on twelve different grounds, including failure of the husband to provide maintenance, desertion for five years or more, the husband's insanity, or the husband's contracting of an incurable disease.

The government's failure severely to restrict employment for women or to exclude women from the workplace has also been striking. There are still few women engineers in industry, but women continue to work in large numbers in factories. The percentage of girls compared to boys in primary and secondary schools is actually higher than before the revolution. And while the percentage of girls in colleges, universities, and higher education dropped after the revolution, it is now running at around 30 percent of all students.* Moreover, restrictions on fields that women can study are being lifted, thanks in part to the efforts of a government-sponsored organization, the Cultural and Social Council for Women. Women are also evident in large numbers in government offices and in the private sector, as secretaries and clerical staff but also in junior and mid-level management positions. In government ministries, there are a number of women serving as directors-general (one level below deputy ministers). Women are running government-controlled cultural and research centers, hospitals, and sports, children's, and youth organizations. The phenomenon is even more striking in the private sector, where women have gone into business on their own, running import-export operations, bookstores, clothing enterprises, catering services, and the like.

The reasons for this striking presence of women in the workplace are numerous. Women were already well integrated into the work force before the revolution; simply put, the process has proven difficult to reverse. Women at all levels—in the universities, the professions, the arts, business, the civil service—refused to be driven out.

Economic need and hardship kept women who had been working before the revolution at their jobs and forced many more women into the work force. Revolution, war, and general economic mismanagement resulted in severe economic dislocation, high rates of inflation, and a decline in standards of living for families across the social and economic spectrum. Civil servants routinely hold one or two jobs in addition to their government work. Two wage earners have become common in both working-class and middle-class families. A strange but not uncommon sight in many government offices and banks provides striking evidence of the absolute need for women to work: women are busy behind desks, while their little children play in a corner on the floor. The lack of day-care facilities forces women to bring preschool and even school-age children to work with them (overcrowding means many schools operate on two shifts and a foreshortened school day). This is one reason the government has been forced, once again, to provide day-care facilities at least at some government ministries.

---

*Statistics from *National Report on Women in the Islamic Republic of Iran Presented to the Fourth International Conference on Women, Beijing, 1995* (in Persian) (Tehran: Office of the President, Office of Women's Affairs, Secretariat of the Committee for the Fourth World Conference on Women, 1995).

Widespread purges of former regime (male) officials, military officers, university professors, civil servants, and others also forced many women into the work force. Many women from such families took over "male" roles and have become the family breadwinners. Ironically, the regime's desire to segregate the sexes has contributed to the professionalization of women. Women worked in very large numbers as schoolteachers before the revolution. But the population explosion and the fact that the Islamic Republic frowns on male teachers' instructing young girls has greatly increased the need for women teachers. The reluctance of traditional women to be examined by male physicians has increased the need for female doctors. In 1993, the government opened an all-female medical school in Qom; and although the intent was once again to segregate men and women (in this instance in the sensitive area of medical education), the need for women professionals continues to argue for male-female equality and to subtly undermine the concept of separate and discrete spheres for men and women.

Moreover, as noted, younger women from the regime's own constituency have proven no less eager than their supposedly upper-class, Westernized counterparts for education, jobs, advancement, and a public role. A striking demonstration of the demand of "regime women" for inclusion and a public role is the large number of wives and relatives of prominent officials and clerics who have been appointed to important positions. In the early 1990s, Fatemeh Karrubi, the wife of the prominent cleric and then Speaker of the Majlis, Mehdi Karrubi, was head of a major complex of hospitals operated by the Martyrs' Foundation. One of President Rafsanjani's daughters headed the Society for Women's Solidarity; another daughter was head of the national council of women's sports organizations and deputy president of Iran's Olympic Committee. Zahra Mostafavi, Khomeini's daughter, headed the Women's Society of the Islamic Republic, another major organization dealing with women's affairs. A'zam Taleqani, the daughter of the prominent cleric Ayatollah Mahmud Taleqani, and Ateqeh Raja'i, the wife of a former prime minister, were members of parliament; Zahra Rahnavard, wife of former prime minister Mir Hosein Musavi, is a much-published columnist and author, writing on Islam and women's affairs, and a member of the Cultural and Social Council for Women.

The regime has also felt obligated to appoint young professional women from its own constituency to head cultural, educational, children's, and —obviously—women's organizations. In 1995, the government announced with much fanfare the appointment of a woman as deputy minister of health. This was the Islamic Republic's first female deputy minister and the

highest position a woman achieved in the civil service since the revolution.
In the 1992 Majlis elections, nine women candidates were successful. Again,
the government's desire to appear "correct" on the women's question was
partly the explanation; whatever their abilities, the women could not even
have stood as candidates without official sanction. The number of women
in high-level public positions does not match the role women were playing
in the government under the former regime. At the time of the revolution,
there had been two women ministers, seven women were serving as deputy
ministers, and one woman was serving as an ambassador. (No women have
been appointed as ambassadors by the Islamic Republic.) Nevertheless, it is
clear that the government feels it must show it is also in the business of
advancing the role of women in various areas.

Having initially ignored and diminished the role of the Women's Organization of Iran, the government again reversed course in the 1990s and has
created a panoply of organizations devoted exclusively to women's affairs
and run either by relatives of prominent officials or by women who rose
through the ranks in revolutionary period organizations. Several have
already been mentioned. Among the others are the President's Office for
Women's Affairs, the International Office for Women's Affairs in the Foreign Ministry, the Office for the Promotion of Rural Women's Activities, the
Office of Women's Affairs at the Ministry of Justice, and the commissions
on women's affairs in each province and in government organizations.

There is no longer a minister of state for women's affairs, but the president of Iran has a special adviser on women's issues; the Council for
Women's Affairs reports directly to the president as well. Most ministries
and major government organizations are required to set up offices for
women's affairs (forty such units had been set up by 1995), and the government sponsors several conferences a year dealing with various issues relating to women. Resistance to such developments continues as well. In the
1992–96 session, the Majlis refused to entertain repeated attempts by
women deputies to set up a parliamentary committee for women's affairs.

Reversal on Family Planning

The government's about-face on family planning also underlines the complex interplay in the Islamic Republic among ideology, gender politics,
Islamic law, and practical considerations. After the revolution, abortions,
which had been permitted up to the first trimester, were banned. This
restriction was in keeping with Islamic law, which does not permit abor-

tions. However, the new regime also shelved the family planning program launched under the monarchy and closed down all the family planning centers. Although Islamic law traditionally frowned on contraception (women, even in medieval Islam, privately practiced various forms of contraception), the indifference of the Islamic Republic to family planning was rooted in ideology rather than Islamic law.

The revolutionary regime was determined to overturn much of what the old order represented, and family planning and population control were regarded with suspicion as Western-inspired. The idea took root that power lay in numbers and that an increase in the population of Muslims was a blessing rather than a bane. When Ayatollah Khomeini called for the creation of "an army of 20 million," he articulated the idea of "a nation in arms," in which every young man was prepared, if necessary, to sacrifice his life to defend the Islamic revolution against its enemies. The "army of 20 million" slogan was taken up as a battle cry by the proponents of expanding the revolutionary guards and creating an army of popular forces. It also became a battle cry for the proponents of population growth.

In addition, the idea of burgeoning numbers of young men (and women) joining the ranks and strengthening the cause of revolutionary Islam fit in nicely with the gender policy of the Islamic Republic. It reinforced the emphasis the new constitution placed on the centrality of the family in the new order. It buttressed the vision of women as mothers and child rearers, contributing to the revolutionary Islamic cause by raising ever-growing numbers of dedicated youth.

The family planning program was thus allowed to languish. On the eve of the revolution, this program was not yet extensive and consisted primarily of providing birth control pills to women who might not be expected, on their own, to discover this method of contraception; a limited program to educate women in basic, natural birth control methods; and an effort to encourage both men and women to limit the size of their families. A negative incentive was introduced in the mid-1970s. Child benefits available to civil servants were limited to two children. However, birthrates were beginning to fall, and on the eve of the revolution population growth was estimated to be running at 2.9 percent annually.

In the postrevolutionary period, birthrates began to climb steeply. In addition to the abandonment of family planning and encouragement of large families, there were other contributory factors: the legal age of marriage had been reduced; polygamy was on the rise; and ration coupons were based on the size of family. The widespread assumption that, under the new dispensation, the Islamic state would provide for the underprivileged persisted. The consequences of these policies and attitudes for population growth became evident in the 1986–87 census, conducted almost exactly a decade after the revolution. The 1976–77 population of just under 36 million had increased by nearly 14 million to 49.4 million. Population growth, estimated at 2.9 percent a year in the decade before 1976–77, was estimated at 3.9 percent for the decade 1976–77 to 1986–87. In the five years between 1987 and 1992, population growth had continued at just under 3.3 percent annually, and by 1991–92, the population had grown to an estimated 58.2 million. Even assuming a much lower annual growth rate of 2.9 percent, the government would have to create each year 600,000 new jobs and build 40,000 classrooms and 500,000 housing units.*

Faced with these prospects, in 1990 the government sharply reversed course. A full-fledged birth control program was launched. The government set up "health houses" to provide women in rural areas with the full range of birth control devices, including pills and diaphragms. Men were offered vasectomies. The main avenues of Tehran and other cities were plastered with billboards lauding the advantages of a small family of four. Religious leaders and preachers suddenly changed tack and began to promote the moral imperatives of birth control and family planning in their sermons and on radio and television programs.

The Battle of the Hairlines

The government's social policy toward women is also in disarray. The signs are everywhere. Men and women are segregated on buses. But in taxis (which in Tehran are shared due to the shortage of public transport) men and women—perfect strangers—sit sandwiched together. Men and women stand next to one another in long lines to do the daily shopping, and, naturally, they talk to one another. The government separates men and women on the ski slopes, but at lunchtime families, both men and women, eat together. On university campuses, boys and girls sit on separate benches. But they mix in cafes and ice cream parlors, keeping a watchful eye out for the "morals police." Sport activities are segregated, but on Fridays young men and women hike together and listen to Western music in the hills above

---

*Statistics from Jahangir Amuzegar, *Iran's Economy under the Islamic Republic* (London and New York: I. B. Tauris, 1994), 61–62.

Tehran, right under the eyes of the sometimes interfering, often helpless, revolutionary guards.

Crackdowns still occur. They greatly discomfit women when they do. But these crackdowns only highlight the erratic character of government policy toward women. In the summer of 1993, for example, the government in a renewed attempt to endorse the Islamic dress code, unleashed its zealots. Young men dressed in black shirts and black pants stopped cars at crossroads, peered down at women's ankles, and hauled away "improperly" dressed women. But the angry public reaction and the excesses of the enforcers caused the government to pull back, and the crackdown sputtered out in a couple of days. A year later, the authorities decided the extra-large sunglasses some women were sporting offended Islamic sensibilities. Women were harassed and arrests were made. But the women went on wearing their sunglasses anyway.

Women, and particularly young women, as we have seen, subtly undermine the dictates of the Islamic dress code: a scarf tossed loosely around the head and shoulders, a robe a few inches shorter than regulations require, a brightly colored headdress, a hint of lipstick, manicured nails—all these are signs of the endless tug-of-war between women and the authorities. The "battle of the hairlines" is evident every day on the streets. Crackdowns bring scarves back over foreheads. The least relaxation by the authorities, and scarves recede inch by inch behind the hairline. A whole new vocabulary has come into being to describe the gradations by which women observe (or do not observe) the Islamic dress code. The *chador* is known as the "superior *hejab*." The term to describe women who show a bit of hair but cannot quite be prosecuted is "loose veiling." Dress that imitates Islamic dress but violates the dress code is "bad-veiling." The vocabulary is an indication that even here, the lines between the permissible and the impermissible are blurring. Regime women who hold public office observe the *hejab*. But Faezeh Hashemi, the president's daughter, has said while the *chador* is preferable, it should not be compulsory.

More than a decade and a half after the revolution, the Islamic Republic is clearly at a loss in dealing with its women. Regime clerics are no longer comfortable, or able, to assert, as they did in the early years of the revolution, an agenda strictly restrictive of women. Instead, leading regime clerics address the women's issue again and again, in mass Friday sermons and in other forums, trying to reconcile a restrictive vision with the idea of equality and freedom, women imagined as mothers and housewives and women imagined as professionals and active members of society, a traditional with a modernist interpretation of Islamic law.

In 1979, the Islamic Republic came to power convinced that the clock could be turned back on Iranian women. The revolutionaries believed that the vast majority of Iranian women were indifferent to what, in short, might be described as women's rights—a concept, they thought, espoused only by Westernized Iranian women and not shared by the majority of the female population. But the Iranian experience tells us otherwise. It suggests that the process of enlarging women's opportunities and role in society, through education, employment, the removal of legal obstacles, the impact of new ideas, including the idea of equality under the law, and mobilization and politicization bring about a deep change in sensibility and expectation among a very wide spectrum of women, across social and economic classes. Once this change in sensibility and expectation takes place, the Iranian experience shows, it is difficult to reverse.

Sources

This chapter is partially based on the following sources:

For a general history of the women's movement in Iran, see Parvin Paidar, *Women and the Political Process in Twentieth-Century Iran* (Cambridge: Cambridge University Press, 1995); Eliz Sanasarian, *The Women's Rights Movement in Iran: Mutiny, Appeasement, and Repression from 1900 to Khomeini* (New York: Praeger, 1981).

For the Constitutional Revolution and the history of the women's movement in early-twentieth-century Iran, see Ervand Abrahamian, *Iran between Two Revolutions* (Princeton: Princeton University Press, 1982); Janet Afari, *The Iranian Constitutional Revolution, 1906–1911: Grassroots Democracy, Social Democracy, and the Origins of Feminism* (New York: Columbia University Press, 1996); Badr al-Moluk Bamdad, *Zanan-e Irani az Enqelab-e Mashrutiyyat ta Enqelab-e Sefid* (Iranian Women from the Constitutional Revolution to the White Revolution) (Tehran: Ebne Sina, 1968); Mangol Phillip Bayat, "Women and Revolution in Iran, 1905–1911," in *Women in the Muslim World*, ed. Nikki R. Keddie and Lois Beck (Cambridge: Harvard University Press, 1978), 295–308; Guity Nashat, "Women in Prerevolutionary Iran: A Historical Overview," in *Women and Revolution in Iran*, ed. Guity Nashat (Boulder, Colo.: Westview Press, 1983), 5–35.

For the Pahlavi period, see Shahrough Akhavi, *Religion and Politics in Contemporary Iran: Clergy-State Relations in the Pahlavi Period* (Albany: State University of New York Press, 1980); Frank R. C. Bagley, "The Iranian Family Protection Law of 1967: Milestone in the Advance of Women's Rights," in *Iran and Islam*, ed. C. E. Bosworth (Edinburgh: Edinburgh University Press, 1971), 42–64; Amin Banani, *The Modernization of Iran, 1921–1941* (Stanford, Calif.: Stanford University Press,

1961); L. P. Elwell-Sutton, *Modern Iran* (London: George Rutledge, 1941); Roy Mottahedeh, *The Mantle of the Prophet: Religion and Politics in Iran* (New York: Simon and Schuster, 1985); *Khoshunat va Farhang: Asnad-e Kashf-e Hejab* (Violence and Culture: Confidential Records about the Abolition of Hijab 1313–1322) (Tehran: Shaqayeq, 1371); *Vaqe'-e Kashf-e Hejab: Asnad-e Montasher Nashodeh az Vaqe'-e Kashf-e Hejab dar Asr-e Reza Khan* (The Event of the Abolition of the Veil: Unpublished Documents regarding the Abolition of the Veil in the Reza Khan Era) (Tehran: Sazeman-e Madarek-e Farhangi-ye Enqelab-e Eslami va Moassesseh-ye Pezuhesh va Motaleat-e Farhangi, 1371); Nasser Makarem Shirazi et al., *Zan va Entekhabat* (Women and Elections) (Qom: Elmieh Press, n.d.); Gholam-Reza Vatandoust, "The Status of Iranian Women during the Pahlavi Regime" in *Women and the Family in Iran,* ed. Asghar Fathi (Leiden: J. Brill, 1985), 107–30; Women's Organization of Iran, *Zan-e Irani dar Gozashteh va Hal* (The Iranian Woman: Past and Present) (Tehran: WOI, n.d.)

For the Islamic revolution in Iran, see Hamid Algar, trans., *Constitution of the Islamic Republic of Iran* (Berkeley, Calif.: Mizan Press, 1980); Jahangir Amuzegar, *Iran's Economy under the Islamic Republic* (London and New York: I.B. Tauris, 1994); Shaul Bakhash, *The Reign of the Ayatollahs: Iran and the Islamic Revolution* (New York: Basic Books, 1984); Said Amir Arjomand, *The Turban for the Crown: The Islamic Revolution in Iran* (New York: Oxford University Press, 1988); Farah Azari, ed., *Women of Iran: The Conflict with Fundamentalist Islam* (London: Ithaca Press, 1983); Mahnaz Afkhami and Erika Friedl, eds., *In the Eye of the Storm: Women in Post-Revolutionary Iran* (Syracuse, N.Y.: Syracuse University Press, 1994); Murteza Mutahhari, *The Islamic Modest Dress,* trans. Laleh Bakhtiar, (Albuquerque, N.M.: Abjad, 1988); Ali Shariati, *Fatima Is Fatima,* trans. Laleh Bakhtiar (Tehran: Hamdami Foundation, 1980); Haleh Esfandiari, "Iran: Women and Parliaments under Monarchy and Islamic Republic" *Princeton Papers in Near Eastern Studies* 2, 1993; Ruhollah Khomeini, *Sima-ye Zan da Kalam-e Imam Khomeini* (Woman as Depicted in the Words of Imam Khomeini) (Tehran: Ministry of Islamic Guidance, 1369/1990); Valentine Moghadam, "Women, Work, and Ideology in the Islamic Republic," *International Journal of Middle East Studies* 20 (1988): 221–43; Hammed Shahidian, "The Iranian Left and the 'Woman Question' in the Revolution, 1978–79," *International Journal of Middle East Studies* 26 (1994): 223–47.

Two

Great Expectations

A DECADE AND A HALF *after the revolution, most of the women I talked to,
irrespective of class and background, expressed disappointment in the revolution. The high expectations they had, for themselves and the country, have
not been realized.*

*The mass of women who joined the great marches and public prayer
meetings in the late summer and fall of 1978 and in the winter of 1978–79
came from the working- and lower-middle-class neighborhoods of Tehran.
Among them were both schoolgirls and older women. These women were,
in part, responding to the call of their clerical leaders to come out into the
streets. Many were galvanized by the figure of the revolutionary leader, Ayatollah Khomeini. Most were moved by the vision of a materially better life
and a more just society.*

*But these women also had reason to believe the revolution would
improve their lot as women. There was the heady experience of being part
of a great political movement. In mosque sermons, in the slogans repeated
over loudspeakers during the great marches, clerics stressed the special
place, the rights, the respect women would enjoy under an Islamic regime.
Except for minor issues, Ayatollah Khomeini and the clerics asserted,
women would enjoy equality with men. If the large majority of women
marched under the Islamic banner and under clerical leadership, this hardly
suggests they marched to roll back the clock on widening educational,
employment, and social opportunities for women.*

*Many middle-class and upper-middle-class women also embraced the
revolution. They left their homes and their government offices to join or
observe the demonstrations, many even taking their children along. In
banks, hospitals, universities, and government offices, they organized and
took part in sit-ins and strikes. Some formed strike assistance committees,
distributed revolutionary pamphlets, and collected money and food for the*

needy. They donated blood and did volunteer work at hospitals. These women imagined the revolution would lead to a more democratic, more open, and more just society. They looked back to the abortive nationalist movement under Mossadegh in the 1950s and imagined the revolution would, finally, realize nationalist aspirations.

The revolution, a businesswoman told me, politicized even the most apolitical among her friends and colleagues. Or, as another put it, after two decades of silence, politics suddenly became the topic of heated discussion everywhere—in hospitals, government offices, banks, classrooms, shops, and streets. There was only one shared goal, one woman recalled—the success of the revolution—and no sacrifice seemed too great to achieve it. There was a sense of oneness, of bonding, recalled a former university professor, when class, position, and family no longer mattered.

Most of these middle-class women had grown up in Muslim households. But they were not practicing Muslims. Their knowledge of the detailed rituals of Islam was superficial. Few understood the depth of religious feeling among the population at large. When the Islamic headdress proliferated among female students on university campuses before the revolution, for example, women professors attributed this display to youthful rebelliousness. They imagined that Islam, clerical leadership, and the invocation of Ayatollah Khomeini's name were merely an instrument to facilitate the overthrow of the monarchy. They believed that after the revolution, the clerics would return to their mosques, the government would be secular, and religion would remain a private matter and of concern primarily to the masses. The left and secular liberals dominated the discourse in the newspapers and magazines that these women read, and these journals depicted the brewing revolutionary movement in classical, European, secular terms. Very few imagined the revolution would lead to the establishment of an Islamic Republic.

The revolutionary euphoria did not last very long. Many of the women I interviewed were shocked by the widespread arrests and executions that followed the fall of the monarchy. This was not the "kind and gentle" revolution they had envisaged. Then came the purges and the dismissals of friends and colleagues, the daily humiliations visited on women at work and on the street. The streets themselves became unpleasant and dangerous. Neighborhood revolutionary committees entered homes, arresting neighbors and family members. The fear of the proverbial knock on the door, one woman told me, was palpable. An elderly woman who had lived in Europe during the Nazi terror recalled that the sound of footsteps on her street in the stillness of the night in Tehran brought back memories of roundups by the German police. The fear was so widespread, a young girl recalled, that when there was a loud knock on their front door one evening, she saw her father walking toward the door holding his hands up, a frightened look on his face.

Some of the women I interviewed imagined that the brutality of the first year of the revolution would be a passing phase. For many others, illusions died within the first year. Their dreams for the revolution turned into a nightmare. They had hoped for a democracy; they ended up with a theocracy. They wanted to participate in a new Iran; they found themselves excluded and ostracized for who they were. As one woman told me, "Of the famous revolutionary triad, 'Independence, Freedom, Islamic Republic,' all we got was the Islamic Republic."

■ ■ ■ ■ ■

Amineh: For me the revolution meant the various declarations and announcements issued by Ayatollah Khomeini during his stay in France, urging Iranians not to kill each other. The expectations of the people from the revolution were palpable for me and a lot of my friends. We felt it. It was the revolution of the masses, uprising by the population. That is how I perceived the revolution.

I was spending the year before the revolution in Paris. I followed the developments in Iran very closely. I carefully studied the leaflets of Bazargan and Bakhtiar. I wanted the National Front to take over;* I trusted its leaders. They were honest, respectable, clean, and patriotic men.

All my life, since my student days, I was against the Shah's regime. The Shah's government was corrupt, and I knew that one day it was going to fall. So when the anti-Shah movement started in 1978, it did not come as a surprise to me. For me, this was what I had anticipated all along. I went back to Iran in the summer of 1978 and became politically active.

---

*The National Front, led by Mohammad Mossadegh, sparked the movement that led in 1951–53, to the nationalization of the Iranian oil industry. Although Mossadegh was overthrown and the activities of the National Front circumscribed after 1953, many Iranians continued to view the Front as the party that spoke for nationalist aspirations. Mehdi Bazargan and Shapour Bakhtiar were both National Front leaders although, after a falling out, they went separate ways.

The turning point for me was not the burning of the Rex Cinema in Abadan in August,* but the killing at Jaleh Square on that Black Friday in September.** I have a vivid memory from that day. I was at home. I heard helicopters flying over my house toward the square. The news of people being shot at and killed, and of some hospitals not treating the wounded, was shocking. I called some friends and we formed a rescue committee. We were all nationalists but also leftists. It was then that I felt the revolution would not be bloodless. I sensed there would be more killings. But what I did not foresee were the executions without trial that took place after the revolution and the takeover by the clergy.

By late September 1978, I was already involved on a day-to-day basis with various revolutionary groups. We were dealing regularly with the clerics. I had met Ayatollah Taleqani, I had listened to him. He had impressed me. Taleqani was a follower of Mossadegh, and for me the revolution meant the fulfillment of Mossadegh's ideas. In those days we met regularly with some clerics to coordinate our activities. In our daily encounters with them, we did not sense any of their fundamentalism. We were not aware of their extremism. As for me, I longed for democracy and a vigorous national culture.

My disillusion came when Ayatollah Khomeini, a mystic, told the nation that those members of the old regime who were arrested were guilty. It was at that moment that I severed my relations with some of my revolutionary comrades. Unlike them, I did not think that the revolution justified executing people without a proper trial and a legal defense. You can say that disillusion hit me very quickly.

■ ■ ■ ■ ■

Mari: The year of the revolution I was teaching at Tehran University. Our university was at the forefront of all revolutionary events. Like many others,

---

*The Rex Cinema fire in Abadan in August 1978 cost a great many lives. Although it appears that the perpetrators were young fundamentalists, at the time the fire was blamed on the authorities and played an important role in further discrediting the Shah and his government in the agitation that led to the Islamic revolution.

**In September 1978, troops fired on demonstrators who violated martial law regulations announced late the night before. The incident also fed antigovernment feeling and was another major turning point in the revolutionary agitation. Although the number killed is not known, popular belief was that hundreds died in the shooting.

I was also swept off my feet by the revolution. I took part in marches, gave blood for the wounded, and was longing for a just and clean government.

My most vivid memory of that period was standing in the university in front of a barbed-wire wall covered with cartoons against the Shah. I don't remember how tall or how wide the wall was. It was so impressive and eerie. After that, I knew the Shah could not last any longer. I had always disliked him, and I was euphoric when he left. I felt the country was mine. I was willing to teach for free. We talked among ourselves about a republic.

I remember the night Ayatollah Khomeini returned to Iran I was very exited and agitated. I could not sleep. His arrival meant that the revolution had finally succeeded. I must confess, I was not familiar with Ayatollah Khomeini's ideas. I had listened to some of his tapes and did not form any opinion. As for Ali Shariati, I found him rather shallow. I could not understand why he had so many followers among the younger generation. I must confess, I was not aware Islam had gained so much ground among the students. I noticed that the number of girls observing the Islamic headdress was increasing in my classes, and quite often these girls would discuss the sociology of Islam. I never considered this a social movement, but rather a show of defiance against the system. Neither the leftist students nor those with Islamic tendencies were very open in class about their ideas. I was too worried about communism to pay much attention to Islam.

The killing at Jaleh Square, that Black Friday, was the focal point of the revolution. I rushed to a blood center and gave blood. I heard about people being shot in the square. I heard about the hospitals being overwhelmed by the sheer numbers of the wounded. I tried to help as much as I could. Look: I was involved in the revolutionary fervor morning, noon, and night. There was no other alternative. How could anybody stand by and just be an observer?

■ ■ ■ ■ ■

Shokouh: I was not impressed for a moment by the demonstrations in the month preceding the revolution. I am a physician. I deal with reality and with needy people. I was not at all political, but I was annoyed at upper-class women who put on a scarf and took part in demonstrations and marches in the morning and went to parties in their usual dresses in the evenings and discussed politics in an abstract way. They were so naive and ill informed. They were followers of a bunch of intellectuals who had no convictions, and they thought they could change the future of the country and the world. I can still remember how adamant they were in their arguments that Islam was just a front, a facade. Everybody went to those marches: university professors, engineers, doctors. If you ask me, the nurses in any hospital are more intelligent than any intellectual you can name. These women worked hard for a living and constantly tried to improve their life. Nurses knew what they had gained before the revolution. They not only came from humble backgrounds, but in their daily work they dealt with ordinary people. They were quite aware of what they might lose.

At the university, I used to see more and more girl students covering their hair and sitting separated from the boys. They were explaining that Islam must be observed and respected. This was before the revolution. I did not pay much attention; one expects students to be radicals.

Of course I was aware of the shortcomings around me. I returned from Europe at the end of my studies. I noticed there was something basically wrong with our society. We had lots of pseudointellectuals. They only talked about improving things in an abstract way, but they did not lift a finger for the country.

Then the revolution became real and the executions started—those horrible pictures one saw day after day. It was frightening. I can never forget the revolutionary courts, people we knew appearing in front of those revolutionary tribunals. It was scary, very scary.

■ ■ ■ ■ ■

Farideh: I was working in the government when the revolutionary movement started. I was very worried. On the one hand, it was exiting to see people so united. On the other hand, I was anxious. I did not know where this was going to lead. I worried that in our country, because the people did not have a political culture, one could easily use religion to explain any ideology and mislead people. Religion can be very positive and it can also be negative. Whenever I asked people, "What next?" their answer was, "We shall opt for a religious government first and then replace it." I did not believe for a minute that religion would simply fade away and that we would have a secular government. The secular opposition was naive to think this was the case.

I watched all the marches. I went to demonstrations and meetings as an observer. I listened to various political groups discussing their expectations and ambitions for the revolution. Not for a moment was I fooled by all this. I remember visiting the faculty of engineering at Tehran University on the day of the revolution. The Mojahedin, the Fadayan, were celebrating their victory;* and I thought to myself, "Give yourself six months, and we shall see how you were deceived and what hit you."

I was a technocrat in the public sector, very apolitical. Because of my position, I knew how bad the financial situation of the country was. People felt futile, useless. Not only did the poor complain, but those who were well off did not stop criticizing the government. Everybody was unhappy. So the victory of the revolutionary movement was exciting, but on me it had a sobering effect. My vivid memory of those days is of young men dressed in revolutionary green uniforms attacking and plundering the military barracks. It was so unreal, it was like watching a movie.

■ ■ ■ ■ ■

Elaheh: I am a university professor in my early forties. The year before the revolution I was studying for my master's degree and I was working in a foundation. One of my colleagues would give us the writings of Ayatollah Khomeini to read. I was not religious, nor was I fond of the clergy. But I accepted the concept of religion as a private belief. I remember that both at the university and at work there were two religious groups, the followers of Ayatollah Khomeini and the followers of Ayatollah Shariatmadari.** I brought this to the attention of one of my friends who was active in the first group; he cautioned me not to mention these groups, so as not to attract any attention to a split among the religious activists.

I did not like the Shah and was hoping for his downfall. I wanted us to

---

*The Mojahedin is a Marxist-Islamic guerrilla organization that operated under the monarchy. After the revolution, the Mojahedin were active as a radical political movement until 1982, when they were outlawed and repressed. The Fadayan is a Marxist guerrilla organization that also operated under the monarchy. After the Islamic revolution, the organization competed with other groups for political power before it was crushed.

**Ayatollah Kazem Shariatmadari, one of Iran's senior clerics in the period before the revolution, took a position that was far more moderate than that adopted by Ayatollah Khomeini.

get rid of the pressure of colonialism. I took part in all the demonstrations against the regime. I was not at all familiar with the clergy. What I heard of their programs did not seem appealing to me. I was hoping for a liberal and independent government with no ties to foreign powers.

Before the revolution, I taught for a year at a mixed high school. The students were very bright. I remember one day we were told that some people were objecting to the nature of this school. They did not want the mixing of the two sexes. They filed an official complaint that the school was propagating prostitution. The school closed down a few months before the revolution. That, for me, was an encounter with religious thinking.

I did not have any illusions about the existing political parties. So once the revolution succeeded and the National Front did not come to power, I withdrew from any kind of political activity. All I wanted after the revolution and the setback of the democratic forces was to leave the country and go abroad and get a Ph.D. I was done with the revolution, the demonstrations, and the killings.

■ ■ ■ ■ ■

Darya: I am a lawyer by training, I am familiar with Islamic law. From the moment there were threats against women in the months before the revolution, I knew we were heading for an Islamic government. Already in the fall of 1977, one heard rumors that the university students were demanding separate transportation for women. There were rumors that unveiled women were being harassed on the streets, and some had acid thrown at them. A few women's centers were also attacked. One felt there was an underground movement with religious tendencies becoming more active by the day. I became quite uneasy when the Shah, addressing a gathering of women in the late 1970s, referred to the religious opposition to women's emancipation by reciting this poem: "Let the moon shine and let the dog bark." We all were expecting some changes, but not a dismantling of that whole system.

My first memory of the revolution was when Ayatollah Khomeini banned the participation of the leftist group, the Fadayan, in demonstrations. I knew this was the end of democracy in the Western sense. Soon enough we found out that when the government talked about "freedom" and "democracy," it meant freedom and democracy within an Islamic context.

When the Family Protection Law was suspended, not only did I sense that the condition of women would regress to what it had been before the passage of the law—namely, back to polygamy, temporary marriage, and divorce instigated by the husband—I also had a feeling that Ms. Farrokhru Parsa was going to be a victim of this new order and that she would be executed.

It was obvious that the Islamic Republic was attacking women and education under the monarchy. The government referred to schools as places of prostitution, especially mixed schools.

I had read Ayatollah Khomeini's books. I knew we were heading for an Islamic Republic, but I thought it would be more like Pakistan, not the government of the Islamic jurists.

■ ■ ■ ■ ■

Gowhar: I am a lawyer. I was a judge, actually one of the first women judges in prerevolutionary Iran. I even presided over a court. But after the revolution, when women could no longer become judges, I was demoted to the rank of a legal assistant. It is like removing the president of a university and making her a janitor.

I was in tune with the revolution. I believed in it. I was young and full of idealism. Today, I look back at those days as sheer stupidity. I was very active in the revolutionary movement. I was a member of the strike committee in the Ministry of Justice. We used to have long discussions, and we wanted to become Sweden or Switzerland. Funny, isn't it?

■ ■ ■ ■ ■

Soudabeh: I am a physician, and in 1978 I was in Tehran working eight to ten hours a day at the hospital. There were demonstrations and marches. I did not take part in any of those events. I stayed in the hospital. Everybody I knew took part in those marches—the upper class, the middle class, the leftist doctors in our hospital. Today the common thing to say is that the university professors and the intellectuals are to be blamed, that by going to those marches they set an example for the people. But, as I said earlier, everybody marched.

In the hospital in those days people were talking nothing but politics. It was difficult to get any work done. We were a government hospital, and we were treating the wounded all the time. I did not care what their political affiliation was. For me they were all patients who needed treatment. Some of the wounded were very worried that we would not accept them if they did not belong to the right political group. I could not understand their concern. For me it was very odd as a doctor to be asked by a patient admitted to the hospital to be treated fairly. Some patients, no matter how seriously they were wounded, left immediately after receiving treatment. They felt the hospital could not give them the necessary protection. I saw myself first and foremost as a doctor, not a political activist, and did not get involved in political debates.

Our leftist doctors were out of the closet, and they and many others wanted the Shah to leave the country. I watched his departure on television. An era came to an end. I, like many others, was hoping for a national government. I never thought that religion would play such a dominant role in our lives. I was not familiar with religious movements.

I have a very vivid personal memory of the revolution. On the day when the military barracks fell, I stayed on duty for twenty-four hours. The number of wounded we treated was very high. We were all working round the clock. At some stage I remember seeing a sixteen-year-old boy who was shot in the head among the wounded. The brain was gone, the artery was cut. But a team of us doctors tried to resuscitate him. I still recall the moment his pulse started beating. We succeeded in keeping him alive. Maybe I stick to this memory because it is so positive, it is life, compared to all the morbid things that were happening in those days.

■ ■ ■ ■ ■

Manijeh: I was a high school student when the revolution started. We lived in Abadan, in the south. We were an ordinary Iranian family with religious inclinations. The family observed the fast, made donations to the poor, etc. My mother's family was more religious. The women wore the *chador*. At school we did not discuss politics. It was as if Abadan were drowning in a sea of silence.

The first time I heard about Ayatollah Khomeini was when he left Iraq for France. My cousins in Tehran were more political. They knew about

Shariati. They read his books and listened to his tapes. They even started observing Islam more seriously.

The crucial moment, the turning point, the revolution—everything—started for me with the fire at the Rex Cinema in Abadan. We lived near the center of town, not very far from the cinema. It was a summer evening, around nine o'clock in the evening. We heard fire trucks and sirens. We got worried and went to the center of town. I saw the movie house surrounded by people. There was a terrible stench in the air. People were shouting and crying and trying to open the fire hydrants. Some said they still could hear moaning from inside the movie house. We went back home. But my uncle was among the men who broke the doors and went into the cinema. Later when he came home he was a mental case. He stayed four hours under the shower. He kept on saying, "I can't get rid of the stench." For weeks he would wash his hands all the time. He had tried to remove bodies from the cinema.

The next day all hell broke loose in Abadan. Rumors started circulating about people being gassed, doors being locked from the outside. Suddenly Abadan became politicized. Leaflets and pamphlets were distributed morning, noon, and night. There were demonstrations, schools were closed. The workers at the oil refinery went on strike.

I don't have any memories of the Shah leaving Iran. I was not concerned with that. But I wanted the revolution to succeed. The day the barracks fell in Tehran, I remember being on the street in Abadan. It was a sunny day, people were distributing the Iranian flag and offering sweets. I thought if there is such a thing as heaven on earth this must be it.

■ ■ ■ ■ ■

Nazanin: I remember the day the Shah left Iran, I was mourning my father's death. I found a red paper flower and wore it in my hair. I wanted to show my joy. I was then working as a social secretary. Today, I am a translator and I write articles for magazines.

For me the revolution started with the fire at the Rex Cinema in Abadan. It did not matter who did it, SAVAK* or another group. It was a monstrous

---

*SAVAK is the acronym for the State Organization for Security and Intelligence, or secret police, under the reign of Mohammad Reza Pahlavi.

affair. After that the revolution was inevitable. I saw the marches, the demonstrations. I was full of sympathy, although I did not take part in those events. For hours I watched all sorts of people passing in front of me—not only bearded men and veiled women but men wearing ties and women with no head cover. I recognized intellectuals, writers, artists. I was choking with emotions.

My sympathy was with the National Front. I had known some of their leaders, and I had found them thoughtful, substantial, and respectable people. But it was a false impression I had. The National Front was not organized, nor did it have a cohesive leadership.

I believed Ayatollah Khomeini would come and settle in Qom. I wanted the revolution to win. I was hoping for some justice and equality. I only saw the secular side of it, not the religious one.

I got frightened the day the military barracks fell. I saw several trucks with young bearded men carrying arms. The people in our district were cheering them. Some even suggested we should slaughter a sheep in front of these trucks in celebration. Suddenly I panicked: this was mob mentality. I was worried that the brakes would no longer work. Once thirteen- and fifteen-year-old gun-toting boys appeared at crossroads, I knew there was no way back and the revolution was lost.

■ ■ ■ ■ ■

Ayesheh: I was running a public institution in Tehran when the revolution started. I could not believe my eyes when I saw those demonstrations. I asked myself who these people were. I was sure they had been brainwashed. How could it be otherwise? Suddenly I had secretaries in the office making the most absurd suggestions, for example telling me not to go to nightclubs or not to behave this way or that way. When I asked them who had ever seen me in a nightclub, they did not know what to answer. Well, I had never been to a nightclub. I am only giving you this example to show you the absurdity of the ideas circulating in our office in those days. The impression I got—just an impression, a feeling—was that the employees were taking their orders from someone, someplace not familiar to me, and were repeating them the next day without giving it a thought.

In our establishment, the work slowdown started in the summer of 1978. The girls who worked for me stopped taking orders and listening to me.

Instead of working from seven to three, they worked from nine to twelve. By September, the atmosphere had become very political. The employees talked openly about the need for the Shah to leave. They also wanted a change in the administration of our institution. I was a seasoned person. I felt that any change, whether local or national, would be detrimental. I worried that the educated class would leave. Not for a moment did I imagine that the religious people would take over. I did not have the illusion that a national government would come to power. After the Shah left, I told my son a chapter has been closed. It would never be the same again.

■ ■ ■ ■ ■

Fatemeh: I was running a private business. Once the anti-Shah demonstrations started, our business was affected, too. We lost a lot of customers. I was worried for my workers, the business, and my customers, so whenever we were asked to close the office, I listened. We used to receive anonymous phone calls telling us to close our doors for a few hours. I never knew who these people were, but I was wise enough not to antagonize them by disagreeing with them. We even had patrols formed by the workers to guard the premises. Looting was not uncommon in those days. As our sales fell, I felt I had to reduce the work force. I did not know that among our seasonal workers we had some with leftist tendencies. They were distributing revolutionary, leftist leaflets. I was warned by some of the old workers that too much political discussion was going on on the floor. Anyway, I managed to give them severance pay and terminate their work. I was fully preoccupied looking after my business and my old workers. I was not at all political and just followed developments as they unfolded.

My first memory of the revolution was when a high-ranking government official took refuge from the mob on our grounds. My workers took him in for a few hours and sheltered him. I knew that the mob might attack our premises at any moment and ransack them, but we could not just let the man go. Later I saw the picture of his executed body in the papers.

■ ■ ■ ■ ■

Atefeh: In 1978, I was in Tehran, running my own private business. I was never interested in politics. I was and I still am a very sensitive and intuitive person. Like many others around me I was swept off my feet by the revolution. The revolutionary fever was contagious, and I caught the bug, too. I had great hopes in the revolution. I was an optimist. I believed that the majority of the people would benefit from it, their lives would improve. It did not matter if my conditions would deteriorate. I wanted other children to have the privileges my children had had.

I believed in the people. The first year of the revolution was the best year of my life and that of the country. There was a deep and palpable feeling of brotherhood, equality, solidarity, and unity among the nation. It was like a dream. But over the years the dream gradually faded away. Maybe if my knowledge of religion had been greater, I would have been more realistic and less of a dreamer.

My strongest memory of those days are the marches, the sea of people covering miles and miles of the main avenue in Tehran. How can I ever forget those scenes, wave after wave of men and women from all walks of life marching next to each other? You felt as if they were walking with an extraordinary self-confidence.

■ ■ ■ ■ ■

Masoumeh: I was in Tehran. I was the chief librarian at a cultural institution. I just could not believe the rapidity with which the revolutionary movement was developing. I could not believe how phony the previous regime was. I remember people were talking politics all the time. I went to watch the marches. What did I see? A sea of people. It was frightening. I did not expect heavenly conditions, but I also did not believe for a moment that there would be such an upheaval.

My first memory of the revolution? They fired my husband, one of the most honorable people in this world. For the newcomers who took power it did not make any difference whether you were decent or corrupt, or what your job was. In their eyes you were guilty by association. He was very stoic about it. He understood the revolutionaries better than I did. He told me and our children that his turn to serve his country was over, and now it was their turn. "Let us see," he would say, "what they can achieve."

Soon after that, it was my turn to be fired. Every day the young people who worked in our office—the same young people who had come back from the United States and whom I had helped to adjust at work and to understand the revolutionary conditions—put out lists of people they thought should be purged. They were members of the newly formed Islamic society. One day as I was sitting in my office, a male colleague walked in and burst into tears. I thought he had lost one of his close relatives. You remember in those days people were being arrested, executed, and so forth? All he could say was that he had seen my name "on the board." I was shell-shocked. I collected my books and my things. I called my husband to come and pick me up. The first thought that occurred to me was, "How are we going to survive financially?" Since my husband had lost his job, I had become the sole breadwinner in the family. From the office I went to the dentist. I had had a previous appointment. On the dentist's chair, I lost my composure. I started sobbing and crying. He never charged me for the work he did that day.

■ ■ ■ ■

Ladan: I was in Iran, working for an educational institution. I was in planning. At the beginning, like a lot of other people, I was sympathetic to the revolution. I was neither attracted to the left nor toward the religious groups. I was for a nationalist solution. With a friend, who was a university professor, we went to one of the marches. Of course we wore the scarf. We saw a lot of our other friends. They were all marching. I was sure that the future meant freedom of speech, freedom of the press, a kind of democracy, even a more balanced class structure. There was nothing wrong with having those aspirations. Bakhtiar or Bazargan were fine with me, it did not make a difference.

My first memory? Well, people you knew were being arrested and executed. But one incident stuck in my mind. It was early evening, I remember. We were sitting in the house of a close relative. Suddenly I saw men climbing up the wall and coming into the house. Not strangers, people this relative had known for a long time. They were the shopkeepers in his street, the butcher, the ironmonger, the owner of a restaurant, and others. They took a lot of stuff with them. They tore paintings. I remember sitting there and watching how they were questioning the man of the house the whole night. They left at dawn. The house was outside Tehran. Very early in the morning, another shopkeeper came. He had brought twenty liters of gasoline and urged the man of the house, who by then was totally exhausted, to leave as quickly as possible. You see the contrast? There were good men and bad men. But our relative refused to leave. He could have gone into hiding. He, like many others, thought that since he had served his country for many decades, he had nothing to fear from the new authorities. Later he was arrested and taken to the school where a lot of the detained people were being kept. There are so many memories, all horrible. I cannot forget any of them. To this day they haunt me.

■ ■ ■ ■ ■

Nahid: I was working in the government. I spent the summer of 1978 in Paris. I followed the riots of Qom and Tabriz very closely. I was in Paris when the Shah gave his famous speech, the one in which he told the people that he heard the voice of the revolution. I thought it was already too late for such talk.

I was in Paris when Ayatollah Khomeini came to Paris. I had never heard his name. I was not a political person and did not follow the activities of the opposition. But all our friends were political. I came back in September. The first thing I noticed was that all the quiet people I knew had become political and anti-Shah. People who up to a few months ago were concerned only with obtaining a better position and promotions became revolutionaries. Our friends were giving speeches and participating in debates. I felt I had fallen behind, and I could no longer reach them. But I also knew we were going downhill.

I was not sure what the revolution was going to achieve. I thought we will have more freedom, but even that notion was too vague for me. I thought maybe we will be able to determine our destiny through free elections. This was a tangible goal for me. People were just expressing their personal wishes and desires without being logical. Everybody had an agenda for his or her own kind of dictatorship.

You ask me about a first memory? How can anybody forget those executions. I felt it was wrong to kill people without trial. I never liked Hoveyda.* I think he is responsible for not having told the Shah the truth

---

*Amir Abbas Hovedya was prime minister from 1965 to 1977 and minister of the royal court in 1977–78. Closely associated with the monarchy, he was executed after the Islamic revolution.

about conditions in the country. He managed to cover up for fourteen years. But when I saw the picture of his executed body on the first page of the paper, I felt sick, very sick.

■ ■ ■ ■ ■

Touran: I was a student in America when the revolution started. I was active politically. In our discussions, we believed that all the various groups in the opposition were instrumental in making the revolution. Of course, I had heard of Ayatollah Khomeini, I had read his writings. We, I mean the students, started returning to Iran in large numbers. We came back with a lot of hope and dedication. We wanted to serve the revolution and the country. We wanted a democratic society, a socialist society. Our model was China. Yes, China. We knew we were better off economically than the Chinese, but who cared? We wanted a classless society. I must be honest with you. I and a lot of my friends did not believe there was repression in China.

The most vivid memory I have is hearing on the radio that the revolutionary forces had taken over the army barracks. They played the song "Ay Iran"(Oh! Iran). I started crying, tears of joy and happiness. I thought we were victorious, that a new era would begin. We had just returned from the streets. We were watching television with my husband and a friend, who was later executed. I will never forget that moment. We were so happy. It was our revolution. Then the executions and the killings started. The killings were not important. Some of those people had to be executed. But the pictures one saw day after day in the paper, those swollen bodies. That was so uncivilized.

■ ■ ■ ■ ■

Ramesh: I was living in America. I was newly married and had a lot of problems with my spouse. I really did not follow the events in Iran. All I knew was that I wanted a divorce and wanted to go back to my family and to Iran. I was not concerned with the revolution. I even did not follow what was taking place in Iran.

Lili: I was a housewife, living in Tabriz. My husband was working in the public sector. We led a very comfortable life. I remember how political everybody had become in those days. You would not believe this—I heard it from educated women—that once the revolution succeeds, our class will be better off because the government will distribute the oil money among us. How stupid can you be? A vivid memory for me was to see my husband's picture in the paper, renouncing his religion. He was not Muslim of course. Well, this was a facet of the revolution you learned to live with.

■ ■ ■ ■ ■

Monir: I was living in Tehran with my family, working as a lawyer. For me the revolution really started when the Rex Cinema in Abadan caught fire, and all those people died, and then the killing at Jaleh Square. By then I knew the revolution had gained momentum and you could no longer stop it—the demonstrations, the marches, the burning of buildings in Tehran, stores and schools closing sporadically. It happened gradually, but also quite fast and calculatedly.

My most vivid memory of that period was the day the Shah left Iran. I was in the south, in the city of Ahvaz. As I was about to enter a public building, I was stopped by a man who pointed to a separate entrance for women. I could not hide my surprise and dismay. He looked at me and said, "We got rid of your pimp king. Soon enough we shall deal with prostitutes such as you." I knew then that everything had changed and was changing, especially for women. I felt helpless and lost, a feeling that has come back to me many times over the last fifteen years. Let me put it to you in a nutshell: because of the revolution, I killed my true self, in order not to perish. And then, I thought, I must come back into a world that I do not know at all, a world that was cursing and undermining all our heritage and all that mattered to me.

■ ■ ■ ■ ■

Nargess: I am a lawyer, and in 1978 I was working for the government. I was the head of a legal office. I believed that we would gain freedom through the revolution. I was a democrat and was longing for a democratic system. For me democracy is as important as water and air. I was always angry at the undemocratic system we lived in. I wanted SAVAK to go.

I followed revolutionary developments very closely. The last few days before the revolution were very exciting times. It was a very special experience to be in Iran. It was like being in a novel. I remember marching with the crowd, being swept away among the mass of people walking down the main avenues of Tehran. I went to the university every day. The various political groups gathered there. I moved from one group to another and listened to their debates. There was freedom under Bakhtiar. The nation was at ease and uninhibited. After the victory of the revolution in February, everything changed. Then the killings and the executions started. Political people you knew were killed. I remember the radio was on all the time, and I was reading every newspaper that was available.

In hindsight, I think the participation of our intellectuals in the revolution was naive and like a game to them. It was as if all the intellectuals wanted was to be let loose. Once they denied these intellectuals their toys, they all started to say, "We were not involved." To me this was the most irresponsible role of the intellectuals.

■ ■ ■ ■ ■

Afsar: In 1978, I was a university professor in Tehran and an active revolutionary. I was among the organizers of a sit-in at my university, I took part in the strike at the university. I was working day and night for the revolution. We were seeking political freedom for our country. Little did we know that we would lose the social freedom we had.

Our sit-in lasted twenty days. I still remember those days with great fondness. We were three groups: the liberals, the leftists, and the Islamic group. Political ideas were still a bit blurred. We all wanted the downfall of the regime. That was our common goal. Beyond that we did not talk to each other. The Islamic group had its communal prayers and meetings and discussions, and we had ours. The left, as usual, was delivering its clichés, and we probably had ours, too. Looking back, I acknowledge that our extremism was wrong. It is much better and more doable to change the society through education than through violence.

My strongest memory of that period is when the people poured onto the university grounds and tore down the Shah's statue. Such happiness, such joy. I felt wonderful. I also remember the day when, for the first time, people approached the soldiers in the streets and offered them flowers. When the bewildered soldiers refused to accept them, the people placed the flowers in the soldiers' gun barrels. I thought to myself, "Having seen this, I could die happily that day."

■ ■ ■ ■ ■

Zohreh: The year 1978 was difficult for me. My husband was very sick, and he was being treated abroad. So I was traveling constantly. I did not have a job, but I did charity work, especially among less privileged women. I was hoping that the revolution would open new doors and frontiers for us. But my disappointment began when the government started clamping down on women. First the authorities lowered the age of marriage, then they blamed the failure of population control on women. The list can go on and on. I found the reaction of the left to women's problems very painful. In those days, I mean after the revolution, I felt very lonely. I kept asking myself, "Why can't I participate in this human wave, which is so elated and triumphant?" I, who was never part of the old regime, nor fond of it. It was very sad to be alone. It was sad to live rationally in an atmosphere where irrationality, excitement, and emotions had taken over.

■ ■ ■ ■ ■

Pouran: I came back to Iran in 1978. I had just gotten my Ph.D. in the United States. I never liked the old regime and was active in the Iranian student movement abroad. For years we had fought among ourselves about what sort of government we would like to have in Iran. I was no longer willing or ready to continue these abstract discussions. I had left Iran when I was thirteen, and I wanted to come back and live in Iran and serve my country. Today this might sound very trite, but that was how I and a lot of young, educated people felt in 1978.

When I returned to Iran, to my surprise I found the people around me, my friends, actually the whole country, polarized over the revolution. My father believed in it, and we had long discussions. My own hesitation was intuitive and not political. I did not like the murmuring about the return of the *hejab*. I went to the marches, but I never felt part of it all. I always saw myself as an observer.

My first encounter with the revolution was when my brother, his girl-friend, and I went to the north. Along the road, we took a wrong turn and we were stopped, actually arrested, by revolutionary guards. They did not listen to our explanations. They just blindfolded us and took us to the prison. They put the women in one cell and the men in another. Their behavior was so shocking that I started bleeding. I screamed so much that they finally took me to the hospital. They questioned us about our activities against the government. It took a lot of arguing to persuade them that we were just simple tourists. That, to me, showed the irrationality of the mentality of some of the people who were taking over.

■ ■ ■ ■ ■

Jila: In the summer of 1978 I was in Germany. I was very nervous and worried about the events in Iran. I did not like the Shah's attacking the oil cartels in his speeches. I knew that one day he would pay for it.

I returned to Tehran in the fall of 1978, just in time to see the demonstrations. To this day I cannot believe that the demonstrations were spontaneous, they were so well organized. As the demonstrations grew in size and numbers, I, too, thought that the Shah had to go. I did not want any killing or bloodshed.

When I saw that the demonstrations were carried out in the name of religion, I knew that the religious people would come to power. While my friends and colleagues were talking about a national government and parliament, I told them I did not think the United States wanted such an outcome. I knew that the United States had a different agenda in Iran. Didn't it once get rid of a nationalist government, through a so-called coup? Later, many of my friends, remembering what I had told them, credited me, as a woman, with a sharper sixth sense.

The day of the revolution, when the military barracks fell, I had a meeting in my office. I was driving, not aware of what was happening in the city. A revolutionary guard stopped me and asked me where I was going. I told him I had a meeting. As I was driving I heard shooting. Then in the office my husband phoned me and told me he was picking me up. I went home and spent the rest of the day in front of the television. Then the killings and the executions started, all in the name of religion. I could not grasp it. I really don't want to talk about it. It brings back such horrible memories.

■ ■ ■ ■ ■

Lida: In the summer of 1978, I was an intern in one of the main hospitals in Tehran. I was working long hours every day. In the evenings and at night people would stand for hours in the streets and have political discussions. One could not be indifferent to what was going on. People who did not have any political experience got involved in the revolutionary movement. I also knew that people were disappearing in our neighborhood. I did not grasp the importance of all these developments. I was too busy with my work to become politically involved. I just did not want people to get hurt or get killed.

Once the shootings started, we got busy with treating the wounded. I remember in the operating room we were constantly operating and removing bullets. The director of the hospital had told us to admit everybody at any time. I remember the staff was working round the clock. I just did not have the time to figure out the political ramifications of what was happening in the streets.

■ ■ ■ ■ ■

Partow: I must be among the few people who did not pay much attention to what was going on in 1978. I was not a working woman. I was a happy housewife raising three children and looking after my family. I was told that the Shah was a benevolent man and that the people liked him. So it came as a shock to me when I heard about the demonstrations. Even when the Shah went abroad, I thought he was just taking a trip and that he would return. Was I innocent, naive, or stupid? I don't know. I lived a sheltered life in the suburbs of Tehran and hardly went to the inner city. Once the revolution unfolded, I started watching the daily occurrences on television—the return of Imam Khomeini, the executions, the proclamations. I was just not prepared for it.

Nayyer: When the revolution started, I was working in the government. I was in the United States for a short visit. I read about martial law in the cities of Iran. I could not believe this was happening. When I came back, I noticed that everything was changing rapidly. To me the changes were the result of the explosion of a nation that could no longer accept the status quo.

For an educated person like myself, on paper, the left and its ideas were more attractive. Its leaders were articulating their views in a more coherent way. I felt the nation, the people, had demands, and the left was expressing these aspirations. I thought the people could not go wrong. When Bazargan was appointed as prime minister, we all continued to work. Gradually some of my friends resigned, but I stayed on. I wanted to serve my country. Frankly, I did not have much choice. My husband had lost his job, and the family depended on my income.

I will never forget the day when I was waiting in the street for a taxi and a bearded man spat in my face. I started crying and cried all the way home in the cab. I stood for hours under the shower washing myself. I felt so humiliated. To this day I don't know why he did it. Was it because of my looks, my *hejab*, my bearing?

■ ■ ■ ■ ■

Sousan: In 1978 I was a university professor, teaching international relations. It was an exhilarating time for all of us at the university. As you recall, all the agitation started from the universities. We were constantly producing leaflets and taking a stand on every issue.

The atmosphere in the prerevolutionary days was such that one believed that the country was moving toward an ideal condition. I remember during one of the marches, when people from different classes were walking shoulder to shoulder, a friend telling me that "for the first time I feel we are all Iranians and equal."

My expectations from the revolution was a government for the people, freedom and independence. I was not familiar with Islamic matters. We did not have a cleric in the family. My knowledge of Islam was limited to what one was told by family and by household help. I don't think that under the previous regime there was a way one could find out openly about the Islamic groups. I had heard about Ayatollah Taleqani, I had great respect for him. I knew he was a member of the National Front, but I had not read his sermons. Looking back, I must confess that despite all my studies, I was quite innocent both in my expectations of the revolution and in the way I analyzed the events as they occurred.

■ ■ ■ ■ ■

Nasrin: I was for the revolution, with the revolution, and to this day I support the idea of the revolution. I never consciously wanted to become political, but in those days you could not help it. I had finished high school and was preparing for the university entrance examination. I was also working as a teacher in the outskirts of Tehran. I was teaching rural girls and boys. I saw their suffering and their needs. I believed the country needed a revolution to address all these problems.

■ ■ ■ ■ ■

Zahra: I was eighteen when the revolution occurred. We were a political family, constantly talking about politics. The revolution did not teach me any lessons I did not know.

I was a first year student at the university. I lived in a dormitory for girls. We talked politics all the time. I had read all the "white-cover books"* and was strong on theory and quite argumentative. We all came from the provinces and had different political outlooks, and these differences created a distance between us, especially after the revolution.

My expectations from the revolution were quite simple. I hated poverty, so I was hoping for an eradication of economic differences. I saw hunger and deprivation as the cause for prostitution among women, so I wished for a classless society where there were no needy people.

There was such solidarity among people. Everybody was participating in the revolution. I, for example, was working as a volunteer in a hospital.

---

*"White cover books" were books published underground, without license from the Ministry of Information. The name derives from the plain, white covers in which they were bound, giving no indication of the publisher or, often, the author.

When the revolutionaries called for blood, I remember I gave blood three times in one month. The atmosphere was such that one felt one had to do anything to make the revolution succeed. Once, in a demonstration at the university, I fell and a man kicked me on the head with his boots. I was blinded for ten days and hospitalized, but it did not matter to me. We were all so enmeshed in the revolution.

In those days I was participating in as many meetings as I could fit into a day. For example, I remember the gatherings of the Writer's Association, and the silly behavior of those who attended. They attacked each other, bitterly swore at one another. I was an eighteen-year-old girl who was witnessing the events in the streets. I had reached the conclusion that ordinary people were pulling the society in one direction, and intellectuals, who were sitting and debating in closed rooms, were pulling it in another direction. I felt our writers had a one-dimensional view of problems and that they were slaves of their own subjective theories, theories that had nothing to do with reality.

My first memory of the revolution is very personal. We were three girls taking private lessons with an electrical engineering student. We were quite fond of him. He used to criticize the previous regime and was very revolutionary. Then one day his name appeared at the top of a list of students working for SAVAK. It was a bitter and very sad moment for me. I will never forget my disappointment.

■ ■ ■ ■ ■

Neda: I was a university professor. I was not at all involved in political activities. I watched the excitement of my colleagues, men and women, and I remember the demonstrations, the marches, the gatherings, the discussions on the streets and in the homes. We were all waiting for something to happen.

Three

Being a Woman before the Revolution

As a woman, I felt. . . I could do anything I wanted," Nayyer, who worked for the government before the revolution, told me. Ayesheh, formerly an administrator, remarked, *"I used to tell my boss, 'If you tell me to move the Alborz mountains, I will not ask you how you want it done, I will ask when you want it done.'"* These remarks encapsulate nicely remarkable shifts in sensibility that appear to have taken place among professional women before the revolution. Professional women of the prerevolutionary period I interviewed displayed a high level of self-worth and ambitious professional goals. They believed that before the revolution few doors were closed to them and had a sense that their professional achievements were the result of individual merit and personal effort. Many, in addition, attributed their professional success to a chance at university education and to supportive parents, particularly mothers ambitious as much for their daughters as their sons.

The professional women I talked to—physicians, lawyers, university professors, administrators, businesswomen, publishers, and book editors—were unanimous in believing that their professional achievements were due to their own capabilities and merits rather than special treatment or favoritism. *"I got where I was because I worked hard and deserved every promotion I got,"* Farideh, a high-ranking civil servant, told me.

These women had experienced what they called "cultural biases," "resentment," and a "negative" attitude on the part of men, which they described as a form of discrimination. But most of these women brushed these obstacles aside as incidental and not difficult to surmount. If class and social background mattered in employment and promotion in the 1950s, these women felt they were no longer a factor in the 1960s and 1970s. Hiring was based much more on education and competence. *"I came from an* ordinary household," Lida, a doctor, told me. "We were five sisters and three brothers. . . . All of us went to university." The universities not only permitted women of middle-class background to pursue professional careers, they shaped these women in other ways. Those from traditional families encountered men at close proximity for the first time on university campuses. At university, many learned to compete with their male counterparts. "They thought we would get our degrees, frame them, hang them in our living rooms, and become good housewives." said Monir, a woman lawyer. "We showed them otherwise."

Regardless of background, most of the women I interviewed credit supportive parents with their chance for an education. In most households, women recalled, brothers received preferential treatment. But when it came to education, parents were willing to support a seriously inclined daughter. In some instances, mothers with very limited schooling themselves were the driving force behind their daughters' education and emancipation. The determination of these women to excel in their work was striking. Again and again, I came across women who were committed to showing that they were equal to their male counterparts.

I had worked with the Women's Organization of Iran before the revolution, when the passage of every piece of legislation relating to women's rights was a struggle. I was therefore astonished by the lukewarm interest displayed by some of the professional women I interviewed in issues relating to women's legal rights before the revolution. Women lawyers who dealt with divorce and child custody cases on a daily basis, for example, understood the importance of the Family Protection Law. But many other professional women, vaguely aware of this law, paid little attention to it. Unlike working-class women, these women felt they could do without the legal protections it afforded. "If I wanted a divorce, I and women like me who came from a privileged class could get it any time they wished," said Shokouh, a physician, and other women agreed with her. "I knew that men could no longer divorce their wives," said a Soudabeh, also a physician. I concluded that many professional and better-off women had come to take for granted the rights and opportunities afforded them before the revolution. For working-class and lower-middle-class women, the Family Protection Law, day-care centers, and family planning programs were of much greater moment and provided a greater sense of security. Today, the necessity for legal protections and rights is felt by women across the social spectrum.

Amineh: I was always very independent, so I never looked at myself as a woman. In the 1960s and 1970s, I followed the work of the women's movement in Iran, but I did not trust the leadership or its approach to feminism. For me the real change came under Reza Shah—through access to education and emphasis on the need for women to have a profession. As far as I am concerned, women like Mrs. Farrokhru Parsa, Fatemeh Sayah, Mehrangiz Manuchehrian, and many others of that generation are the founding mothers of any emancipation Iranian women achieved. They are true pioneers. They did not talk about "liberating" women. They cared for family values, they wanted education for women. They did not seek personal gain. They devoted their lives to the cause of women. It was possible for women like my mother to accept them as their leaders.

We used to discuss women's issues with my friends but in the context of obtaining the right to study and work. We talked about freedom. We also knew that men did not think much of women. I saw this all the time, even among educated men.

As for the Family Protection Law, I believe it helped the less privileged class. At least they got access to courts and women lawyers. The women lawyers were more effective than the law. It was they who knew how to represent the illiterate and poor in court and win their cases. As for the middle- and upper-classes, despite the law the men still managed to do what they wanted. My own brother-in-law forged some papers and divorced his wife. I know that the Women's Organization pushed for the passage of a new version of the Family Protection Law, but it reaped the fruits of the efforts of earlier women activists. Basically, I did not have much faith in the organization, nor did I like its leadership. I believe the leaders did not speak the language of the ordinary Iranian women.

■ ■ ■ ■ ■

Mari: I was always aware of my gender. At the university where I worked, I knew men and women had equal chances for advancement. But I also knew that women did not have much of a chance of becoming chancellor or even vice-chancellor of a university. Even the chancellor of the women's university in those days was a man.

For me it always mattered that I should prove myself as a woman. I was aware that I was competing in a man's world. I was not interested in managerial positions. I wanted to write, to publish, and I was given the opportunity to do so. You could not have lived in Iran and not felt that the society gives certain advantages to men. But among the teaching staff at the university, you also felt a sense of equality. Academic advancement mostly depended on one's merits.

I grew up in a privileged family, surrounded by boys. At home I felt that my brothers were my father's favorite, so I decided to beat them by excelling in my studies. I must admit that my father's attitude also shaped my character. Of course since I was sent abroad for my schooling, I did not feel discriminated against as a young girl.

I also married a man who was very supportive of my studies and work and who provided me with the possibility of devoting a lot of my time to my academic work. Very few women were given the opportunities I had.

Before the revolution I remember talking about women's issues with friends, especially with you. In our family, you had quite a reputation as a feminist. Let me tell you an anecdote. I remember one morning my husband held a button in his hand and asked whether you, Haleh, would object if I sewed on his button.

I also followed the activities of the Women's Organization and thus knew about the Family Protection Law. I feel it was an important step forward in the life of Iranian women, regardless of what class they came from.

■ ■ ■ ■ ■

Shokouh: I spent the first seven years of my life in Europe. I went to elementary and secondary school in Tehran. I had a European upbringing. We grew up with boys and did not feel at all discriminated against as women. My family are all educated and professional, even the women, so it was not out of the ordinary for me to go to Europe and study medicine. I got married when I was a student. It was my decision. My husband returned to Iran before I did. I stayed on and finished my studies. I was always an independent woman. I came back to Iran, started my private practice, worked in a government hospital, and taught at the university. I felt the system wanted women to make progress and be in the forefront. I remember an old man, a patient of mine, once said to me, "God bless Reza Shah who made it possible for women like you to study and become doctors and treat people like me." It was very moving. He was so old and I was so young. In those days it was very easy for women to work. Not so today.

Being a physician and seeing patients from different classes, I became familiar with the problems women faced in this country. I knew vaguely about the Family Protection Law, but I was not familiar with its contents and the details of the law. For people like me, divorce was never a problem. If I wanted a divorce, I and women like me who came from a privileged class could get it any time they wished. But the real shock was when I found out I needed my husband's permission to leave the country. I did not know there was such a thing as the Passport Law. And they did not change it; it exists to this day. On the whole I believe that women were treated unfairly before and after the revolution. Women must have economic independence. For me that is the key to equality, freedom, and emancipation.

■ ■ ■ ■ ■

Farideh: I was born in Tehran, in a merchant family. I was educated in Tehran. At the university, the girls were more brilliant. Perhaps they shone more because the male students came mostly from the provinces and were less sophisticated. At the university, I remember there was a lot of mixing between girls and boys, but this was not the case socially off campus. Once you left the college you did not see the boys.

After graduation there was work for everybody. Some of my classmates became teachers, others joined the private sector, some like me went to work for the government. I rose rapidly in my job. I stayed with the same institution for twenty-two years, until after the revolution when I decided to retire. I don't think in all the years I worked I was treated either unfairly because I was a woman or with favoritism. My promotion was based on the quality of my work and my merits. I got where I was because I worked hard and deserved every promotion I got.

As a woman, neither I, nor the women who worked with me, nor my female friends felt any shortcomings or discrimination. I was a single woman, living on my own, in my own apartment. Neither my family nor my friends were troubled by it. I was seen as an independent woman who had the right to choose to live any way she wanted. Meeting men and going

out with them was also not a big issue. In all the years I worked, I did not
come across a man who wanted to start a personal relationship just because
we were working in the same office.

I was aware of changes in the family law, but I had not seen the text of
the Family Protection Law. It did not affect me. I was not sensitized to it. I
felt women had found their place in the society, and they knew how to handle their husbands. So it was of no concern to these women to discuss
women's issues.

Looking back, I think the Family Protection Law was crucial for the
lower-class women. But middle-class women? No, it made no difference to
them. But when after the revolution the law was suspended, then women of
all classes started worrying.

■ ■ ■ ■ ■

Elaheh: As a woman before the revolution, I always thought that since I
was from a modest family with little or no monetary support and since Iran
was a dictatorship, all doors must be closed to a person like me. Then I saw
this was not the case. I was at the top of my class at the university, and I
won a government scholarship to go abroad to continue with my studies.
Looking back I think women were shown some favoritism. The atmosphere was such that, as a woman, you could accomplish more than your
male colleagues.

■ ■ ■ ■ ■

Darya: In my career as a lawyer, I always had to prove to men that I was as
well versed as they in legal debate. I made sure they understood that I feel
equal to them, that I didn't feel weak or at a disadvantage. I never feared
men. Not once in all my life did I believe that a man has the right to violate
my gender, my womanhood. For me there was no conflict between my gender and that of a man. I did not see any difference between myself and a
man. Only when women were deliberately belittled and humiliated because
of their gender and due to the culture we live in did I feel we were discriminated against.

I had a modern upbringing. The men in my family were educated at Dar-ol-Fonun.* Graduates from that school believed in serving their country. They were Westernized to some degree.

I was born and brought up in Tehran and went to Tehran University. I studied law. When I entered the Faculty of Law there were fourteen, maybe fifteen, girls and seven hundred boys. Our classes were coed. But we did not associate with our male classmates outside the university. I think we women were much more mature in this way. We wanted to prove that we would avoid behavior the university would disapprove of. Anyway, the boys were far too socially inferior for us to associate with them. We didn't go to movies and restaurants together.

When I graduated from the faculty of law, I first became a teacher. Many years later, I started practicing law. In my family I never felt discriminated against because I was a woman. I was given a free hand to choose my husband. I insisted that my marriage contract stipulate my right to seek a divorce and contain a notarized permission to travel separately from my future husband. I had better suitors than my present husband, but none agreed to my demands. That speaks for itself, doesn't it? It shows the pattern of behavior among most educated Iranian men. When I discussed these conditions with my present husband, I was surprised to find that not only did he not object, but he had intended to make these suggestions to me.

I became interested in women's issues by witnessing the misery of the ordinary women who came to our house. I studied law because I wanted to find out what legal obstacles we faced as women. I read a lot about the activities of women in other countries, and I studied various women's movements, the obstacles they encountered and their achievements.

After I got my law degree, I joined the Women's Lawyers Association. In the association we discussed the legal problems of Iranian women. We also published a booklet describing existing legal discriminations against women. So when the Family Protection Law was introduced, I was quite familiar with it. Later, I was on the team that drafted the expanded version of the law. My sense is that we were very bold and took great risks preparing that law.

---

*The Dar-ol-Fonun, founded in 1851, was the first of the modern, European-style schools established in Iran. In the nineteenth century, many of the country's leading civil servants were graduates of the school. It continues to count among best secondary schools in the country.

Gowhar: I went to law school and graduated at the top of my class. In high school I was not a very studious person, nor was I obedient. But I gradually settled down, and at the university I proved to be better than any boy. I was among the first women judges hired by the Ministry of Justice. I was the youngest presiding judge in court. All this means that I never encountered any problems as a woman before the revolution, neither at work nor in society. I behaved like a man. I did not wear makeup, nor did I act coquettishly. I wanted people to look at me as they looked at a man and to act toward me as they would toward a man; and I therefore did a man's work. I tried to impose my will on my colleagues, and I was quite successful at it. I must admit that since, as a woman, I did not have any problems under the previous regime, I believe that other women had the same experience.

I dealt with the Family Protection Law every day in my court. I believe the Women's Organization failed to educate women on their legal rights. It did not do enough. Its legal classes were limited in number. Of course women who came to the Family Protection Courts knew about the Family Protection Law. But after the revolution, when the law was suspended, very few women noticed because it was done in a very subtle way. That is why there was no protest against this decision at the time. But gradually, as the number of unilateral divorces increased, women became aware of the lack of any legal protections, and then they started to act. They managed to force the government to reactivate some parts of that law. I think women today are more familiar and knowledgeable about their rights than under the previous regime. Maybe women had to lose the privileges they had to learn to fight for them and become more militant about their rights.

■ ■ ■ ■ ■

Soudabeh: I am a physician. I studied at Tehran University. I made it on my own. I believe that before the revolution women had all the opportunity and freedom they desired. But there was also a lot of corruption and pressure to conform, which created many inconveniences for women.

I think in those days if you were a woman and were looking for a job, the man who wanted to hire you first tried to make passes at you. At least this is the impression I got, although of course this was not my experience. I got my job entirely on my own merits and I must confess not once did a man at work try to hint at the least bit of impropriety toward me. I still would say that in those days the general attitude in employing women was to prefer looks to knowledge. Maybe this was the case only among the people I knew, but that is my conclusion.

In the hospital I felt that nurses were mostly hired because of their looks and that their appearance was also their stepping-stone to advancement. I personally resented this attitude very much, and I kept my distance from my co-workers. I felt no matter what class they belonged to, women were considered as dolls and objects by their male colleagues. What bothered me were those women who played up to men and found this behavior becoming and used all the feminine ploys to advance. Having said that I must admit that my aloofness was not an obstacle to my advancement.

I did not talk to other women about their problems. I knew in general what the Family Protection Law was. I knew that men could no longer divorce their wives. Women who worked in the hospitals constantly talked of the difficulties they encountered in their daily lives. They were happy to get the right to divorce and have some kind of legal protection. I feel lower-middle-class women benefited more from the Family Protection Law than the lower-class women who were brought up to obey their husbands no matter how they were treated. But I remember in the late 1970s the attitude of these women was changing, too.

■ ■ ■ ■ ■

Manijeh: Before the revolution I was a high school student. In our household there was total equality among my brothers and me. I was the oldest and a girl. My parents believed that the education and upbringing of their first child were very important because she could be the role model for her sibling. My parents insisted that the youngest children should respect the older one. The work at home was equally divided between us. If I was asked to do the dishes, my brother had to dust. I remember he would cry every time he was told to do housework. It was so degrading for him; he was a boy, and in our culture boys are not supposed to do housework.

I grew up in Abadan. The atmosphere was more relaxed than in other provincial towns. As a girl, I could move about freely. At home we never discussed the problems women had in society. My mother ran the family with an iron hand. There was extraordinary harmony between my parents.

They always made sure that I, as a girl, should never be at a disadvantage. I think I even developed a superiority complex.

■ ■ ■ ■ ■

Nazanin: I grew up in Tehran, in a Westernized, educated, and civilized family. I went to a French school and studied in England. I got my master's degree in French and English literature. My father always wanted me to have a proper education. He wanted me to be economically independent of my future husband, but at the same time he also wanted me to remain feminine. I never got married, but there was no pressure on me. My family respected my decision.

Neither of my parents showed any favoritism toward my brother. We were brought up as total equals. I never felt at a disadvantage because I was a woman. On the contrary, I felt superior. Even at the age of seven or eight, I noticed the difference between me and my friends. I was more worldly and had traveled abroad.

After returning to Iran, I started working as a social secretary. I met a lot of foreigners. At work, I was treated as equal to my male colleagues. Actually there was an advantage in being a woman. I was more respected. I always felt that working as an Iranian woman with foreigners added to the respect they had for my country and that my being there was a credit to Iran's standing. I saw myself a professional, capable, and hardworking person.

I wrote on women's issues, but not from a feminist point of view. I found visits to Iran by feminists like Germaine Greer and Betty Friedan in bad taste.

I was aware of the Family Protection Law. It was an impressive achievement. I knew women faced problems in obtaining a divorce, that they lost custody of the children to an alcoholic father, uncle, or grandfather. I believe the lower classes were the main beneficiaries of this law.

I give a lot of credit to the Women's Organization of Iran for this and their other programs. I was told that the Women's Organization of Iran not only did research on the condition of women, for example, in the red light district of Tehran or in the prisons, but also that it acted on these reports to improve conditions for women. My problem with the Women's Organization was that I did not want Princess Ashraf as the representative of Iranian women. It was explained to me that having the princess was a sure way of securing funding for various projects. I accepted this argument. I must confess I thought the leadership of the Women's Organization of Iran too sophisticated to be able to deal with the existing problems of women in Iran. It was just an impression I had.

I would have loved to talk about women's issues with my friends, but they preferred to talk about trivial matters. If a topic did not concern them, they did not pay attention to it. Foreigners were more interested in our social problems, and they asked more questions.

■ ■ ■ ■ ■

Ayesheh: I was born in the provinces. I finished my elementary and high school education in my hometown. Some of my classmates came to school wearing the *chador*. This was not the case with us. Our home was not religious, but religious ceremonies were observed. For example, food was given to the poor in the name of Ali, or during the month of Ramadan people were invited to break the fast at our house.

I had three sisters and one brother. My mother insisted that all her daughters become educated, but she showed her favoritism to our brother. I had an enlightened grandmother who was an avid reader of magazines. I remember my mother scolding my sister because her skirt was too short and my grandmother reproaching her for not being in tune with the fashion of the times.

After I finished my high school, I went to England and studied midwifery and worked in a hospital. I lived in England for ten years.

As soon as I returned from England I started working in a government organization. I saw myself as a very successful and capable woman. I felt everything was possible for me and within my reach. The word "no" did not exist for me. I used to tell my boss, "If you tell me to move the Alborz mountains, I will not ask you how you want it done, I will ask when you want it done." I felt I had the power to achieve the impossible. I felt the world was mine, and my capacity for work and my audacity increased by the day. I was planning, managing, and executing new projects all the time.

I had two hundred women working for me. Most of these women, who came from simple backgrounds, were aware of the Family Protection Law. They all thought that these laws had always been there, just like they took their education and social mobility for granted. They assumed that their legal and political rights were part of their natural rights. I followed the activities of the Women's Organization very closely. I knew it was instrumental in legislating laws pertaining to the status of women. I felt involved in any gain women made in Iran, all the way from the passage of the Family Protection Law to women getting decision-making jobs. Even ten years before the revolution I felt there was total equality between men and women. A lot of people will dispute this, but this was my impression.

■ ■ ■ ■ ■

Fatemeh: I grew up and went to school in Tehran. My father had his own private business. Among the children it was I who from the very beginning showed an interest in the business. I went to Europe and specialized in confectionery. It was quite an experience. I started as a simple apprentice on the floor of the bakery factory and learned my way up. Look, we talk about women being treated differently in Iran. I remember the floor manager in Europe trying to discourage me from staying there. He believed that this was not a profession for women, let alone for a woman from the Middle East. He used all sorts of ploys, from asserting that women's fingers are too delicate to insisting women could not stand on their feet seventeen hours a day, in order to get rid of me. I was very persistent. I finished my studies, and my father decided to modernize our factory and our premises. He left it all to me. I was in my early twenties. It was a big responsibility. I knew I could handle it, and to my father it really did not matter that I was a woman.

My father retired two years before the revolution. In all those years that we worked together, I never felt that my gender was an issue, neither at work nor in society. I felt women had the same opportunity as men, provided they showed professionalism, capability, and efficiency.

I was never concerned with women's rights until I came face-to-face with the problem of getting a divorce. It was then that I became aware of the first version of the Family Protection Law. I used the law to get my divorce. It was during that process that I saw how unjustly women were treated and how little recourse they had to redress in the courts. I therefore think that the Family Protection Law made a big difference in the lives of Iranian women.

Atefeh: In those days I never felt there was any limitation to what I could achieve. Of course it made a lot of difference what sort of background you came from. I grew up in an affluent family. My parents were divorced, and my mother lived abroad. I was educated both in Iran and in Europe. I never felt any difference between women and men. In my family we were given the same opportunity.

After I came back, I started my own business. I was subcontracting work to carpenters, furniture makers, electricians, and the like. Not once did I feel they resented my being a woman. There was a mutual respect between us. In those days I don't think there was anything I could not do because I was a woman.

I was married and familiar with the existing family law. I remember always telling my husband that he should make a will and leave the custody of the children to me. This was before the passage of the Family Protection Law. I knew that if he died our life would not be the same, while if I died nothing would change for him and the children. I urged the men in my family to make sure to leave the custody of their children to their wives. Since the law did not provide for the mothers, I felt it was up to the men to do it. Some listened to me, others did not. Not only did I talk about these issues with my women friends, I urged the women in the Women's Organization to do something about the child custody law. The guardianship of minors office in the Ministry of Justice was a nightmare. Once the Family Protection Law was passed, I believe all women benefited from it. It came as a relief to all of us. Even today they had to reintroduce some sections of the family law. This alone shows the importance of that law.

■ ■ ■ ■ ■

Masoumeh: I had a great sense of fulfillment before the revolution. As far as I was concerned I never felt handicapped as a woman. I felt superior to the people who were around me. I loved my job. Before the revolution I had worked only in two places, and both jobs gave me a great sense of satisfaction. As a woman, I knew I could study, work, travel, marry the man I loved, lead the life I wanted. It was perfect.

I came from a broken home and had a difficult childhood and a tense relationship with my stepmother. I was witness to my parents' divorce, so naturally I was aware of the problems women had getting a divorce and

knew of the Family Protection Law. Of course, the law made a big difference in the lives of our women. As far as women's issues go I am much more
attuned to them since the revolution, not that we did not talk among ourselves in the past. But today it is so different. The issues are so much more
tangible, so palpable, they have become part of our daily life.

■ ■ ■ ■ ■

Ladan: I was always an independent woman. I went to a French school. I
came from an emancipated Westernized family. I have been working all my
life. I remember there was a time when I taught in the morning, had my own
radio program for women, studied in the afternoons, and looked after my
husband and my children. What more does one want from a woman?

I saw myself as an avant-garde woman, more progressive than the other
women around me. There was a time when all my friends were working as
secretaries. They had been abroad and had acquired secretarial skills. Later I
came across professional women, I mean women who held other kinds of jobs.

I never felt discriminated against because of my gender. Maybe I never
held a position threatening to men. I knew about the problems other women
had. I was superficially familiar with the Family Protection Law. I knew that
a man could no longer marry a second woman or unilaterally divorce his
wife. I was aware of the family planning program, too. You were the only
person I talked to about women's issues, feminism, and the problems
women had. My friends were really not at all in tune with these subjects.
When I grew up, women accepted the idea of being totally submissive to
men. I rejected this approach. I got engaged to the man I loved and married
him only after I had gone abroad to study. As a woman I wanted equality,
independence, and freedom of action.

■ ■ ■ ■ ■

Nahid: I grew up in a traditional but educated family. I went to school in
Tehran and studied in Europe, like my brother. We both got our Ph.D.s. I
never felt any difference between myself and my brother. We were given the
same chances.

I worked for the government and for a brief period was working in the women's movement. We did research on family matters and women's issues. We discussed women's problems with each other. It was part of our work. I was quite familiar with the Family Protection Law. I don't accept for a moment that the lower-class women and the religious middle-class women were not aware of this law. On the contrary, they knew that there was such a thing as the Family Protection Law and that it made a lot of difference in their lives. They needed the protection of the law. But women like us solved our differences and problems with our husbands mostly by mutual agreement. What I find fascinating is that the majority of women I talk to, I mean women in my class, think that the Family Protection Law was introduced very recently. They are quite taken aback when I tell them that it was passed before the revolution, was suspended by the current regime, and only later reintroduced in a different format. I don't think the previous regime was good at explaining what it did, nor was it good at advertising its achievements, especially when it came to women.

■ ■ ■ ■ ■

Touran: I came from an upper class, affluent family. We were two sisters, we lost our parents at a very early age and became orphans. We were the wards of our maternal aunt and uncle. I went to a French school and did my university education in the United States. In the States, I became involved in the Iranian student movement, actually in the radical left-wing movement. A cousin of mine, who was my childhood idol, introduced me to political activity. She always impressed me. I remember she came in her nurse's outfit to her wedding, and after the wedding ceremony was over she returned to her work. To me this was very cool. I always had an admiration for strong women and disliked weak women.

I returned to Iran in 1968 for a brief stay and worked at a research institute, doing social research. I came face-to-face with the plight and misery of ordinary Iranian women. I felt Iranian women were oppressed and their rights had gone to waste. It was totally irrelevant that I was an independent woman, that I could go out with boys, that I would choose my own husband, that I was well off. To me what mattered was that I wanted to do something for other women, but what I could achieve was so limited in scope that it was almost suffocating. I found out that society did not treat me equally even though I did not feel any shortcomings in my own life, nor did I see myself as inferior to any man.

I remember after returning to Iran in 1968 going to get my father's pension. He had served in the army. I was asked whether I was married. I said no. They told me they had to do a medical examination to make sure I was a virgin.

After I went back to the States to work on my dissertation, I followed the women's movement in Iran closely. I was quite familiar with the Family Protection Law, but I did not approve of it; it did not go far enough. To this day I have not changed my mind. I still insist that this was not a progressive law; it did not sufficiently improve the rights of women. There were enough influential people around in those days who could have pushed for a better law. Maybe the number of qualified women who were willing to work in such a reactionary atmosphere was limited. I thought then and think now that the Women's Organization and the laws it introduced were more of a showpiece and did not have much substance.

For me, issues relating to women were at the forefront of my activities. I was constantly arguing and discussing women's rights with my colleagues on the left. My view was that we should reject the argument—common among left-wing groups—that the issue of women's rights was of secondary importance and that discussion of the women's question should be postponed until the country was free. In our group, the women who were more independent agreed with me, but those whose eyes were glued to what the men were saying followed the party line. I feel these women were backward in their outlook.

I believed the revolution was an opportunity to obtain equal rights for women. In those days I gave a lot of speeches explaining this position. In my speeches I argued that the existing laws were not progressive and since women and men were equal, women should be treated with total equality. I urged women to fight for their rights and not wait for the men to give these rights to them. I believed in advancing, not retreating, and I pushed for this cause all my adult life.

■ ■ ■ ■ ■

Ramesh: I grew up in a traditional family. My mother had nine years of schooling. I lost my father when I was very young. My older brother was the man in the family. He was narrow-minded and a fanatic. He worried constantly about me. I was very pretty. I felt he could not wait to marry me off. I was bright and a good student and wanted to study, but there was so much pressure from my family that I finally got married at an early age. I just wanted to get away from all that pressure. It was a disastrous marriage. The divorce was messy and long. I blame my family more than society.

After the divorce, I felt like a loser. I had lost all my self-confidence. I was back at my mother's house and miserable. I got a job as a secretary and studied French. It took a while for me to be myself again. But I did not trust any man. I felt men just wanted a passing relationship with me.

Through my own marriage I became aware of the disadvantages women have in our country and the power men can wield over them. To this day I blame my brother for my failed marriage, and my mother for not standing up to him.

I was so naive that even when I wanted a divorce my husband was able to make me sign the wrong papers and take away my dowry money. This is proof that I knew nothing of the Family Protection Law. Well, I was young and was told that women should be submissive and obedient.

■ ■ ■ ■ ■

Lili: I am a secretary in a private office. My employer is related to my husband. Otherwise my husband would not let me work, although we need the money.

I was nineteen when I got married. My father was a very strict man, but my mother, with the little education she had—she had been married off at the age of thirteen—was an emancipated woman. I remember at one stage when things were rough in our marriage, she not only supported the idea of my getting a divorce, she was willing to look after our three children so that I could marry the man I was in love with.

My family wanted me to marry my cousin, but I really disliked him. They were against my marriage to my present husband. His family was not thrilled either. I just wanted to get out of my parents' house, in order not to marry someone they chose for me. It was my decision to marry my present husband.

Both my husband and his family claim they are broad-minded, but on our wedding night they insisted I produce the famous handkerchief to prove my virginity.*

We started our married life with two suitcases and in two rooms. I started working, too. We both worked for the government. Then we moved to the provinces and we had a big nice house and I stopped working. After the revolution we moved back to Tehran.

I wish I had gone to university. This was my biggest mistake. But in those days, if you lived in a strict traditional family, the only way to escape was to get married.

I believe that Iranian women were and are now at a disadvantage. I never dealt with women's rights issues. I was young when I got married and then I had my children. The issue arose for me when I wanted to divorce and found out that, because I was instigating the divorce, my husband would automatically get custody of the children. That was so unfair. I did not discuss either my private dilemma or general topics relating to women with other people. Today it is different. I am aware of most of the laws pertaining to women's rights. I have a daughter, and her future matters to me.

■ ■ ■ ■ ■

Monir: I am a lawyer, I studied law at Tehran University. I grew up in the provinces. My family was traditional. My mother wore the *chador*, but I was free to dress as I liked. My mother had had a traditional education, but she wanted a Western-style education for me and my brothers. She did not discriminate between me and my brothers. On the contrary, she invested more in me and sent me to Tehran to study at the university.

When I came to Tehran, I was exposed to boys at the university. I had never been in such close proximity to boys. We were thrown together. It was a different world for me. You might say I experienced culture shock.

I never felt unequal to the boys, but their self-confidence in class was greater than ours. We women first imitated, and then acquired, their self-confidence, but we were never their equals. In their eyes we never were their equals. They never took us or our studies seriously. They thought we would get our degrees, frame them, hang them in our living rooms, and become

---

*Traditionally, on the wedding night, the "bloodied handkerchief," produced and shown to the family of the groom, served as evidence that the bride was a virgin.

good housewives. For them, we were models in a store display window. We showed them otherwise.

We were not political at all, but then Al-Ahmad published *Westoxication*, and we were electrified by it.* Yet to this day I believe the biggest transformation in the university occurred when they built a mosque on campus. Suddenly, with the call to prayer, the university changed from being a Western enclave to something Asian. More and more religious students gravitated toward each other and isolated themselves from us. Then of course we witnessed the phenomenon of Shariati and the Hosainiyyeh Ershad.** And the rest you know.

I became aware of women's problems when I joined a women's magazine and started answering the "letters to the editor." Women wrote about the difficulty of open relationships with men and of sexual relationships and clandestine affairs that made them uncomfortable, virginity, wife abuse, and all the hardship and discrimination they were encountering in their daily lives. I gradually started writing about these problems for different magazines. I also worked as a lawyer in the public sector. In those days I felt I could work anywhere I wanted and reach any goal I set for myself.

■ ■ ■ ■ ■

Nargess: I finished high school in the provinces. I took the university entrance examination at the Faculty of Law. We were thirty-five women in the entering class. I remember finding the atmosphere at the Faculty of Law so exhilarating. Our teachers were the best jurists in the country. The program was based on the French system. We even had to read some of the books in French. But when I think what has happened to the law school today! It resembles an adult literacy class rather than a university.

I was playing on the volleyball and basketball teams. The girls had to wear slacks and tunics with long sleeves, but no scarves on our heads. Still,

---

*Jalal Al-Ahmad, intellectual, novelist, and essayist, created a sensation in 1962 with his book-length essay, *Westoxication*. The essay criticized the tendency among Iranians to imitate and privilege all things Western and called for the reassertion of an authentic Iranian identity. The book was banned but circulated underground as a "white-cover" book.

**Hosainiyyeh Ershad was a religious center where in the late 1960s Ali Shariati and others lectured, often advocating an Islam in keeping with modern-day problems. The center enjoyed wide popularity but was subsequently closed down.

it looked funny. I remember one day one of our female classmates appeared in class wearing a pantsuit. It created such an uproar, our section was almost closed.

The girls had few problems in socializing with the boys on campus. It was not so for the boys. Most of them came from the provinces; their cultural perspective was narrow, and this was their first encounter with women in such close proximity. They reacted to our presence by not taking women seriously. For them, we were pretty little objects.

After I graduated from the university I started working for the government. In all the years before the revolution I did not for a minute think that I could not reach the goals I had set for myself. There was no limit to what I could achieve. My gender was never an issue. For example, I remember I was sent to a religious town to look into the accusations of womanizing brought against an official. Nobody in that town was surprised to see me. I had a group of women lawyers working for me. I would send them on business to the provinces. Not once did I hear them complain of mistreatment because they were women. In those days if you were not political you were free to do what you wanted and as a woman you had every opportunity that a man had.

As far as the Family Protection Law, well, I was a lawyer, so it is obvious I was quite familiar with it. I never thought the Family Protection Law progressive, but it was a major development in women's rights. I don't think upper-middle-class women were aware of the contents of the Family Protection Law. The Women's Organization's effort was to educate middle-class and lower-class women. They wanted to "pull up" those women. I don't disagree with their goal. But I still think that the law could have been bolder.

■ ■ ■ ■ ■

Afsar: I grew up in Tehran and went first to a French and then to a Persian school. All my life I was a very self-confident person. I wanted to study painting in Europe. Nobody in my family could stop me. When I returned to Iran I started teaching at the university. In the fifteen years I taught there, I never had a problem because of my gender. It never occurred to me that people would discriminate against me because I was a woman. As a woman I felt then, as I feel now in both my private and my public life, that I could assert myself. It was I who chose my two husbands; it was I who used the

Family Protection Law to initiate divorce proceedings. I never saw a reason to discuss women's issues with my friends, since I never felt any discrimination as a woman.

As a woman I feel I can go into a lion's den and come out unharmed. I never allowed people to treat me unequally to men. I am against the idea that men and women are different. I believe people should be judged according to their merits, not their gender. I do not like separating women from men. For example, I do not approve of an exhibition of paintings by women only or an award for the best woman writer, woman artist, or musician. Having said that, I don't want any injustice inflicted on women, either. I believe men and women should shoulder responsibilities equally.

■ ■ ■ ■ ■

Zohreh: All my life I was an activist for women. I grew up in the provinces. At sixteen, I became a member of the women's council. I was also working as a journalist. At the age of eighteen I became a member of the International Society of Women Journalists.

I got married at seventeen but continued to go to school. I never felt that as a woman I could not achieve my goals in life. But I also knew, through my social work, of the hardship and sufferings of lower-class women.

My official involvement with the women's movement came to an end in 1963. It was after the White Revolution. I was against the Crown's granting women the right to vote. I believe individuals must grow aware of the rights they lack and then fight for them. If you succeed, then you learn to defend your rights. This was the case with the veil, too. I remember that every year, on the anniversary of the abolition of the veil, in the provinces women wearing the *chador* were taken to place flowers at the statue of Reza Shah. I thought to myself, "How ironic." Neither the officials who dragged these women to the ceremony, nor the women who participated in those events, knew what they were doing. Please understand me correctly. I was not against granting women the vote or women having choice in the matter of *hejab*. What I objected to was that in both cases, these changes came down from above, from the Crown.

As far as the Family Protection Law goes, I remember the relevant government offices in the provinces being reluctant to implement the provisions of that law. The courts were male-dominated and showed favoritism toward men. The head of the local judiciary in the city I lived in refused to grant child custody to the mother despite the Family Protection Law. I am sure that lower-class women knew that they could no longer be divorced on demand, or they could obtain the custody of their children, but they did not know how to go about it. There was a lack of awareness or maybe the law was not attuned to the needs of the people it was meant to serve.

I don't recall the women I associated with being interested in discussing social issues, let alone the status of women. I felt these women wearied of my company. Appearance and superficiality mattered to them. It was a strange atmosphere. You could not carry on a serious conversation with anybody, men or women.

■ ■ ■ ■ ■

Pouran: Before the revolution I was a student in the United States. I did not think about my gender, nor was I interested in the status of women in Iran. I believed once I finished my studies I could work and live wherever I wanted. I left Iran when I was thirteen, and I always dreamed of returning one day. I was involved in the student movement, we argued all the time among ourselves. I must confess that I always felt that being a woman was an obstacle. This was not a political conclusion, it was just a sense I had.

■ ■ ■ ■ ■

Jila: I was the president and one of the founding members of a consulting company. It really didn't make any difference whether I was a man or a woman. I was always blunt and outspoken. I was judged for my work rather than for who I was or what my connections were. Not for a moment did I think that I would have been treated differently had I been a man. Of course there were occasions when men's behavior in meetings was arrogant and rude, but they themselves knew that this was not professional or acceptable. I suppose it gave them a bit of confidence to be rude to a woman who was professionally and socially superior to them.

I grew up in the provinces. My family was educated and affluent. I never felt any difference between myself and my sisters, and my brother. We all went abroad to study.

I was familiar with the problems women had in a traditional way. We had to settle family disputes in our village and, since my sister was running a woman's organization, she would tell us heartbreaking stories about women whose only recourse was to turn to her. Once I became familiar with the Family Protection Law, my mother and I and my sisters started explaining the law to the women in our village. How else could they learn of these laws?

I don't think in the late 1960s too many ordinary women, especially in rural areas, were aware of such laws. I don't know what happened later. I did not follow women's issues any longer.

■ ■ ■ ■ ■

Lida: I was born in the south of Iran but grew up in an old, lower-middle-class neighborhood in Tehran. My father was a schoolteacher. We were five sisters and three brothers. You would not believe it, but all of us went to university and are professionally very successful. I was the second daughter and somehow became a surrogate mother for my siblings. My father treated all the children equally, but for my mother the education and upbringing of the boys were more important. Her attitude caused the girls to develop a stronger and more independent character than she anticipated.

I was a student before the revolution. I studied medicine. Because I was at the top of my class, my father paid university tuition for only one term. My whole education was free, and I was receiving a generous stipend for pocket money, which enabled me to buy clothing for my younger brothers and sisters.

I never felt any difference between me and the boys, especially at the university. We were all competitive but very supportive of each other as well. We exchanged notes and studied together, but we did not go out with boys. Not for a moment did it occur to me that women are less progressive than men or suffered from discrimination.

I was not concerned with women's issues so I neither heard nor was aware of the Family Protection Law. But once I started working in the hospital as an intern, I came into contact with women's grievances and their daily problems. But I don't remember discussing the repression of women with any of my friends. I really was too busy with my studies. The status of women was not my problem.

Partow: I am a secretary and a technician. I work in a hospital. I work on the computer. This is my first job. Until the revolution I had never worked. I grew up in Tehran, in an old neighborhood in a traditional family with my ten sisters and brothers. We were very supportive of each other. My mother is the boss in the family. She has the final word on everything.

I met my husband at a cousin's house and fell in love with him. I was fifteen, and he was twelve years older. My father was against my marrying at such an early age. He wanted me to study. I was young and naive. My husband provided me with a wonderful life: a house, a car, domestic help. We traveled to Europe. It was like a dream. But we lost everything in the revolution.

My husband could not take the pressures resulting from the revolution. He left us. No, he abandoned me and the three children and went to Europe. We could have gone with him, but I knew I could not live in a foreign country. I am not officially separated from him, but in reality we live apart. Overnight I became the sole breadwinner of the family. I took a typing course. My sister found a job for me at a hospital. I was lucky to have a boss who is kind and understanding and compassionate. He told me to learn computer programming and earn more.

As a married woman, I never had any problems. I was busy raising three children. I was getting pregnant all the time. I went to a gynecologist because my husband thought I should have my tubes tied, but when the doctor suggested that my husband should have a vasectomy, to my surprise he went along with this proposal and had the operation.

I was not aware of the Family Protection Law. All I knew was that men could no longer divorce their wives. I tell you the law is no guarantee. Didn't they reverse all these laws after the revolution?

Immediately after the revolution, my brother-in-law tried to stop my sister from continuing her university studies. They almost got divorced. Finally my father intervened, and they went to a notary's office where my brother-in-law signed a notarized statement that he would not stand in the way of my sister's studies. Today, since I have a teenage daughter, I keep up with the law as much as I can understand it.

■ ■ ■ ■ ■

Nayyer: As a woman, before the revolution, I felt I could do anything I wanted if I were capable, that nothing was impossible for me. I knew I could make any decision I wanted, could move in any direction, take any steps I desired. Every goal I set for myself became attainable. I was free to lead the kind of life I thought suited me.

I grew up in a traditional family. My mother was a remarkable woman. She wanted her children to have a proper education. After I finished high school, my father wanted me to get married, but my mother did not allow it. At home I never felt discriminated against. I was leading a man's life.

I was working in the government. My job involved a lot of traveling, just like my male colleagues. I felt like a man and acted like a man. There was a companionship between me and the men who worked with me. Some men hated my assertive manner. My husband does not like it either.

I became familiar with the women's movement and the issues women were discussing in the 1970s. Until then I did not know much about the Family Protection Law. I already had the right of divorce stipulated in my marriage contract, so this was not my problem. I knew it made a lot of difference to other women, especially those from the lower classes. We middle-class women felt the absence of the Family Protection Law after the revolution. I remember a friend telling me that because of the Family Protection Law she had not insisted that the right of seeking a divorce should be written in her marriage contract. After the revolution when the Family Protection Law was suspended, no matter how much she tried, since her husband did not agree, no court would grant her a divorce. There was nothing she could do. Before the revolution I did not discuss women's issues with my friends, but since the revolution that is all we talk about. We discuss all aspects of a woman's life, family rights, personal obligations, coming to term with one's sexuality, learning about one's body, marital rape, promiscuity, and depression.

■ ■ ■ ■ ■

Sousan: As a woman, I always saw myself as sitting on top of the world. When I was growing up I did not feel discriminated against. My parents treated their sons and daughters equally. I always appreciated the fact that I was sent abroad to study, just as my older brothers had been. I handled my own expenses. We all received the same amount of money. My brothers, though older, were not told to look after me. But one incident stuck in my mind. Mother bought a car for my brothers, but not for me. This bothered me, but my father tried to make up for it. As soon as I returned to Iran at the end of my studies, he gave me a car.

The opportunities women like I had in those days were extraordinary. I came back from England and was offered several jobs. I chose to work at one of the ministries. After a while I transferred to the university and taught international relations. It was quite obvious to me that in England, somebody in my position would never have the same chances. I had my home, my car, my job. In short, I was put on a pedestal.

While abroad, I did not follow women's issues, nor did I discuss them with my friends. But I read a lot on Iran. I believed that all the change and the progress in Iran that I read about was superficial—until I came back, started working, and saw how much the country had progressed.

I remember at my ministry I was asked to write a report on women in Iran, Turkey, and Pakistan. I got interested in that subject. I studied the Family Protection Law and watched its development. I also remember when my older sister got married—this must have been before the Family Protection Law—my father insisted that she should have the right to divorce stipulated in her marriage contract. But her future husband was willing to grant the power of attorney to initiate divorce proceedings only to my father—to another man—and not to his future wife. Women's rights and their status was of no concern to me or my friends, so we did not talk about them. My friends were a bunch of upper-class fun-loving people. But after the revolution I got totally enmeshed in the position and legal status of women in the society. To this day I pursue the subject very closely. How could it be otherwise? What has happened has affected all women. It is no longer a problem of class or privilege.

■ ■ ■ ■ ■

Nasrin: Before the revolution I was in high school. I lived in the provinces with my family. My father was a civil servant. He was a religious man, so religious that when after the revolution I put aside my *chador* for an Islamic headdress, he stopped talking to me for four months. As a young schoolgirl, my sisters and I all wore the *chador* even when we went to school. Today, I feel comfortable in both the *chador* and the *maghnae*. My parents did not discriminate between their daughters and their only son. We were free to go and come as we wished. I was an avid reader and used to take part in serious discussions with men. As a woman I did not feel any limitations. On the contrary, I felt I was moving ahead.

I was aware of the existing cultural problems. The men I saw did not talk about women. I had heard about the Family Protection Law, but it did not concern me. As a Muslim woman, I accepted the dictates of the Koran as they were put to me. Let me put it this way: I accepted religion as it was put to me. Today, having worked in depth on women's issues, my views are very different from what they were fifteen years ago. I am familiar with existing discrimination against women. If you ask me, the discrimination starts at birth and continues through life. Our religion makes it possible for women to be treated on an equal basis with men. It all depends how you interpret the law.

■ ■ ■ ■ ■

Zahra: I was eighteen when the revolution occurred. I finished high school at sixteen and went to university at seventeen. I was accepted at the Science and Technology University, but I wanted to study art. That was upsetting for my parents. My father was the grandson of a prominent cleric, and my mother was religious and said her daily prayers.

I was born and grew up in the provinces. My father was a doctor; my mother had a high school diploma. We were four girls and two boys at home. My mother differentiated between her daughters and her sons, but my father did not. He was an enlightened man. He never let his daughters feel inferior to his sons, but my mother always quarreled with her daughters. She kept on repeating that boys know much more than girls. This attitude was quite upsetting for us. To prove her wrong we tried to excel in school.

In ninth grade I got the highest IQ score in school. I was sure I would have an extraordinarily bright future. It did not make any difference that I was a woman.

I was too young to know about the Family Protection Law, but I was not unaware of the problems women had in our society. My major in high school was mathematics, and since no girls' school in our town offered a mathematics major, I and a few other girls studied at the local boys' high school. We were not welcomed at that school. The boys and even the school principal did not stop creating difficulties for us. We felt discriminated against daily. You know what we did? We formed a group and called it the

Amazon Girls. The idea was to organize a solidarity front and confront the daily heckling and teasing by the boys. We all knew that being a girl meant being at a disadvantage, but since it did not affect us directly, we did not talk about it.

■ ■ ■ ■

Neda: Before the revolution, I never felt there was an obstacle in my way. I belong to a generation of women that no longer had to go from their father's harem to the harem of their husband. This was due to the changes of the last five decades preceding the revolution. I, for example, came from a provincial family. I took the university entrance exam; I got the highest test score; and throughout my years at the university I was at the top of my class. I won a scholarship to go abroad to continue my higher education. My father did not feel comfortable that his unmarried daughter should go abroad alone. So I gave up the idea of going abroad and got a teaching job and married a classmate of mine. In those days, if you came from a middle-class, educated family it was left to the girl to marry or to stay single. We could choose our own path in life. The following year my husband applied for a scholarship for me to go and study abroad, without even telling me. That is how I went to Europe and got my doctorate.

When I came back, I felt all the doors were open to me, I never felt that my gender was an obstacle to my progress. The respect we got depended on our merit and capability. In later years it became fashionable to hire women. I personally did not approve of such a trend. I felt women deserved to be judged on their own merit and not because they were women.

Four

Revolution as "Earthquake"

THE WOMEN I INTERVIEWED *experienced the revolution as an "earthquake," a "hurricane," which created devastation all around them and wreaked havoc with their lives. For one reason or another the men in many families lost their jobs, stayed at home, and became demoralized. It was left to women to find work, earn a living, and hold the family together, both economically and psychologically. Women considered members of the old social order found themselves the targets of the revolutionaries, who were eager to discredit and ostracize them. As one civil servant remarked, "From the very beginning the new administration tried to make it very difficult for women to work. You either were one of them, . . . or there was no room for you."*

But the women adapted without, they felt, compromising their principles. They refused to stay home. Those who had not held jobs before the revolution found work. Those who were already working continued to do so, in their old jobs if possible, or fashioned new careers for themselves when they had been purged or dismissed or quit themselves in exasperation. At work and on the street, they resisted the pressure to conform. They found ways to adjust to the new situation. "I continued being the president of the company," Jila, an engineer by training and currently a businesswoman, remarked. "But I no longer attended meetings with the new people." She just sent her male employees to meetings with the revolutionary authorities. Mari, a publisher, adopted the same approach. She sent a man to the Ministry of Guidance to get clearance for books published by her company. Zohreh, another publisher, makes it a point to argue with the officials of the ministry over censorship and the right to publish herself. She relates with amusement (and some satisfaction) that at the ministry she is referred to as a "witch" who uses "feminine ruses" to get her way.

Women showed greater flexibility than men in redefining their profes-

sional careers. A political science professor, dismissed on frivolous grounds, decided against taking her superior to court and started her own business. One well-to-do woman had never worked before the revolution. But her husband abandoned her and the children after the revolution and went abroad. She took on two jobs, became the head of household, and raised the children herself.

Women look back on these years of struggle and adjustment with mixed feelings. "Do you want to know what the revolution did to me?" Zahra, a young film director, asked. "It robbed me of my youth." For many women a sense of wasted years is combined with a sense of achievement. After all, they endured, they had been tested and had proven themselves. "As for me," Masoumeh, a businesswoman, said, "The revolution turned me into a woman who is more independent. . . . I am a different person. I have become bitter, cold." Nahid, another businesswoman, struck a more positive note. "They no longer intimidate us," she said, speaking of the revolutionary authorities. "The day we were no longer afraid to shout back at them and they retreated was the turning point for us."

For some women, the revolution, of course, opened up opportunities. The revolution was dominated by a certain group whose women also demanded a share of its fruits. Like the men of the revolution, they were eager to take over the positions occupied by men and women of the old regime. Pouran, a young university professor who had been studying abroad and was in the opposition before the collapse of the monarchy, thus sees the revolution in a different light. The revolution, she says, "opened some doors to people like me." Nasrin, a young revolutionary, told me that had it not been for the revolution, she would never have become the editor of a woman's magazine.

■ ■ ■ ■

Amineh: It was as if you played havoc with my private life. My husband taught at the university. He continued teaching as long as he lived. He died a few years ago. I am still trying to settle his will. Day after day, I get up in the morning, take the bus downtown to the various government offices, and deal with the bureaucracy. So much paperwork! You have to be made of iron not to have a nervous breakdown. For example, just this morning I was told they lost my identity card. Without an identity card you don't exist in this country. The bizarre aspect of it all is that when I gave the man my identity card, I told him to be careful not to misplace or lose it. Your daily life here is nothing but aggravation.

In my professional life, for a long time I was not able to write at all, let alone to write plays. Creativity requires strong nerves and a lot of concentration. I have been under considerable pressure, and there is no way I could sit behind the table and just concentrate on being creative.

After the revolution I had to reorient my life. I started doing new research and gradually decided that writing books was more feasible for me than writing and producing plays. I wanted to write books that were accessible and understandable to ordinary people, your everyday reader. Do you know what that meant for me? I had to put away in storage all the work I had done in the decades before the revolution and start afresh. What a waste! I don't think I will ever go back to that work. I even don't know where my notes are. That chapter is closed.

■ ■ ■ ■ ■

Mari: The revolution left its imprint on all our lives. I was a university professor. Assuming you were not dismissed, the choice was to put up with the humiliation or to resign. I decided I wanted to work. Besides, why give the revolutionary authorities the satisfaction of quitting a career that I had built over many years. The women who stayed resented being called prostitutes just because they worked under the old regime. I remember the deputy director of the department rudely telling me, "We want to make sure that the prostitutes will depart."

Gradually we stopped shaking hands with men. As the faculty thinned down and new people were hired, the friction increased. The problem was no longer that you were a woman. Your social background and your cast of mind became objectionable. The revolutionary authorities accused me of projecting a courtly image. They even lied to me. They told me that the students had signed a petition requesting me not to teach. I spoke to the students. I discovered that because the *hezbollahi* fellow who was teaching the same course had no students, they were using this ploy to get rid of me.

Today, university administrators are stuck with the new faculty that they hired. The good students don't want to take courses with them. We senior faculty are suddenly more respected. Our training, our knowledge, is superior. The authorities can no longer intimidate us, and they know we are not dependent on them. On the contrary, they need us.

Shortly after the revolution, I went into publishing. We printed forty-five books in thirteen years. Of course we had our falling out with some of my colleagues and the Ministry of Guidance. I never go to the ministry. I send a man. I say to myself, "Let him deal with the censors." Some of their directives are too funny for words. For example, in the books we publish, we cannot speak of a man and a woman kissing or use some ordinary words like "embrace." Just absurd.

Our office has become an interesting place. We have lectures, discussion groups, gatherings, and guest speakers. Although the publishing house is not a money-making endeavor, it is rewarding.

In my private life, there were changes, too. My mother was taken to prison just because she belonged to a prominent family. After she was set free, she went to Europe and has not returned to Iran since. My husband lost his job at the university. After all the years he had served the university, this really came as a blow. Accusations were constantly thrown at all of us. The revolution taught us to fight and to survive. Maybe at the beginning we contemplated leaving the country, but never seriously. We are too deeply rooted here. In hindsight, I am so happy we stayed. Both my husband and I find life much more fulfilling and rewarding in Iran than anywhere else.

■ ■ ■ ■ ■

Shokouh: How can the revolution not have affected my life or anybody's life? I was teaching at one of the government hospitals. I was dismissed from my teaching job at the university for not being dressed appropriately. My patients rented a bus and went and demonstrated in front of the office of the chancellor of the university. I was treating these patients with a new medication, and they were showing some improvement. The chancellor sent for me. I refused to go, but then I was threatened. I went back to work, at first reluctantly. I did not want to work for the new authorities, but I was scared.

It wasn't just me. My husband was called in for questioning, too. He was always very apolitical; he loved his work, his research, his practice. I was very worried for him. I remember receiving a phone call from a friend telling me not to let my husband go to the hospital. They thought his life was in danger, but I could not stop him. Eventually the new people at the hospital made him so angry that he left his teaching job at the university. For years he just attended to his private patients, took up gardening, and stayed home. Such a waste! The pressure on him was so great that he became very sick.

I was ready to leave the country. We had both studied in Europe, and I knew we could be very successful no matter where we went. Despite all the problems he had, my husband refused to leave Iran. He is a dedicated nationalist, and his aim in life is serving Iran. I stayed because of him. At first I was very angry. I felt I was falling behind in my profession: I could not go to conferences, I could not keep up with the latest developments in my field. Our friends were leaving. I felt alienated and lonely.

I am fully aware that my family needs me. They would die without me. I have to take this into consideration all the time. In the past I felt I was just trapped here because of them.

I have fought all the obstacles the regime put in front of me: the humiliation, the pressure, the sense the authorities tried to inject in you that as a woman you are a nobody. Despite all the upheaval in my life, professionally I am the best in my field in the country. I felt such a victory when a few years ago the government gave me a prize for my scientific research. Government officials had a ceremony, and when they called my name, I got up and walked down the aisle in a traditional tribal costume, holding my head up. As I was walking, people gave me an ovation. I felt like telling them, "You have not succeeded in breaking my spirit." I treated the soldiers who were burned by chemical weapons during the Iran-Iraq War. I think that as a doctor and a citizen I have done more for these people than they have done for me.

I see myself as a successful career woman. I have also started a business, and I am very good at it. I make a lot of money, and in my own right I am quite well off.

Looking back, I think my husband made the right choice by staying in Iran. Work here is more satisfying to me, my ego is better served here. I have a much more comfortable life in Iran. I travel whenever I feel like it, and I do what I like both in my private life and in my professional life. Today, although I still have the option of leaving, I tell myself that what keeps me here is that I can be of service to the people.

■ ■ ■ ■ ■

Farideh: I had to change my life-style after the revolution. My financial situation deteriorated. I was a government employee living on my salary. I had my own apartment, but I was a woman living alone. My immediate family had gone abroad. A very close friend died after a heart operation. I was very lonely. I felt all the purpose I could muster came from within myself; there was nothing coming from the outside. The atmosphere was bleak. Talk was of death and martyrdom. No music, no theater. Everything around you was black.

Before the revolution I played tennis and I skied. After the revolution I stopped all sports activities. I could not bring myself to ski when people were dying at the front. After the revolution, being a single woman became a problem. You were considered "loose," even a prostitute, as a woman, let alone if you were not married. You lived from one half-hour to another.

In my professional life as an economist the changes were striking. For a while I had to work with a group of novices who also were *hezbollahis*. It was a horrible experience. The rest of the time I worked with my old colleagues. Some changed. They started backbiting and grew mean. I often asked myself why I was putting up with all that pressure, but I wanted to serve my country. I felt an obligation to teach the new people who were taking charge, not for their sake but for the sake of Iran.

When I finally decided to retire, even on my last day at work I was still debating whether I had made the right decision. I wanted to leave; at the same time I wanted to stay. I wanted to be with these people; I also wanted to be away from them. I did not know what was right and what was wrong.

I remember during the first parliament of the Islamic Republic, I went to the relevant parliamentary committee to explain the budget to the deputies. Outside the parliament building, there were chickens and roosters, and in the parking lot there were many BMWs. In those days the deputies were housed near the parliament building. There were several checkpoints, and we were searched bodily. Our pencils, lighters, cigarettes, and keys were removed. We had to take off our shoes and socks.

The members of the committee were all men. They avoided looking at me. Those who looked gave me angry stares. Once I started talking the atmosphere became less tense. I had the upper hand. I was a technocrat who knew her material, and they had never dealt with the budget ·before. I decided that I had to teach them how a budget is drafted and written. I continued with my explanations outside the committee room in the corridor. They came up to me and asked questions. My knowledge and my tongue were my weapons. That was all they had left me. Toward the end, I started teasing them, and by making their lack of knowledge obvious, I was taking my revenge.

Elaheh: I can't say the revolution had an immediate effect on my life. It did not wreak havoc with my life, nor did it upset my plans. I was supposed to go abroad to continue my education, and so I did. But the shock came when I returned to Iran. It was a very difficult adjustment. It was like landing on a different planet. I found out I no longer knew anybody at the university, nor did I want to be part of the existing departmental politics. I just wanted to teach.

Before the revolution you felt there was a set of rules and principles that the teaching staff felt obligated to follow whether they believed in them or not. But what did I encounter in the mid-1980s when I returned from Europe? Total chaos: people would come and go and teach as they liked. Nobody felt any responsibility either toward the students or the administration. I remember observing to a relative that there was not much difference between the post office and our department.

■ ■ ■ ■ ■

Darya: How could I not be touched by the revolution? Me, of all people! We lived with the events, we saw them unfolding before us on a daily basis. I quit my job and watched helplessly as all the progress and achievements in the field of women's rights were being reversed. It was a personal loss. You suddenly felt you were becoming a different person. It took us several years to put together a semblance of a normal life.

■ ■ ■ ■ ■

Gowhar: I was a revolutionary, so I was at one with what was happening. I continued working as a judge until the law prohibiting women from judgeships was passed. Then I and all the other women judges were demoted to legal assistants. I accepted this new position. What else could I do? I was not a quitter. The universities were closed, so there was no possibility to teach. The Bar Association would not licence any new lawyers. I was not going to work in a store. And I wasn't alone. We were forty women working for male judges. Then the government passed a law that allowed women to take early retirement, after fifteen years of service. I used this law, and the excuse that my husband did not want me to work, to retire. This was five years after the revolution. I started from zero. It was as if I had just graduated from the university. I was determined to be very successful again, just to spite these people. I remember being told by one of the judges I worked for, "It is a pity you are a woman." This remark was so insulting, it wounded me deeply. Until that day I had never thought of myself as a woman. It was then that I made up my mind to become a thorn in their side. I was going to work myself to death to prove to them that I am excellent in everything I do.

Today I have my law practice, I act as a consultant to various companies, I teach at the university, and I publish legal books. My first book was published by the Ministry of Justice—the same ministry that demoted me because of my sex.

■ ■ ■ ■ ■

Soudabeh: The revolution did not have a negative effect on me, neither on my professional life nor my private life. As far as my professional life goes, I would have made the same progress with or without the revolution. I worked hard before the revolution, I worked hard during the revolution. In short, I am a conscientious, professional person who takes her career very seriously. I have never allowed people to stop me. I also never gave any excuse to the authorities to block my advancement.

Our private life did not change either. Of course one is sensitive to the new society one lives in, and in order to survive you adjust to it. What I am saying is that the adjustment was not difficult for me.

■ ■ ■ ■ ■

Manijeh: The revolution turned me from a carefree young girl into a responsible mature person. I cannot separate the war from the revolution. I come from the south. I was in Abadan when the Iran-Iraq War started. I worked as a first-aid volunteer in the hospital. The situation became so chaotic that I found myself doing anesthetics in the operating room. The doctors had barely time to cut off limbs. The nurses were so scared that they could not urinate. We felt we were abandoned and forgotten by the rest of the country.

When the Iraqi soldiers reached the outskirts of the city, I decided to leave. I had lost twenty-five pounds and was living on salt crackers. There was nothing else to eat. Later, in Tehran, I was hospitalized for malnutrition.

I got myself into a trailer truck, which took me to the city of Bushehr. I then took the bus to Behbahan. I will never forget that when the bus stopped in front of a bakery and we went to get bread, the baker pulled the shutters down and refused to sell to us. To him we were people who had abandoned their city and were running away. Nobody knew what the population of Abadan had gone through. Not even my parents could understand my state of mind. They had left earlier for Tehran.

I arrived in Tehran a week later. When I saw the rows of empty buses at the bus terminal, I started to cry. They could have sent these buses to transport all the war refugees stranded along the road.

My father had lost his job. We were all living in a room at the home of one of my mother's relatives. My father would go out every morning to look for a job and would return home empty-handed and depressed. People did not hire war refugees. They recognized us as southerners by our dark complexion and our accents.

I decided to work to contribute to our income. I never told my parents. I took a baby-sitting job. If my father ever found out, he would die of shame. After six months I switched to a job in a lab. At first I was cleaning out the bottles. I then became a lab technician.

I wanted to study in the States but was denied a visa, so I went to a university in Tehran. It was important for my father. I did not want him to feel that he had failed to provide for his children's future.

In those days the atmosphere at the university was terrible. You had to be very careful. Everybody was watching everybody else. An atmosphere of fascism reigned. I put up with it for the sake of getting a degree. I accepted the reality that I could no longer have too many ambitions and ideals. It was very sad for a young woman.

■ ■ ■ ■ ■

Nazanin: The revolution changed everything. I had a profession, I lost it. I stopped working and went to England to get a master's degree in French and English literature. When I came back to Iran I did some teaching at home, but then decided to write for Persian literary magazines. I worked to avoid depression. Since the revolution, depression is so widespread in Iran. As Voltaire said, the antidote for melancholia is working. I believed one had to work—to write and make a statement.

I witnessed too many of my friends losing their jobs, staying at home, and falling to pieces both physically and mentally. I, on the contrary, did not go to pieces, nor did I feel wretched. Of course, I had a difficult and frustrating time, but it was my choice to stay in Iran and to prove to myself that I could survive. I saw how uprooted my compatriots who were living abroad had become. I did not want that kind of a life. I had to make compromises after the revolution, and I accepted that.

The joy of life has gone from my generation. We no longer laugh; laughing is considered ugly and vulgar.

■ ■ ■ ■ ■

Ayesheh: The revolution made a tremendous difference in our lives. I quit working my government job in 1980. For a person who had been working since she was eighteen years old, this was a personal sorrow and a tragedy. I saw everything that I had built come to a standstill. I asked myself, "How can they do without people like me who worked honestly and were dedicated to public service?" It was a very difficult time. I have my own attitude in life. I had my principles, my own way of thinking. I could not change them.

At first, after I quit working, I would get up every morning, get dressed as if I were going out to work, and go into the kitchen and stain my good clothes cooking and cleaning. My spirit was in mourning and my mind cried out. I realized that as a woman I could no longer be what I wanted to be.

My husband worked in the private sector. He, too, had to limit the scope of his activities. Everybody was trying to keep a low profile and not attract attention. It was as if everyone's work and life had become clandestine. It was so sad.

I forced myself to join the private sector. The adjustment took its toll on me. To this day I wish I could be back where I belong, in my old government job.

There was a major change in my private life. I got married in 1978. My husband is a very civilized person. We share the same outlook, the same feelings, and the same thoughts. These should have been the best years in our lives. They turned out to be the hardest years. My husband went into a deep depression. I had to help him surmount this depression. I pretended it was easy to survive and start all over again. A number of our friends had left or were in prison. I could not make any new friends. To this day, I pull out my old friends from the bottle of my memory, and I live with them.

■ ■ ■ ■ ■

Fatemeh: The revolution affected all our lives. I can't name one person who remained unscarred by it. We had to be on our guard all the time, at home and at work. I took over the business from my father two years before the revolution. He decided to spend half the year in Europe and half in Iran. His presence meant a lot to the business. After the revolution, my sister and her family left; my younger sister was still living abroad; and my parents decided to spend even more time in Europe. We stayed because my husband did not want to leave and our child was very young. I just did not have the heart to sell the business, abandon the workers, and go. So I stayed and became responsible for the family assets as well as the business. I had to provide for the whole family. I had to do a man's job. Suddenly I had to deal with the *komitehs* and the relevant government offices. At first it was very difficult, but if you don't have a choice you learn very quickly how to operate within a new system.

Despite the pressure and the hardship of dealing with the revolutionary authorities and the war, I decided to expand the business. I was working six days a week, twelve hours a day. When you work that much, there is very little time left for yourself and your family and friends.

My private life changed insofar as my immediate family was no longer here. So I lacked the support that the family always gave to me. Some of my close friends left. Of course I felt the vacuum, but I adjusted to our new pattern of life. There was too much to worry about every day to consider whether it would have been better to leave. In hindsight, I am glad we stayed. I have a comfortable life here, and I enjoy my job. In a way you learn to handle these conditions and these people, of course with a lot of aggravation. The revolution taught me to fight back and also to negotiate.

Atefeh: The revolution was like a hurricane passing through my life. It created havoc. These were unusual times, and people showed their true colors. For example, I spent some time in jail. A lot of my friends did not even go to visit my child who was staying with the maid.

I went to jail because of a complaint lodged by our gardener. I used to have a large garden outside Tehran. There were two gardeners working for me. One stayed faithful to me and to this day works for me. The other schemed to take possession of my property. The months I spent in jail were the most miserable, difficult time of my life. I hope nobody will ever experience such a thing.

But it is amazing how one adjusts to a new environment. At first I slept on newspapers and covered myself with newspapers. Gradually I got a clean sheet. I asked the jailer to give me a broom so I could sweep the cell. Then I asked to work in the kitchen. I just could not sit idle. The way I conducted myself was surprising to the authorities. Not once was their behavior insulting. I believe you can live according to your own standards under any conditions.

When I got out of jail, I was a different woman. I worked with a vengeance to exonerate my name, get my property back, and put my life back in order. A number of my close relatives had left. Among those who stayed behind there was a coolness toward me. My optimism about the revolution was off-putting to them. They conceived of me as a revolutionary who felt animosity toward them. While this was not the case, I constantly worried about their well-being.

Because of the war, my business was very slow and almost came to a standstill. It was a trying time. I started selling my personal belongings to make ends meet. I lived from one day to the next.

■ ■ ■ ■ ■

Masoumeh: The revolution wreaked havoc with my life. First, my husband was dismissed from his job, then I lost mine. We had been living on our salaries. We had no private resources to fall back on.

We sold our car, then I sold my wedding ring, then the piano and the fur coat. One morning I opened the closet and there was nothing left to sell. My father in law was helping us. For several years, we received 5,000 *tomans* a month from him. In those days, this came to $250. Today it comes to $20.

You see, our problem was how to survive from day to day, where to get money for the next day's expenses. The cost of living was rising daily, and I was trying to budget the little money we had.

All this did not take place in a normal time and atmosphere. There were arrests, executions. Our friends had left or were keeping a very low profile. Everybody was scared. One was afraid of an unfamiliar face or an unrecognizable voice. Every knock on the door made you jump. You thought, "Maybe this time they are coming for me."

Let me tell you a story. Once or twice a week we used to gather at a friend's house not far from the infamous Evin Prison. We sat on her balcony and usually read poetry. We could also see the prison's wall. Between two of our gatherings, a friend was arrested and was now behind those walls, while we still sat on that balcony on a cool Tehran spring night. It was not a normal situation. You could not pretend to be casual, not even in the privacy of your home. You did not have control over any aspect of your life.

It was then that I decided I had to take the children and leave Iran. I knew there was no way my husband was going to join us. I always compare him to an ancient plane tree, with roots several hundred years old in the soil of Iran. You cannot uproot such a tree without killing it. But he suddenly got very sick, and I could not abandon him. So I decided to stay and adapt myself to this new life.

I started knitting. I even bought a knitting machine. It did not work. The pressure on me to produce and to sell made me very nervous and sick. It was a failed project. I was desperate to earn money.

My husband had started a small publishing company with a couple of friends. This was his profession. He did not know what else to do. The idea was to put out "how to" books. Our first project was a simple cookbook, and it sold quite well. We went door to door, office to office, bookstore to bookstore and sold the book.

My husband and I were also doing some translating, but we really could not meet our daily needs with the little money we made. It was at this stage that I received a call from a woman I had known when I was working in a publishing house. I remembered her as an ordinary person, but very bright. I had come across her on the street shortly before the revolution. She had changed a lot. She was carrying a miniature poodle and was quite dressed up. She told me she had a couture salon and was making and selling dresses. She had also moved to an affluent neighborhood.

This woman, who had heard about our situation, offered me a job to come and manage her workshop. She was then producing children's clothes and had a group of women seamstresses working for her. She paid me 4,000 *tomans*. I accepted her offer. At least I knew that every month we would have a steady income.

Working in that salon was very trying for me. The women seamstresses, who came from very simple backgrounds, commented on my looks, my dresses, my manners and gestures. For them I was a woman cut out from the German fashion magazine, *Burda*. In my free time I volunteered to sew buttons and press clothes. I spent a whole year in that workshop. Gradually I became sick and developed an ulcer. I was crying all the time, I was losing weight and could not sleep. I knew this could not go on for much longer. The publishing business was not making any money either. I had to find a job in my own field. I wanted to be my own boss and to work at a job that was both satisfying and would allow us to earn a living. It was then that we decided to invest with a few silent partners in a bookstore.

I was doing a man's job as well as a woman's job. I found the premises, dealt with the real estate agent, the electrician, the builder, the plumber, and so on. I remember telling one aghast plumber at six thirty in the morning that if he, as a man, had two balls, I as a woman had four. I did all the leg-work. But with the authorities my husband was the front man, the person whom they met and dealt with.

For the first four years we both ran the business. But after that, I decided that my husband would be more productive and do more interesting work by not coming to the bookstore. I wanted our place to be a center for literary gatherings; my husband wanted people to come in, buy a book, and walk out. I did not want to be treated like a shopkeeper. I mean, I did not want people to come and bargain about the price of a book. There were unpleasant incidents, too. I remember a friend of mine, a man I had known since my student days in Europe and who used to come to our store regularly, telling his little daughter to count the change since Ms. Masoumeh was in the habit of not returning the exact change. I will never forget the humiliation I felt. He left, and I burst into tears.

On another occasion a man walked into the store. I took one look at him and knew he was an average *hezbollahi*. They are so recognizable.

The man introduced himself as someone who as a child had read all the articles I had written for a literary youth magazine and had followed my literary career. I took one look at him and thought to myself, "I should have both my hands amputated with a kitchen knife for writing the articles that turned you into what you are today, appearing in front of me with this beard!" Eventually we became good friends. He was studying law while working in a school. Today he is an attorney in one of the provinces.

You see, as women we carry all the burden. We are professionals par excellence, and then we go home and become the average, ordinary housewife. We cook, we wash, we clean, and we raise our children. In the old days I used to work, but I had a woman at home looking after the children and the house. She left after the revolution. She wanted to go, and we could no longer afford to keep her.

The revolution turned me into a woman who is more independent than I ever was. I learned to struggle. Today, as my mother says, even when I sit on a chair I don't lean on it. I am a self-made woman who was forced to remake herself, to reconstruct her life. I am a different person. I have become bitter, cold, bad, and inside me there is a fist ready to strike back.

■ ■ ■ ■ ■

Ladan: I must confess I suffered a lot. The revolution brought about a terrible upheaval in my life—not only in mine but in the lives of the people around me, friends and family. But we managed to put it behind us and we came out on top. We never knew whether we would make it to the next day.

Important decisions had to be made every day. I was forced to change direction. At the peak of my professional career, suddenly I had to start all over again. Among other things, the school where I was teaching changed hands; it was no longer a mixed school and the teachers were all dismissed. I am a very competent person and not helpless. I'm fluent in several languages, so I started working from home. We sold the house I had loved so much and moved into a smaller place. We even sold our country house to send the children to school abroad. I don't regret having done that. Today, the children are very successful young professionals. But I feel that my husband has still not adjusted to the situation. He works, but he is like a man working under duress.

■ ■ ■ ■ ■

Nahid: The revolution created a class of people who felt alienated and like strangers in their own country. Of course over the years this has changed. Today we are once again who we were. The day we were no longer afraid to shout back at them and they retreated was the turning point for us.

In my case I had to change jobs because of the revolution. After working for many years in the government, I started my own business. That alone was quite an adjustment. To deal with the revolutionary authorities and the people who came to your office, you needed iron nerves.

In our private life, all our friends left. Our children left and did not return. Members of the family kept a very low profile. You could not help but worry for your next of kin. One was anxious all the time. Let me give you an example. We were twenty-five women who met socially once a month. After the revolution only five of us were left. In short, we felt very vulnerable.

■ ■ ■ ■ ■

Touran: Would it be an exaggeration if I told you the revolution caused a major change in my life? I spent three years and two months in jail for my leftist political activities. My professional and private life became a total mess. I had taught briefly at the university before being purged. Then I worked as a translator for a newspaper. I resigned from that job. Today I work from home. I do research for various organizations.

In my private life the damage was greater. I did not see my child for more than three years. My husband was detained, too. We are so vulnerable as a family, so fragile. We stopped being politically active. But every time there is a political incident, we feel uncomfortable. We try to keep a very low profile.

■ ■ ■ ■ ■

Ramesh: The revolution did not affect my life. There were changes in my private life, but not as a result of the revolution. I wanted a divorce, and after the revolution it became more difficult for a woman to obtain a divorce. But my brother managed to obtain a divorce for me.

I got remarried and I lead a most comfortable life. I wanted to study, passed the university entrance exam, and got accepted. I will graduate in two years and will probably start my own business. In brief, the revolution did not make much of a difference in my life.

Lili: The revolution changed everything in our lives. I lived apart from my husband for three years. He stayed in the provinces, and I moved with our children to Tehran and lived with my in-laws. I was so scared for him. He visited us every ten days. It was my decision not to live alone and to move into a building where we had family. In those years I was rebuilding our lives. I lived very sparsely and tried to save as much as I could. From the day we came to Tehran I wanted to work, but my husband insisted I could get a job only with someone he knew. He mistrusts strangers.

I saved and suffered the inconvenience of living with my in-laws so that we could buy a house. We managed to buy a house, and, once more, it was I who decided to rent it out. I am doing all this because I want a better future.

Finally, I found a job with a relative and my husband no longer objected to my working. Now I have taken a second job to add to our income. My husband is quite accommodating, but, unless I tell him, he does not take any initiative on his own. For example, if I ask him to do the dishes he will do them. Otherwise, the dishes will sit in the sink until I come back from work. We live in a male-dominated society. Nevertheless, men like my husband are so dependent on their wives. My husband trusts my judgment in managing our finances, but he is very suspicious about whether I am faithful to him. His attitude borders on fanaticism.

The revolution left its impact on our private life as well. I almost left my husband for a man I fell in love with. But my husband told me he would not give me custody of the children. It was a type of blackmail. I did not want his family to raise my children, and I did not want my children being told that their mother abandoned them. In hindsight, I think the right decision would have been to marry the man I really loved.

Today, I am a disillusioned woman. I don't see any future for myself. I know I missed my chance. I no longer desire anything for myself. I want everything for my children. Having said that, I consider myself a successful person and compare myself to a mountain that endures through all the four seasons.

■ ■ ■ ■ ■

Monir: I wish I had been twenty years old when the revolution occurred and not thirty-five. I could have better understood the impact of such an upheaval on society and on our private lives. All I know is that instead of harvesting all the seeds I had planted, I was forced to start from scratch.

This should have been a period of my life when I could sit back and enjoy the results of working so hard for so many years. Instead, I had to make a new life and start at the beginning.

I killed myself in order to survive. People like me were being attacked for who they were and what they represented. Our Western education, our values, our outlook, everything we stood for was turned into an indictment, cursed, and destroyed. As a woman and as a lawyer, I and many other women like me did not know who our accusers were, why they were doing this to us. Every time I went to the Ministry of Justice I trembled like a willow tree.

At the ministry and in the courts, they did not acknowledge our presence. The atmosphere was being poisoned against the legal profession. They showed plays on television depicting lawyers as collaborators of the secret police and military tribunals. It was as if one were witnessing a conspiracy to destroy and defeat the lawyers. I stayed on and acquiesced in being humiliated—not because I was fighting the system. No! I had to earn a living. I knew that my absence or presence in the court made no difference, but there I was day after day.

I remember on many occasions when I went with a woman client to the special courts they had set up to look into family disputes, the presiding judges would instruct me not to talk so much or would tell the client she had no need for a lawyer. They made me feel so small with their insults.

I decided I had to understand their lingo, so I started studying Islamic law with a vengeance. I had to acquire their weapons. Even so, we—the handful of women lawyers who, lacking any choice in the matter, continued to go to the Ministry of Justice—ended up either as legal assistants or doing odd jobs for male lawyers.

I offered to do *pro bono* work, but clients had no confidence in a woman lawyer who would represent them in a court presided by a cleric. My aim was to get over my fear of arguing cases based on Islamic law. Today I have become quite good at it. I have managed to have a sentence of stoning reduced to whipping, a death sentence reduced to a prison term, and so forth. Look, one day I died, and then I decided to come back to a totally unfamiliar world and survive in it.

■ ■ ■ ■ ■

Nargess: Because of the revolution, I had to give up my administrative job and join a research unit. But after two years I was called back and was given the position of deputy director of the same office I had been running before the revolution. The authorities needed my skills and services. Once the law enabling women to take early retirement was passed by parliament, I retired. My excuse was that I needed to take care of my family. In today's Iran no male employer will argue with that. I then went into private practice and started my own law office.

Our private life was not spared either. My husband was unemployed for a while. Today he works in the civil service as an administrator. We just did not have any choice. We needed both incomes to survive. Financially, the revolution was a setback for both of us. Had it not been for the revolution, I would have advanced rapidly in my profession. Today, as a woman lawyer, I feel I am standing still. I find it very difficult to function in the present Ministry of Justice. I love my profession, but I feel my hands are tied both by the law and by its executors. To my sorrow I must admit that I might have to give up my job. I just can't take the unjust pressure any more, and I feel I will no longer be successful in my career.

■ ■ ■ ■ ■

Afsar: The revolution was bad for people of my generation, both in our private lives and in our public activities. We had just started being productive, and then it all came to a halt.

I was dismissed from my job as a university professor. Not only that, but I was permanently discharged from any government employment. The revolutionary authorities accused me of being a propagandist for antigovernment groups. A lot of nonsense, all false accusations. I started publishing a magazine; they stopped the magazine, too. I managed to work for six months as an adviser to a government organization. My new employers learned of the discharge order, and once again I was dismissed. Now I do market research for a private company. It has been many years since I have been creative as an artist. I am a woman in my mid-fifties, and I feel very, very tired.

■ ■ ■ ■ ■

Zohreh: Because of the revolution, you constantly had to explain to people who you were and what your background was, and not only that you were not different from the revolutionaries but that you were one of them. I could not sit idle. I wanted to be active again. The condition of women and what was happening to them mattered a lot to me. I got together with a group of women who shared similar views on women's issues. The women belonged to various political groups but were there because they felt their personal survival as women was at stake.

We were the first women to analyze the Law of Retribution and its consequences for women. We had already expressed our concern to the way the constituent assembly, which drafted the constitution, had dealt with women's issues.

I remember the leftist members of our group being under a lot of pressure to follow the party line. On several occasions when they refused to toe the line, they were accused by men of working with *taghuti* women. I mean, it was the men who became irrational and unprofessional.

At some stage after the revolution I decided to start my own publishing house. So far we have published eighty books. Some of my books deal with women's issues. For example, we try to show how women cope in a totalitarian system. We publish books that deal with feminism. I find such books of great importance, especially when women are under so much pressure in the society in which they live.

I have to deal all the time with the men at the Ministry of Guidance. Unlike a lot of women entrepreneurs, I did not delegate this task to my male colleagues. Because I get my way, I have been told by the men in the ministry that I use feminine ruses or that I am a witch. I am a serious person and I fight for my rights. I have made sure that nobody keeps me waiting outside closed doors. Of course I have my reasons. I want to serve my country, and I want to be successful, and I fight for my goals.

■ ■ ■ ■ ■

Pouran: I came back to Iran during the revolution. It was a big change for me. I had been living abroad for many years. At first I felt lost and helpless. My husband was working, and I stayed at home. I became a nagging wife. I decided to go to work. I took a teaching job at the university and started writing literary articles. After a while it was I who was very busy. My husband started to resent my work.

The revolution opened some doors to people like myself who had just come back from abroad and had been in the opposition. I resented preferential treatment, especially if being a woman came into it, too. Anyway, I discovered that such treatment did not last long. When my first literary piece criticizing an established Iranian author appeared, rumors started circulating that the real author of the literary piece was a man, who used my name as a pseudonym. Until very recently nobody took me and my work at all seriously. It is only now, after fifteen years, that I feel I have established myself as a serious scholar in my field.

At a professional level, at the university, I don't have clashes with my colleagues; they respect me, but they don't treat me as an equal. When I first started working, they did not ask me to participate in committee work. The excuse was that as a woman I had a lot of housework to attend to. It was really insulting. I consider myself the most important member of my department, and they bypass me. On one occasion, I was even refused leave to go to a conference on the assumption that I might not observe the *hejab* while abroad. I went to see the president of the university and became emotional, burst into tears, and accused him of not respecting my scholarship. I am sure a man would have dealt with this matter more rationally, but I am an emotional person.

I have American training so I confront people and I am aggressive in presenting my views. A number of women in the department try to be self-effacing and meek.

In my private life, my husband and I have reached an understanding. He respects my work and does not mind if I take time off to go abroad to do research and leave the children with him. As the children grow older they resent my not being at home as much as they want. The dilemma of a working woman is the same everywhere, but it weighs more on you if you live in alien surroundings, under less than friendly conditions.

■ ■ ■ ■ ■

Jila: Show me one person among our class of people who was not affected by the revolution. Show me one of us who remained untouched by the revolution. There is no such thing. We all had to make some sort of adjustment—some of us more, some less.

Lida: My professional career developed under the revolution. For me these have been successful and rewarding years. I am among the few women in charge of a hospital. I have a booming private practice and consider myself among the best in my field.

All this did not come easily to me. In the early years of the revolution, when I was doing my residency, the director of the hospital was very happy with my performance. He always referred to me as "the little satan." I am physically small but very clever. Then everything changed. Rumors were circulated that my husband was a revolutionary guard and that I was at the hospital to spy on my colleagues. Everybody avoided me. The authorities withheld my salary for six months and stopped my promotion. Anonymous letters were circulated about my character. Finally my husband stepped in. To see his wife insulted was too much for him. It took him six months to sort things out and set everything right for me. He has been my support all along. One day, in my private clinic, I received a call from the chancellor of the university appointing me as the director of the hospital. I told him I did not have much experience in running a hospital, nor did I have the support of the staff.

My appointment created an uproar. In my first meeting with the teaching staff, the former director referred to me as the handpicked puppet of the chancellor. His wife would tell me to my face how ugly I was. For two weeks the hospital did not have a teaching staff. They all refused to come to work. Finally the chancellor gave them an ultimatum: either they would return to the hospital or he would dismiss them all. Of course everyone showed up.

Today I run this place like a dictator. I have put an end to gossiping and promotion through connections. I have put an end to the interference of the Islamic society in how this hospital should function. I run this place with an iron fist and don't allow any outside interference.

■ ■ ■ ■ ■

Partow: The revolution was like an earthquake in my life. It destroyed all I had. Our living standard deteriorated rapidly. First we sold one house we owned, then a second house. Then we sold our car. My husband lost his job. He was sitting at home glued to the radio. He had a nervous breakdown. He could not bring himself to work. Like most Iranian men he was spoiled.

My husband could have joined a family business, but he preferred to go to Europe. I knew this was a wrong decision and refused to go and stayed behind with the children. We have been living apart since then, but neither of us is interested in a divorce. In our society, it is easier and more respectable to be a married woman—even if one is only nominally married—than to be a divorcée.

I, who until the revolution was an ordinary housewife minding my own life, suddenly had to raise three children in the absence of their father.

In an indirect way the revolution gave a purpose, a direction, to my life. I suddenly had a goal in life—to prove to everybody that I could manage our affairs. I am a serious person and was not going to be defeated. In a way, I feel liberated because of my economic independence. Today, if my husband returns, I won't take him back. I prefer to face a future of loneliness than to be party once again to a married life with a husband I can no longer depend on and trust.

■ ■ ■ ■ ■

Nayyer: My whole life changed as a result of the revolution. My husband lost his job and stayed at home. I had to earn enough to sustain him and our children. A true role reversal. We are the only generation of Iranian women who must think and be concerned about what will happen to our husbands if we leave them. Overnight we had to think like men but still act as women. We had to provide for the family, but we also had to conceal this role in order not to offend our men. The attitude of Iranian men toward their women is: "This is the way we are, take it or leave it." What they mean really is: "Put up with us."

Many times I felt like leaving home, but I knew that without me the family would be lost, so I stayed. Now I am angry, and I feel trapped.

When the revolution took place, I was working for the government. A lot of my friends took early retirement. I decided to stay on. I believed in serving my country. From the very beginning the new administration tried to make it very difficult for women to work. You either were one of them, complied with the image they projected of women, or there was no room for you.

In the government offices, the scarf became a must. I remember receiving a written notice, signed by the secretary of one of the deputy directors, telling me not to sit behind my desk any longer because I had been seen at a meeting with a bit of hair showing under my scarf. It was so humiliating. It made me livid. I picked up the phone and scolded the secretary for daring to write such a note. I packed my bags and went home. The officials treated it as leave with pay. After six months I was summoned by one of the directors, who gave me a pep talk about the importance of the *hejab* and how women should not behave like dolls. He accused me of not yet embracing the *hejab* fully since my neck was showing. My hand went automatically to my neck. I believe there was less than half an inch of flesh showing. Once again I felt so small, so humiliated.

With their arrogance and behavior, the authorities turned us into quarrelsome and fighting women. It became a daily struggle not to be intimidated by the men. I went back to work as an educational consultant. I constantly had confrontations in the office. I was accused of ruining the atmosphere in the workplace. The authorities drove me to hysteria, and finally I was forced to retire in 1985.

I was forced to reeducate myself. I took a course in management, a course in accounting, and I learned typing. I started working in the private sector. The adjustment was very difficult for me. It meant working for another person with no independence. I became experienced enough to start my own business. I went into partnership with another woman and took orders for rare books. I am now running the business myself, but it is not enough to sustain a family. I do some writing and translating, anything to add to our income.

I am not going to give up. I took the university entrance examination and I passed it. I want to study law. My days are long and exhausting and at home I don't have the privacy I need. I feel like a buffer zone between my sons and their father. They see that he does not work. How can they show him the respect he demands from them? I have turned into a punching bag, receiving the blows of my children and my husband. Sometimes I become so very angry that I feel like smashing my fist into the metal wall of a bus. I don't have a punching bag to hit.

■ ■ ■ ■ ■

Sousan: The revolution affected my professional life more than my private life. I was a university professor teaching international law. Very soon after the revolution a substantial number of the teaching staff left, not only from our department but from many departments at the university. This was an excessive reaction and the wrong attitude. It harmed the university. Then our center dismissed one of the women professors, and some of our male colleagues were purged. I applied for leave without pay and made sure the administration understood this was a protest move.

After a year I was asked to go back to work. I refused and was dismissed. This was in 1985. I had signed too many leaflets, including one against the Law of Retribution. We lawyers did not feel the Algiers Agreement* was a fair deal.

The purge in those days took place on three levels. The first purge affected former ministers, members of parliament, in short high-ranking officials of the former regime. The second purge dealt with people who were involved in activities against the revolution and the government. The third purge was directed at people like me who were critical of certain decisions of the government, but always within the framework of the constitution of the Islamic Republic. Of course, I could have taken my case to the civil ser-vice tribunal, but I decided against it. I had made up my mind to leave the university. By that time the faculty of law had once more become a male stronghold. Some of my colleagues made peace with the new administration and went back to teaching. Some were asked to sign an admission of guilt. I wanted no part of it.

I started a small publishing business with some friends. We concentrated on printing simplified legal texts. It was not a money-making endeavor, so I decided to go into private business and open a store. My father had a store. I took over the store, painted it myself, fixed it up, and started sitting behind the counter and selling books and educational material. Today, I even exhibit paintings and sell them for the artists.

In those days, like today, people dropped into the store, looked around, chatted, and left. Very soon after I had opened the store, I noticed a young *hezbollahi* keeping watch from across the street. At that time one was con-stantly on one's guard: you had to deal with the *komitehs*, the *hezbollahis*,

---

*Under the January 1981 Algiers Agreement, Iran agreed to release the American hostages held at the American Embassy in Tehran since November 1979. The United States agreed to release several billion dollars of frozen Iranian assets, and a tribunal was established at the Hague to adjudicate claims by the nationals and governments of the two countries against one another. The number of American claims against Iran were much greater than Iranian claims against the United States.

the white Toyotas with the *khahara* (revolutionary "sisters") in them. Any of these people could take you in for questioning.

The *hezbollahi* guy started coming to the store and looking at the books. I knew he was also listening to the conversations. One evening after the last customer left, he came over and asked me who these men I talked to were. I told him I did not know their names and explained to him that a store which sells primarily books is not like a grocery store. You browse, you look, you talk, and then you might buy a book or just leave. He said he was fascinated by my attitude and the way I talked to men. He told me that, except for his mother and sister, he had never talked to a woman before. He also added that he always thought that women who worked and talked to strange men were not honorable. I will never forget his remark that my behavior was "just like that of a man." I said to him, "For me there is no difference between a man and a woman. It is you people who have introduced the element of sex in relationships between men and women." We became friends. I guided him in his readings and lent him books. At some stage—I don't recall when maybe it was last year—he told me that he did not let his father marry off his sister at the age of sixteen, that she finished her high school and was applying to go to university. It is moments like that which makes the troubles I encountered just disappear.

My private life has not changed much. My old friends are around. We go to the same kind of parties we used to go to before the revolution. I still live in the house I grew up in, in the same neighborhood, and through my business I meet new people.

■ ■ ■ ■ ■

Nasrin: Unlike other women you have talked to, the revolution was not an earthquake, nor did it create an upheaval in my life. We were a traditional family and welcomed the revolution. I am who I am because of the opportunities the revolution gave me and people such as myself.

■ ■ ■ ■ ■

Zahra: In my professional life, the revolution gave me the opportunity to work in the film industry. Families found it easier after the revolution to permit their daughters to work in films, since the Iranian film industry was purged of all the corrupting prerevolutionary elements. It is now a better and cleaner working environment.

On the one hand, women are protected; on the other hand, women cannot advance beyond a certain level. I recall one of the people in the Ministry of Guidance asking me whether I was planning to push ahead of the men, simply because I was trying to make more than one film a year.

The revolution changed the course of my private life. It actually ruined it. I was going to marry a man I was in love with, but he left the country because of the revolution.

I was eighteen when the revolution took place. It robbed me of my youth. I never had the chance to discover and to develop my emotions. I had barely discovered my psyche as a woman when I was forced to fight my inner feelings and suppress being young. I remember I used to have long hair. I was told by a boy that if I want to be a true revolutionary I should cut my hair short. And I did.

Today I am happily married. I direct films and am also a partner in a construction firm. I have not encountered any discrimination in being a woman. Actually I don't allow any man to block my way. I have learned to fight for my rights and get what I deserve.

■ ■ ■ ■ ■

Neda: I suffered in my private life and had to make basic adjustments in my public life. I don't want to talk much about my private life. All I would like to say is that it was not easy to live away from one's husband and daughter. My husband had to leave, and we felt our daughter would get a better education abroad. I stayed because I wanted to continue teaching in Iran. It was very hard not to see them for several years.

It was no easier in my professional life. We women professors had to prove to the revolutionary authorities that women of our class were not "corrupt," that we were hardworking, knowledgeable. We felt a responsibility to project a proper and correct image of what the Iranian woman was before the revolution.

Let me tell you there were occasions when I was driven to despair and went and stood under a tree on campus and cried. They bothered us a lot.

Students would come up to us and would ask, "Are you still around?" We constantly worried that they would post our photographs on the wall, as "corrupt" individuals.

There was a group of us women professors who suffered all possible humiliation and yet we stayed on. Actually, the women professors who quit the country and left owe us. Over the years we have learned to deal with the people who are now running the show, and they have learned to respect us.

Five

Resistance

ASKED HOW THEY WOULD DEFINE *women's resistance against the impositions of the state over the last seventeen years, most women answered with one word:* hejab. *Despite cajoling, threats, physical punishments, lashings, verbal scoldings, insults, and monetary fines, women take special pride in having resisted the Islamic dress code. The dress code has become a principal battleground between the state and women, and the battle over dress has assumed political significance. Through the dress code, the state endeavors to define and symbolically control the role of women. By flaunting the dress code, women not only seek to score points against the authorities; they also strive to assert autonomy over their own persons.*

Women, of course, cover their hair and wear the required neck-to-ankle robe in public. But they find subtler ways of getting around the dress code. Today the robes are shorter and come in a variety of colors. In wealthier north Tehran, raincoats and overcoats have replaced the robe. Instead of the maghnae, *which fits tightly under the chin, women wear loose, flowing scarves. Young girls around the campus of Tehran University wear colorful scarves, disclosing the tip of a pony tail or flaunting their famous* kakols, *a fringe or bob of hair showing beneath the scarf, in the face of revolutionary guards. It is not uncommon in Tehran to see, beneath the folds of a* chador *flapping in the wind, traditional women wearing Western-style suits and dresses.*

Men and women at all levels of society and regardless of class, occupation, or social background admire the women who stand up to the government in this way. "I don't approve of showing your hair," a religious woman told me. "But I can't stop admiring these young women who are so bold and wear their hair so provocatively." A driver who takes me around when in Tehran routinely points out to me women showing their hair or wearing a touch of makeup or colorful robe. "Look how they defy the authorities," he tells me. He drew my attention to his own eight-year-old daughter: as soon as the little girl gets into the car with me and away from her religious mother, she snatches off her scarf and pulls a puff of hair down over her forehead, in imitation of the young women she sees on the streets.

For many of the women I interviewed, the imposition of the dress code has become an infringement of their freedom of choice, a violation of their private space and civic rights. "They just don't understand that you cannot perform surgery . . . with a maghnae strangling your throat," said Shokouh, a physician. She recalled that she used to wear the scarf only when men came into her clinic. She then started wearing a turban that covered her hair but exposed her neck. Some zealots waged a complaint against her. Today she wears a loose scarf; she finds it unbecoming yet more daring than the authorities wish to impose on her.

Pouran, a university professor, recalls that she left her first teaching job because she refused to wear the hejab. But today she appears in class with a scarf on her head, its ends tossed around her neck. She has been reprimanded many times for showing some hair while moving in class and lecturing. She is no longer bothered by the criticism of the authorities. She has threatened to resign, but they need her and want her to stay.

Ramesh, a woman in her thirties who just completed her studies at the university, told me the hejab reminded her of her own mother and of the resentment she felt when her mother picked her up from school wearing the scarf. When I first wore the scarf, "I thought I had become like my mother," she said. Yet she wears a maghnae when she goes to university. The government underestimated the resistance of women if it thought that it could keep educated women at home by imposing the Islamic dress code on them, she said.

Women feel they have also resisted the impositions of the state by their continued presence at work and on the street and their insistence on getting an education. "All over the country women try to make up for the disadvantage of being a woman by studying," Monir, a lawyer, remarked.

The policy of the government, explained Amineh, a writer, was constantly to beat women over the head and refer to women as an incarnation of Satan. The women decided to fight back, she said. They continued to work and study and make their significance felt in society. Ayesheh, a former government employee, compared Iranian women after the revolution to "the Great Wall of China." Nothing deters women from achieving the goals they have set for themselves if they are persistent in getting an education and then a job, according to Lida, a physician.

I asked one interlocutor to summarize women's resistance for me. Sousan replied: Women have resisted, "first, in the way they have altered the hejab; *second, by pursuing education; and third, through their enduring presence in society—whether at work, in ration lines, or at Friday prayers."*

■ ■ ■ ■ ■

Amineh: I started wearing the scarf before the revolution. I wore it with my jeans. I remember it was a few months before the revolution. I went to visit my sister who was a friend of Fatemeh Sayah, an early Iranian feminist. My sister took one look at my skimpy head cover and said in disgust, "It seems they easily put the scarf back on your heads. Of course you did not struggle to have it removed." It was so moving, so touching. For me that skimpy scarf was just symbolic. Then one day, after the revolution, I was attacked with a metal chain by two *hezbollahis* in one of the city squares. It was then that I found out that my skimpy scarf was not the *hejab* they were expecting from us. It was no longer a game.

By their sheer presence women have resisted this government. Iranian women were working both in the cities and in the villages before the revolution. But when they came face-to-face with a religious government that told them they are no longer needed, that they are the cause of corruption in society, they are Satan incarnate, they felt they had to impose their presence on this government and the society it was creating. The government not only clamped down on women. It was constantly "hitting women on their heads."

Women were looking for a way to fight the system. They tightened their belts and worked many times harder. They had to show that they were better than men and could excel even when privileges were taken away from them.

■ ■ ■ ■ ■

Mari: In Iran today being a woman is an issue. A lot of young girls and women are conscious of what it means to be a woman. To be a woman means to "matter." It makes a difference if you are actively engaged or remain passive. The government prefers women to stay home. But women fought this policy for sixteen years. They are aware of being an underprivileged class. They suffered more than men, and they are more responsible when it comes to dealing with problems.

Women stood in lines, they worked, they looked after the house and the children with no private help or public support. Have you noticed the number of children who accompany their mothers to work? Look at the problems these women have. Elementary schools work in two shifts, so after school is finished, the women take the children to work. Even nurses take their children to the hospitals.

On the whole the resistance of women has been admirable. I feel women are under two sets of influences: first, the impact of the achievements of women before the revolution; and second, the repercussions in Iran of the women's movement in the West. They are familiar with the movement through women's magazines, both Iranian and foreign.

I notice that the girls at the university are quite aware of these two trends. They work very hard, they are ambitious and are achievers, they compete frantically with their fellow male students. I find it amusing that the boys don't like to be outshone by girl students. But I also fear the possible implementation of a policy to set up universities for girls, thus introducing segregation at the university level. Having said that, I believe girls will fight this trend, just as they resisted other government pressures on them in the past.

■ ■ ■ ■

Shokouh: Women are the only vocal group in the society. They have resisted this government by not observing the *hejab*, by showing up at work. The government's policy was to force women to swallow any shit, to humiliate women. But it failed.

In the past, I ran into a lot of trouble because of the *hejab*. It is so aggravating to constantly worry about your *hejab* and *roupoush*.

One day I was walking along Gandhi Avenue. A van stopped and revolutionary guards, men and women, forced me into the back of the van. They are known as *khahara* and *baradara* ("sisters" and "brothers"). One of the women pulled my scarf down and saw my earrings. She asked me whether I was not ashamed of looking "like a prostitute." I told her she should be ashamed of talking in such a tone to me, a woman who could be her mother and who is a university professor. I told her she should be more respectful. In the end, we intimidate them.

On another occasion, when I was summoned to appear before a revolutionary court for not observing the *hejab* in my private practice, I told the presiding cleric that he must be thankful that women like me are still around. I told him, "I am among the few specialists left in the country who treats the chemically wounded soldiers of the war." I always went to the court alone, without my husband. The authorities let me go after lecturing me as to how I should dress. They just don't understand that you cannot perform surgery on a patient wearing a loose robe with wide long sleeves and with a *maghnae* strangling your throat.

■ ■ ■ ■ ■

Farideh: The *hejab* just crept into our lives. I remember shortly after the revolutionaries took over, a circular was sent to the women in our ministry asking us to observe the *hejab*. We asked for a meeting with the minister. It was strange to see him sitting cross-legged on the floor, surrounded by papers. We told him we did not see why we should be forced to wear the *hejab*. We told him we would march to show our disapproval of this decision. He asked us to wait and promised he would bring it up in the Council of Ministers. Nothing came of it. We started wearing the scarf here and there, and within a few months it became compulsory.

I remember attending a meeting in parliament wearing an ordinary scarf. At lunchtime, as a woman, I was asked to join the women deputies in a special section, separated by a curtain from the male deputies. The women deputies wore black *chadors*. One of them asked me whether I was uncomfortable wearing the scarf. Didn't I feel self-conscious being looked at by men? Another woman deputy talked to me about how corrupt the women of the prerevolutionary period were. I was quite amused because she was not aware that she was making this remark to a professional woman of that period. I found it very strange that none of these women asked me what I was doing there or what my expertise was. I am told that such an attitude no longer exists among the women who are in decision-making positions.

I believe that women of all classes have put up a fantastic resistance: by their sheer presence, by working, by looking after their families, by standing for endless hours in lines to do the daily shopping. I know of women who worked in an office and sold china during their lunch hour to make ends meet. The women of the lower classes have become more aware of their roles, too. You can no longer push them around. They are also asserting themselves. There is a constant battle to prove yourself as a woman. I think our women are lionesses.

■ ■ ■ ■ ■

Elaheh: I don't know what you mean by resistance. All I know is that the government has had great difficulty in imposing the proper *hejab* on women, at least in a city like Tehran. In the provinces more and more girls have to wear the *chador* to go to university. Otherwise, they would be excluded from higher education. The desire to become educated is so strong among the younger generation, even the girls who come from very religious families, that you can't help but describe it as resistance against submitting to traditional values, which prefer that girls stay at home. Of course, once you have an educated class of women coming from traditional religious backgrounds, the government must provide them with work, and their presence is a sign of resistance to the barriers dominant in our society.

■ ■ ■ ■ ■

Darya: If I want to evaluate the resistance of women, I have to do it within the framework of the society we live in. After the revolution, the emphasis was on the needs and the demands of the people rather than on defending women's rights. Women struggled individually, they continued to prove on an individual basis that they are alive. It was women who held the family together, it was women who had to earn a living. They were not only responsible for the economic needs of the family, but they took over the task of maintaining the continuity of our traditional and cultural life. For example, they made sure that Norouz and Chaharshanbeh Souri were celebrated.* You remember how the government tried to discourage people from observing these festivities?

---

*Chaharshanbeh Souri is the eve of the last Wednesday of the Persian year (and therefore observed on Tuesday night). The occasion is celebrated by jumping over a bonfire.

Women like us, I mean professional women, were alone. Neither the traditional class, nor the left, nor the intellectuals cared for us. Do you recall any of these groups ever expressing an opinion when women's rights were disregarded? We were expecting the intellectuals, who had mostly been exposed to Western education, to be at the forefront and to be progressive. They not only did not give us any support, they abandoned our cause. It was women who fought tooth and nail and step-by-step, who managed to inch their way forward. That, for me, is resistance.

■ ■ ■ ■ ■

Soudabeh: At first wearing the scarf was a matter of choice. At work, we were told to dress modestly. We continued wearing our ordinary clothes and put a scarf around our head. Then it became obligatory, and I did not want to fight it. I told myself, "This is the uniform of the society I am living in, the uniform is a coat, trousers, and a scarf."

There were demonstrations against the *hejab*. A group of nurses and women workers from our hospital went. They were beaten up. I was very angry. Some of our women doctors were dismissed because they used to take off their coats and scarves as soon as they got to the hospital. In those days nobody dared to challenge the decision of the administration to dismiss these women doctors, neither men nor women. Actually the teaching staff at the hospital accepted all the new rules and regulations. What else could they do? Women had tried to show their opposition, but one saw what happened to them.

If you ask me, women accepted the *hejab* but not the Islamic *hejab*. Look at the *kakol*, look at the different colors of the scarves, and the *roupoush*. On the other hand, there are also many women like me who don't have a problem with the *hejab*.

Today I feel women have finally found their rightful place in the society. This was achieved through perseverance and presence. They proved they are indispensable. Recently, even those women who were purged are being called back. For me this represents the ultimate resistance and victory of women.

I think women have demanded to be respected, and they are granted the respect they deserve. Maybe I look at things differently. I never wanted to give anybody the excuse of insulting me and acting disrespectfully toward me. I see myself as a professional woman in a country that has certain social rules. I go along and live in peace.

■ ■ ■ ■ ■

Manijeh: The resistance of women has been extraordinary, whether in the way they dress or their studies or their role in the society. I believe women sometimes react to events unconsciously, sometimes intuitively. You have a culture and a tradition weighing heavily on your head. For a while you put up with it and then you rebel against it. That is when you become aware that because you are a woman everybody is doing injustices to you. I feel quite often when we women reach a moment of decision in our lives, we suddenly are forced to pull back. Take the example of women who want a divorce. They hesitate because they lack the necessary security in such a traditional society.

Today the number of girls from traditional families who go to university has increased. These girls know that a high school diploma is no longer sufficient for a career. Once at the university they discover their capabilities and start making demands both in their private life and when it comes to work. They want an active role in the society, with or without the *hejab*.

I was seventeen when the revolution occurred. I had never worn a scarf. When it was introduced, I accepted it but I did not like it. I, and many women like me, wear it because it is a must. The *hejab* can never deter a person like me from working.

■ ■ ■ ■ ■

Nazanin: Women admirably resisted all the hardships the government inflicted on them. I divide our women into several groups. I find women of lower-class background really impressive. They are survivors, they gave courage to their husbands, they are bold and hardworking.

Women who work in government offices are very brave. They put up with a lot of insults and denigration. At some stage the guards searched their bags before allowing them to enter the building. There was a case when, during the fasting month of Ramazan, the guard found food in a woman's bag. He kicked her in the stomach. She was pregnant and as a result lost her child.

Among our class, there are women who were forced to work after the revolution. We never had the tradition of a woman becoming the breadwinner in the family. As women become more assertive and aggressive, their husbands come to feel small, belittled, and humiliated, and the children are confused and don't know any longer who is the mother and who is the father.

Of course there are also the affluent, spoiled women, obsessed with expensive clothing and jewelry, and they live lavishly. Their main concern is the *hejab*. When a nation went through a war, how can the *hejab* be the most important issue? I really don't understand why a woman's personality is broken because she is wearing the *hejab*.

In 1981 I returned from a two-year stay in Europe. I noticed more and more women wearing the scarf, and then we all started observing the *hejab*—at restaurants, in shops, behind the wheel. Gradually the scarf became thicker and the makeup on our face faded and we did not wear nail polish.

Yet look at our young girls, how brave they are, the way they dress, their *kakol*, the way they push their scarf back. The symbol of their resistance is identifying with Michael Jackson and Madonna.

■ ■ ■ ■ ■

Ayesheh: I believe women more than any other group resisted the government in this country. In many families the only breadwinner is the woman. In spite of all the obstacles and difficulties, women continue to work, especially in government offices. The revolution has failed to keep women at home. Today women are everywhere. They cook, or they sew at home and sell their products. The revoluton turned women into businesspeople. To everybody's surprise, a lot of women who before the revolution were ladies of leisure came out of their homes after the revolution and saved the family.

Don't forget it was women who faced up to corporal punishment and verbal abuse. Women were called prostitutes and sluts and dolls and puppets. Women received lashes and were thrown out of offices for the way they looked and for their behavior. Let me give you an example. We have been going to ski at Shemshak for the last thirteen years. You should see how these young girls appear on the ski slopes. They must spend hours in front of the mirror fixing up their looks. They know that they might be arrested by the *komiteh* people a few steps from their cars. Yet they still do it.

I believe our women stood tall like the Great Wall of China. They were "hit on the head," but they bounced back, and they proved that they would not allow their spirit to be broken. They will not be denigrated.

■ ■ ■ ■ ■

Fatemeh: I think women resisted by not giving up. Women were quick to see that they have to be a presence in society. They did not have much of a choice. You either stayed on and made your presence felt, no matter how difficult and harrowing that experience was, or you went home and sat and waited for a miracle to happen.

As a woman you were forced to go out and get what you wanted. You had to fight the officials every inch of the way. Of course women were humiliated, but in most cases they ignored the harassment and stood up to the pressure.

Take the imposition of the *hejab* on women. Almost sixteen years after the revolution this is still a problem for women, the government, and the revolutionary organs. In short, I think the increasing number of women at the workplace and in public places, and the inability of the government to deal with it is a telling sign of women's resistance.

■ ■ ■ ■ ■

Atefeh: I don't regard women's presence in the society as a sign of resistance. Women were present then, and they are present now. But in my opinion, the way women defy observing the complete *hejab*, the way they dress, the way they wear their makeup is the symbol of women's resistance. I am personally too old to put up a resistance against the *hejab*. Not that it is not important for me. But it is not a central issue in my daily life. I don't want to be insulted, nor do I want to be humiliated by being told that my scarf is not worn properly.

I am full of praise for the desire of women to be educated. Maybe because women are so conscious of living in a society they feel is against them, they react by working twice as hard as men and setting difficult goals for themselves and achieving them. I personally don't know a single woman or a young girl who is not working for a living.

■ ■ ■ ■ ■

Masoumeh: Our being here is our resistance. Our daily life is our resistance. Our encounter with men is our resistance. If you are an intelligent woman, and if you are familiar with the condition of women in progressive societies, being humiliated daily as we are here is very painful, and it turns you into a fighter.

I believe being a woman in Iran today is a triple negative. Let me explain what I mean by triple negative: first and foremost is the problem of *hejab*. I mean a bunch of unmarried young kids, I mean boys, regardless of their age, are asked to keep an eye on women, to see whether they are dressed properly or not. You are faced with this treatment. Yet you hear the government talk about the "special status" of women and the respect women should be accorded. This only creates more humiliation for women and belittles them.

Second, the way women are treated at home. As a woman you not only work outside the house, but you are expected to perform all the duties of a traditional housewife, too. I mean, household chores are your responsibilities—chores such as cleaning, cooking, washing, shopping—and you are not supposed to expect any help from your man, and you won't get it if you wanted it.

Finally, belonging to a minority of educated, open-minded women in a traditional society is a negative. Educated women such as I suffer constantly from the way we are treated, but we fight back. At the beginning we were in a daze. Now we have gained the upper hand. The government not only has to deal with us but has its hands full with its own female constituency. Therefore you have all this talk about women's "special place" in society and the government advocating its own version of women's rights and stressing the necessity of active participation of women in society.

Ladan: Today in Iran, to be a woman means to struggle. Women don't have the right to choose what they want to wear. In the universities they cannot study any field they want. In the courts they are discriminated against. There are not too many women in decision-making positions. Those who are have to adhere to the position the government takes on women's issues.

As a woman, regardless of what class you belong to, you have to worry constantly not to give the authorities an opportunity to insult you. It does not matter if, professionally, you are a successful woman. You are vulnerable because of your gender. At any moment, you can be stopped in the street by an eighteen-year-old brat who takes objection to your scarf, your glasses, even the way you hold yourself.

In short, this is a society that favors men. Having said that, I will add that women have been fighting this attitude for sixteen years—not only educated women but also the women who come from lower classes, especially these women. The revolution pulled them out of their homes. Even if their husbands want them back in the home, they cannot do it. Women have taken over a lot of responsibilities from their men. These women spend several hours a day standing in line for food. They have to deal with the school authorities, they have to pay the bills for water and electricity. They are on the streets quite a lot. They talk to each other. There is an awareness in these women that makes an impact on their attitude toward their husbands. The government has unconsciously politicized the mass of Iranian women.

Why do you think the government reintroduced parts of the Family Protection Law? Because it wanted to keep its own female constituency happy. The government did not care whether the middle-class or upper-class women felt miserable or discriminated against. But it did matter to them that ordinary Iranian women should not feel abandoned by the revolution.

■ ■ ■ ■ ■

Nahid: At first I felt like a stranger in my own country. Everything around me was changing so rapidly. As a woman, I was scared—I mean, as a woman of a certain class. We were referred to as *taghuti*. That word was so damning. We were all that the revolutionary authorities condemned and repudiated. They pointed their fingers at us; we were exposed to senseless accusations. I recall I was so scared of being insulted and humiliated. You become so defensive.

In the beginning people like me did not dare to answer back. We avoided having any contact with the revolutionary authorities. Today we go after what we think is right, we shout at them, we intimidate them with our behavior and with the way we dress and act. Of course we observe the *hejab*, but not the way they want it. We throw the scarf around our head; our youngsters show their *kakol* and wear colorful clothes, so all the young girls do the same. This is our resistance. Our sheer being there is the symbol of the resistance of Iranian women.

I believe that the revolution made women more conscious of their rights and gave them an economic independence, maybe through sheer necessity. Whatever the reason, women will resist any kind of social reversal. I am not talking about women like myself only. I include the lower-class women, too.

The development of lower-class women is very important. These are the ones who have and will transform the society. For years these women had to stand in line for several hours every day to do their daily shopping. When you stand in line, when you go to the Friday prayers, when you go to religious services for the martyrs of the war, you talk to each other and you hear about the latest developments. All this exposes ordinary women to a world outside that was not as accessible to them before the revolution.

Today a number of such women study in religious centers. They are ambitious. They will follow the trend toward a modernized attitude to religion. They will have an impact on the society. In my business I deal with women from the traditional classes. They are religious, but they resist superstition. They share the same ambitions of educated Westernized women. They want to become teachers, doctors, administrators. They demand equal opportunities and press the government for this. To me, this is resistance.

■ ■ ■ ■ ■

Touran: I postponed and resisted wearing the scarf as long as I could. I did not shop in stores that sold only to women who observed the *hejab*. Once I was walking in the park with my husband. A hezbollahi came up to us and told me to wear my scarf. I refused. He turned to my husband and said, "Have you no honor?" My husband answered, "Don't talk to me, talk to her." The guy started shaking with rage and calling my husband shameless and all sorts of names. In the end, almost in the last minute, I, too, like everybody else, started observing the *hejab*.

For more than sixteen years the system has been trying to impose the *hejab* on women. That alone is the proof of women's resistance. The continuous presence of women in their places of work despite all the obstacles created by the regime is a very important matter. Women have not budged an inch. They use every opportunity to make a statement. They appear helpless, but they bring a lot of pressure on the regime, so that the government is always forced to react to women's demands.

■ ■ ■ ■ ■

Ramesh: Despite all the punitive measures against women, the daily humiliations, the constant bothering, the governmental authorities are not able to frighten us or to intimidate us. We are different from their women: our looks, our behavior, the way we speak, and the way we dress. They not only did not change us, but their women are trying to imitate us. I wish we were better organized. We don't have a leader. Our resistance is individual. I remember the last time grocery prices went up, there was talk that women should stop buying certain items for a week. I myself did not go to the store, but I sent the cook. He told me there were lots of women shopping. I only know of one university professor who complied with this decision.

I resent the *hejab*. It reminds me of my mother and how I objected to her coming to pick me up at school because she wore the scarf. When the *hejab* was once again introduced in our society, I was twenty-four-years old and I thought that I had become like my mother.

After the revolution when I first came back from the States, and I heard Bani-Sadr* talking about the "rays" women's hair projected, I could not believe my ears. In those days the talk was of women wearing black and even the *chador* becoming obligatory. I knew the authorities could not impose it on Iranian women. They did not impose the *chador*, but they forced the Islamic dress code on us. At first I tried to go out as little as possible. But you can't give in to these pressures. That is what they wanted— for women like me who do not feel comfortable wearing the scarf to stay home. We defied them by wearing the scarf and being everywhere.

---

*Abol-Hasan Bani-Sadr, the first president of the Islamic Republic, was one of the ideologues of the Islamic revolution and, in exile in Europe before the revolution, wrote widely on Islamic government, "Islamic economics," and similar subjects.

Lili: The resistance of women has been wonderful. Look around you. There are women everywhere. I mean working women. Take the sheer number of girls at different universities. They study much better and much harder than boys. Girls are achievers, their goal in life is to succeed, and that is their form of resistance.

Let's take the problem of *hejab*. Do you think the government was able to create a uniformity in *hejab*? Of course not. Look at the variety in the headdress in the streets, the different colors and shapes of the *hejab*. I am not even talking about what women wear in the privacy of their homes. Look at the women who wear the *chador*, even they wear a T-shirt and jeans under it. Hardly a week passes by without a statement by someone in the government about women's attire. If the authorities had solved this problem, why do they talk about it so much it?

■ ■ ■ ■ ■

Monir: The resistance of women took different forms. Political groups acted according to their objectives. They tried to accommodate both sides. For example, the left was very cautious in how far it would go in supporting women's rights. Its leaders did not want to antagonize the leaders of the revolution. They kept on changing their position. Nobody paid much attention to what they were saying.

The faceless masses of women—the educated and the less educated ones, and those who belonged to political parties and were active in the revolution—were shocked on several occasions by the decrees the government issued regarding women. The first shock came when the *hejab* was introduced. Then came the suspension of the Family Protection Law. Then women were harassed in the workplace and on the streets. At first there was group resistance. Then the resistance became individual, and of course it led to purges from government offices.

The greatest resistance by women was their continued presence in their places of work. Ordinary women workers were left alone. The government targeted women who had certain skills and who were specialists. These women were humiliated for being women, but their expertise could not be attacked.

The resistance of women has manifested itself by the sheer number of women in higher education. All over the country women try to make up for the disadvantage of being a woman by studying.

For me wearing the *hejab* came gradually. I first wore a wide band over my head. It looked quite strange. Then I started wearing loose clothes. Finally I wore the robe and the scarf. I remember my *chadori* mother getting very angry. It is very demanding on your personality to be stopped by men who are young enough to be your sons and be reprimanded about your dress and hair cover. At first we feared them. Then we ignored them. Now we have learned to argue back, and we frighten them. Today women of all classes are much bolder than before. They have hardened and are more aggressive, and they pass their aggressiveness on to other women.

■ ■ ■ ■ ■

Nargess: The most fundamental struggle of women was manifested through the issue of *hejab*. I don't believe there is one woman who has not been insulted for not observing the proper *hejab*. Now things have changed. There were times when men on motorcycles would slash women's hands or sleeves with a sharp razor as punishment for their appearance. Of course, there were collective arrests of women, appearances in front of revolutionary *komitehs*, and other such humiliating encounters. The most fascinating aspect of it all was that women ignored this treatment and continued to defy the authorities. We working women had to wear the *maghnae* at work, especially if we worked for the government. I remember at first it was difficult for me to keep the *maghnae* on my head. It was falling off all the time. I was officially put on notice for that. The Islamic society at work had sent in a written complaint about my *hejab*. Today I dislike it, but I wear it at work. What started with a skimpy silk see-through scarf is now a piece of black cloth strangling your neck, forced on women who have to work. But in the street, the government is losing the battle over the *hejab*.

■ ■ ■ ■ ■

Afsar: Before the revolution, I always wore a large scarf around my head when I went to the villages, but I was against forcing the *hejab* on women.

I did not accept it willingly. Even when Ayatollah Taleqani came to the university to meet with some of the faculty who had gone on strike, I appeared in my jeans and no *hejab*. But the day when Ayatollah Khomeini arrived in Tehran and we stood in the street waiting for him, I covered my hair.

I remember being assaulted by a male motorcyclist in the street for not observing the *hejab*. I grabbed him by his collar and told him to mind his own business. I am full of admiration for these young women who show their *kakol* despite all the punishments the government inflicts on them. On the whole women stayed strong all these years, while men crumbled and did not know how to cope. By their sheer strength and perseverance women resisted the government.

■ ■ ■ ■ ■

Zohreh: I believe the resistance of women is instinctive. I mean, when a young woman puts on some lipstick and goes out into the street, it is an individual decision. She wants to prove that she has an independent mind. We each act independently from the other. When I went to visit a relative at the Qasr Prison, I wore the *chador*. That *chador* gave me the power to scream at the guards because I had become like one of them. Each of us finds a way to show our resistance to the daily harassment we face. The end result is what matters—namely that the government can't turn back the clock on women's social progress and development.

■ ■ ■ ■ ■

Pouran: For me the imposition of the *hejab* was and is a problem. I resigned from Tehran University over wearing the *hejab*. I remember we were at a large meeting at the Faculty of Law. Soroush and Farsi* were among the

---

*Abdol-Karim Soroush and Jalal ad-Din Farsi were among the ideologues of the Islamic revolution. Soroush, trained in both Islamic and Western philosophy, became a critic of clerical domination of the state in subsequent years and advocated an Islam compatible with democracy, pluralism, and toleration.

speakers. I looked around. Except for me and two other women, all the other women wore a scarf on their heads.

I argued against the principle of imposing a dress code on women. I told the audience that I felt humiliated being forced to wear the *chador* for the sake of earning 20,000 *tomans* a month. In those days Leila Khaled, the Palestinian guerrilla fighter, was the heroine of the revolution. I asked them whether she was wearing the *hejab*. Farsi answered that Iranian women "are always in the forefront and one step ahead of events." I was accused of being irrational and emotional. I started crying. A cleric got up and chastised the people who had called me emotional. After that incident another woman professor and I left the university. It took them a year to accept the fact that I was not going back to teach. I stayed home for four years. Except for a handful of people, everybody went along with the *hejab*, including the left. I remember the Marxist magazine, *Paykar*, printing a cover picture of a woman in a *chador* standing in front of the red flag!

To this day at some universities your standing depends on whether you observe the *hejab* properly or your hair shows. I know of incidents in which a member of the Islamic society peered through the classroom window to see whether women faculty were wearing their scarves properly when teaching. It is absurd, because when you walk in class and you talk and you gesticulate, sometimes your scarf moves, your hair shows, your wrist becomes exposed. Then you are summoned and reprimanded. You feel that not only as a woman but as a human being your rights are trampled under their feet. These days we women have learned to intimidate the authorities by being aggressive and standing up to them. Suddenly they find our class, our background, and our upbringing frightening.

There is a dichotomy in the resistance of women, as in all the other aspects of our lives. On the one hand, the resistance of women has been very intuitive and was not always the result of a conscious decision. On the other hand, contrary to our expectations, some of our women intellectuals, who were in a position to set a good example, did not do so. They suffered much, but they did not really contribute anything to our society.

The real struggle was put up by ordinary women—women who had to go out on a daily basis and earn a living and suffer all sorts of humiliation. The economic problems of the family were passed on to women, and they had to find solutions. What is irritating is that women struggle and men make fun of them.

Jila: The revolution proved to us that women were more resilient than men. Women did not quit their jobs, while men did. Women resisted wearing the *hejab* as long as they could, while men stopped wearing the tie immediately. When women were dismissed from their work because of the *hejab*, men should have walked out in protest. But no. They were so meek, they encouraged women to go along with the new dress code. I remember, it was in the early years of the revolution, I went to a meeting in one of the ministries. As chair of my company I was explaining our project and pointing at the chart I had prepared. Suddenly I noticed that all the men avoided looking at me. You see, under Islam they were not supposed to look into the face of a strange woman. I stopped in the middle of a sentence and said, "Since I am not used to talking to people who don't look at me, I will ask my colleague Mr. so and so to continue." As far as the men are concerned, we women are not human beings. Otherwise they would look into our eyes.

You know why women have been so resistant all these years? Because the government started prying into their private lives. Women don't like to be told how to dress, how to behave, how to work, and be punished for not observing these guidelines.

■ ■ ■ ■ ■

Lida: Resistance by women is a cultural matter. The more women are educated, the more they want to be visible and wish to prove their abilities. Competent women don't allow men to hold them back in the society. They stand up to men. To me, this is resistance. We live in a patriarchy. In our societies boys are preferred over girls. Religious and traditional families don't encourage their daughters to go to universities, but if these girls are persistent in getting an education and then a job, nobody will be able to stop them. This is resistance. For me, resistance is being active in the society in which you live, it is being an achiever, a doer, and getting what you want, regardless of whether you wear the *chador*, the *maghnae,* or the scarf.

■ ■ ■ ■ ■

Partow: The women in Iran today are more resistant than in the past. I respect them more. They are more capable, they shoulder most of the day-to-day responsibilities. If you go out in the streets very early in the morning, you will understand what I mean. You see a lot of women going to work, shopping, standing in bus lines. I feel women have set a goal for themselves, and they want to reach that goal. They want to improve their standard of living. We live in a society and in a culture that is trying to kill the spirit of women, to take advantage of women's patience, but the authorities don't succeed. Take the problem of *hejab*. They forced women into wearing the *roupoush*. What happens is that under that baggy *roupoush* women wear miniskirts, jeans, or leggings. They want us to look dirty, disheveled, and shapeless, and women resent this interference. So they react by wearing more color and fashionable robes and showing a *kakol*. Let me give you an example. I used to wear white sneakers at work. One day I was called in by the authorities and was told off by a woman for my sneakers. For a few days I wore black shoes, then I went back to wearing my white sneakers. I decided, "It is none of her business what sort of shoes I wear."

We live in a patriarchal society. There is nothing in favor of women. Even in the bus you have to stand in the back. I remember one day I was very tired. The men's section in the bus was empty. I stepped under the bar dividing the two sections and sat in an empty seat. The driver stopped the bus and refused to leave until I went back to the women's section. Quite humiliating, isn't it?

In our society, from the moment you are born, you are taught that as a woman you have to acquiesce. But today even women like me who have only a limited amount of education reject this concept. The moment you are not economically dependent on a man, you can decide more freely about your way of life.

■ ■ ■ ■ ■

Nayyer: Do you want to know how women have resisted these many years? Very simply by constantly making demands on the government. To be a woman in this society, regardless of your social class, is very difficult. As girls we were told not to talk back to men, not to raise our voices, not to react to insults. In short, as girls we were not supposed to attract any attention. The revolution, the daily humiliation, changed this attitude in women of my generation and even the younger generation who are bolder than us. Today, despite our melancholy, we have to fight back in order to survive. In our daily encounters, we still have to prove that we are respectable women and not prostitutes.

Let me give you an example. I was riding a taxi. A man and a woman were sitting in the back seat. When the woman got out she swore at the man sitting next to her and slammed the door. The driver asked me what was wrong with her. I told him the man must have harassed her. Without a pause, he answered that she must have instigated him. I got angry. I told him, "During a whole lifetime your mother, your sister, your wife, and your daughter are faced with such behavior and abused daily, but they are afraid to complain precisely because of attitudes such as yours. Tell your women-folk," I added, "next time a man abuses them they should scream." He apologized to me. But, you see, not for a moment had it occurred to him that the man was at fault.

We are dealing with a fundamental social problem. When these people took over the regime, all they knew about women was that you sleep with them and you control them. Once they came to power, they saw that women have a different role to play, a major role. They started responding to the needs of women and to the pressure exerted on them by women in general and their own women in particular.

Unlike some of my friends, I am for all the measures the government introduced in the field of women's rights. I am in favor of the Bureau for Women's Affairs. I don't think the *ojrat-ol-mesl* law is a bad thing.* I think women's magazines and women's groups are important in shaping opinion. Women's magazines provide a forum for discussing women's legislation and women's problems. It will take time to implement these laws. Men and women have to believe in these laws for them to succeed.

■ ■ ■ ■ ■

Sousan: If it were not for women, we would have been deprived of the little social life that is left for us. The revolution incapacitated our men. It is the women who work, earn a living, run the family. This is not exclusive to one class. It includes women from all different strata of society.

---

*The law authorized the courts to require a husband who chose to divorce his wife through no fault of her own to pay her compensation for the years she served as mother and housewife.

For me the resistance of women has been so impressive. I see this resistance manifesting itself in the following manner: first, in the way they have altered the *hejab*; second, by pursuing education; and, third, through their enduring presence in society—whether at work, in ration lines, or at Friday prayers.

The *hejab* inched its way into our daily life. I remember being stopped in my car by revolutionary guards and asked to wear a scarf. I took out my Hermes scarf and wore it loosely around my head. Even when the scarf became a must, as long as I was teaching, I refused to wear the *maghnae* or a black scarf. Today, I continue wearing an ordinary scarf around my head. I don't play their games.

■ ■ ■ ■ ■

Zahra: Women's resistance has been unsurpassed by anything I have known. They held their families together with tooth and nail. Women took over the functions that men abdicated. They have proven to be strong, either by their participation in the prerevolution marches or by resisting the *hejab* or by showing the *kakol*. Women, by their passive resistance, have shown they are less compromising than men.

The last time I appeared in public without the *hejab* was when I worked as an assistant to a film director. This was many years ago. Several revolutionary guards showed up and stopped the filming. Their excuse was that the women who worked there were not observing the *hejab*. The next day we all appeared with our heads covered. We were not going to let them use the *hejab* as an excuse to deny us working on a film.

■ ■ ■ ■ ■

Neda: Women have shown in the last fifteen years that they are a power the government has to come to terms with. Despite all their problems, women stood up to the restrictions imposed on them by the authorities. They withstood the *hejab*, they fought the daily humiliation in the street and in the workplace, and they made the government give in on a lot of issues.

When the revolution took place, I was considered one of the senior professors at the university. One day as I was walking on campus, a young man approached me and said he could see "the shadow" of my hair. I told him he was young enough to be my child, but he went on cursing and using foul language. I was very shaken. I went to see the head of the department. He didn't take any action against the man.

I could have quit, but that would be playing into the hands of the authorities. I and other women like me stayed and endured the humiliation and fought our way back. We proved ourselves. Of course we had to work twice as hard as the men, but we did it. Some of the women professors left, even those who were very revolutionary. I remember a woman colleague of mine who was very active in the revolutionary movement telling me that for her the issue of *hejab* was so unimportant that she was ready to wear a blanket over her head forever, as long as the revolution succeeded. Of course, for her it never came to that. She left for Paris, and we stayed and covered our heads. I don't think our problem is the *hejab* in its present form. What worries me is that they might force the *chador* on us. I think I would draw the line then and there.

I think women have proven to be very capable. Look at me. I have seven books and twenty-six articles, and still the university authorities refuse to give me a promotion, all because I am a woman and have proven my superiority to them. These people know that by our sheer endurance we defeated their policy against women and proved it a failure.

Six

A Solidarity of Sorts

THE REVOLUTION HAS CLEARLY CREATED *a sense of common identity among women: they are subject to a common dress code, are harassed in common by the revolutionary committees or "morals police," and are the subjects of the same set of laws applied specifically to women. But this sense of common identity takes complex forms. For example, the women I interviewed speak routinely of women as having shown resourcefulness, courage, and competence since the revolution. They speak of women as having understood much more quickly than the men the gravity of the predicament of their families in the aftermath of the revolution and as having proven far more competent in dealing with a new set of postrevolutionary problems. But these women rarely think in terms of gender solidarity; the term itself is not part of their common vocabulary; and some vehemently deny it exists.*

Women speak of the "oneness" evident among women in the early years of the revolution and during the Iran-Iraq War. In government offices, they find it easier to deal with, and feel they get much better treatment from, female than male civil servants. They tell of attending fashion shows or art exhibitions organized by women and buying what they can afford in order to help another woman stay on her feet. They recount occasions when a female neighbor would alert another that ration cards were being distributed at the local mosque or that the revolutionary committees were prowling the neighborhood.

But these women rarely speak of a woman's network or of female solidarity. Rather, even when speaking of mutual support among women, they think in terms of family, friends, or, on occasion, women of "my class." They all found that family and close friends were always there to help in times of difficulty. Masoumeh spoke of women of her "class" and added: "I personally know I can rely on each and every single woman friend I have." When a bomb shattered the plate-glass windows of her house during the

Iran-Iraq War, she said, it was her women friends who rushed over to paste newspaper and cardboard across the shattered windows. Several women told stories of women friends helping them find a job, lending them money, discreetly assisting them to sell valuable household items, or making them presents of groceries.

On the other hand, some women complain bitterly about the lack of solidarity among women, attributing it to the limited opportunities available to women and the resulting competition for good jobs and opportunities. A few speak wistfully of a "lost" solidarity: women bonded during the early revolution and the Iran-Iraq War, when they stood in ration lines together, suffered food, fuel, and power shortages in common, and lost sons and husands on the front. Once the war was over, said Zohreh, "everyone starting looking out for herself." Lili, a secretary, said that when she was offered a job as a computer technician, her predecessor not only gave her no assistance, "she did all she could to undermine me. You call that solidarity?" There were the usual complaints of backbiting and backstabbing among women.

Most of these women believe firmly in equal rights and opportunities, economic independence, and freedom of expression and movement for women. They are equally determined to achieve and retain total autonomy over their bodies. But very few refer to themselves as feminists, apparently associating the term with the excesses of the feminist movement of the 1960s. Some see themselves as feminists at heart, in the sense that they are committed to women's rights, but feel unable to articulate or act on their beliefs in the prevailing family and social environment. Nayyer told me, "I think as a feminist, but I lead a traditional life. As a feminist, my values are clear, but I have to ignore them in my daily life." Many women, she felt, were in the same situation. They compromise their ideals to preserve peace in the family.

Several argued for situating the concept of women's rights and equality in the Iranian cultural context. Neda, a university professor, saw herself as an advocate of women's equality but at the same time remarked that in a traditional society like Iran's, "feminism is incomprehensible." Monir, a lawyer, said she rejects Western-style feminism but would consider herself a feminist if it meant "equality." She added, "To me, my chadori mother who wanted me to study and be an independent woman is a feminist." Another woman did not see herself as a feminist yet shares what she sees as feminist ideas: equality under the law, a refusal to regard women as inferior to men. Most reject a militant feminism. Zohreh, an activist woman, while embrac-

ing feminism, for example, objected to what she described as "pants-wearing women."

There are also women who speak proudly of themselves as "feminists" and want to see women fight for their rights. Masoumeh, a militant feminist, recalled she read somewhere that "feminism is . . . hating the woman you don't want to be" and added, "I don't like passive housewives who live to obey their husbands."

■ ■ ■ ■ ■

Amineh: I believe women are an integral part of Iranian society. Therefore their behavior and reactions to events are just like men's. I mean, when there is pressure and hardship, women show a sort of solidarity with one another; men do the same thing. For example, during the war you really saw women standing by each other and helping out other women who were in need. When there is no danger of external attack, there is no solidarity. This is a matter of attitude rather than gender characteristics.

■ ■ ■ ■ ■

Mari: I have never thought about whether I am a feminist or not. I don't differentiate between men and women. Theoretically, I approve of equal rights between men and women, but I am aware of the fact that men and women have different physical problems. I also think that there is a male support system in our society and culture—that is, father, brother, and husband who will not abandon women.

I also see a strong support system among women. I don't refer to it as solidarity, just a kind of understanding and sympathy for each other. It can be as simple as telling each other where to find a chicken or standing in line for a friend or standing up to discrimination in the place of work. Since women cannot talk to men in the office, they talk to other women. This talk automatically creates a bond. I personally would recommend and hire women for jobs.

Shokouh: I consider myself a true feminist. I believe women are superior to men. They have more vitality, they are more real. I think feminists should push for total equality between men and women. A friend once put it in a nutshell. She said, "The day we can pinch a man's bottom, we women will have reached total equality." I wish men and women not only had equal rights but equal living conditions, too. Women in this country deserve better treatment. They need to be respected and appreciated more for all they do.

■ ■ ■ ■ ■

Farideh: Solidarity exists between women. You feel women want to help each other, but it is all on an individual basis. There is no network. When I was still working for the government after the revolution, I tried to train the revolutionary women who had joined our office. They were very receptive and were learning fast. When I wanted to retire, they tried to dissuade me. They knew that once I left they could have my job. But they wanted me to stay. They made it clear that there was a bond, a solidarity between us, that they appreciated all I had done for them. Of course, there are those who try to stab you in the back. That is part of the working game. Men stab you in the back, too. Why should one exaggerate this behavior when it comes to women?

Generally speaking, I don't consider myself a feminist. In Iranian society, how can I be and act as a feminist? I think we have to work for the advancement of men and women equally. I am not against equal rights for women, but I think there is a need for fundamental work at a grass-roots level for men and women. One has to do long-term planning in order to raise the level of education, culture, understanding, and intellect in people, so that they should not easily submit to a bully government that has no roots in the society. There should be proper laws that address the needs of both men and women equally.

■ ■ ■ ■ ■

Elaheh: I am not familiar with the concept of solidarity among women. I must confess I lead a very secluded life, and I am very careful because I am a single woman. I don't mix much. But I remember when a woman professor was fired from our department, not a single woman on the faculty raised her voice to ask why this was done, let alone protested. I don't think women even understand the concept of gender solidarity. Of course, at work, since you cannot interact with the men, you are drawn toward your women colleagues. Women don't show you the same animosity men do. We live in a society in which all have to look after their own well-being, so automatically this condition leads to competition and animosity or indifference.

I don't know what feminism is; therefore, I don't know whether I am a feminist or not. All I know is that I am a woman who feels trapped in a society that is dominated by men and this society is totally alien to my way of thinking. As a woman, I feel isolated and abandoned.

■ ■ ■ ■ ■

Darya: I don't see any solidarity among women as a group. This is not a gender issue. I don't see any solidarity among men either. Society has become atomized. People are more individualistic. They are aware of their common interests, but they are concerned with their own well-being.

Of course, women understand each other's problems. For example, when the husband of a poor woman becomes a drug addict or the husband of a middle-class woman takes a second wife, they sympathize with her. But that is an emotional solidarity.

When women don't have any social security or any protection under the law, they start competing with each other. They denigrate each other. They see other women as a threat, especially women who lack a profession. Women of a certain type are criticized for caring only for their looks, dressing up, having plastic surgery, buying gold. I don't blame these women. In a country where until a short time ago the husband could divorce his wife after fifteen years of marriage and leave her without support, her looks are her capital.

■ ■ ■ ■ ■

Gowhar: I do not approve of slogans, nor am I a follower of clichés such as feminism. I believe in total equality regardless of race, religion, or creed. I do not tolerate discrimination in society. If feminists want to separate the problem of women from that of society, then I am not a feminist. I believe that any change must be fundamental, and it has to come through education both for men and for women.

■ ■ ■ ■ ■

Soudabeh: There is no such thing as solidarity among women. You know why? Because the society is such that we each have to look after our own interests. The prevailing attitude is, "Why should I care what the other person does?"

My personal experience at work is that women act against women more than they do against men. If a woman is excelling at her job, other women try to bring her down. Of course men can behave in this manner, too, but the percentage among women is greater.

I feel my male colleagues accept my success at work and in my scientific research more easily than my female colleagues. The women constantly send you negative vibes. Let me give you an example. I was invited to go abroad to a conference. My request to go was denied. I found out that a woman colleague had reported to the authorities that I did not observe the *hejab*. Of course, I confronted them. I went to the conference. But that incident left a bitter taste in my mouth.

Of course, I am a feminist. What a question! For me, a feminist is a woman who works and looks after the well-being of her family. At work I see myself equal to a man. I work just as hard and as much as they do. But I also have the delicacy of a woman. When I come home, I forget my professionalism and become a wife and a mother. I am at ease in both worlds. There are a number of working women who ignore their families. I do not approve of such an attitude. I also believe there is a physiological difference between men and women, so I don't have any problem with women being barred from becoming judges. I am among those who believe that when women have their monthly period their condition is not stable enough to judge cases.

■ ■ ■ ■ ■

Manijeh: In my own way, I consider myself a feminist. In my work I constantly deal with issues relating to women, so I have to take a stand, make a choice, clarify my position. It is only in the last few years that I started reading about feminism. There is a lot for me to learn. I want to know the latest theories, and I would like to follow the debate among feminists. Basically, I don't see why there should be any difference between my world and that of men.

I know there was a lot of criticism of the movement when it started in the 1960s. I am personally against militancy, but I also think that every movement must be militant in its initial stage to succeed. Then it has to settle down and follow a middle-of-the-road course. Women have different outlooks on issues that relate to them. I compare the movement to a tree with many different branches.

■ ■ ■ ■ ■

Nazanin: I have seen solidarity among various classes of women, I mean women belonging to the lower classes or the bourgeoisie. They shop for each other. They look after each other's children. They stand in line for each other. On the whole, I am skeptical when it comes to friendship between women, but I don't want to generalize. Among certain groups of women who share the same interests, there is a strong bond and friendship.

As far as I am concerned, the feminist movement started in the United States. It became a burning issue for women to be part of the movement. I did not like the extremism of that movement. You remember the bra-burning and communal living! I did not see, then or now, why one should take refuge in these kinds of arguments to improve one's legal status. I believe whenever women had a reasonable case to make, men went along with it.

In Iran, before the revolution, I started writing antifeminist articles. Both Iranian and American men used to tell me they agreed with me. I believe men and women are different, psychologically and physiologically. "Vive la différence!" I do not approve of women who look like dolls, but I don't see any contradiction between being feminine and intelligent at the same time. The feminist movement has put me off, and to this day I am annoyed by the stand the extremists take. I think feminism left women all alone, and one morning women found that they were lonely, that the men no longer called them.

Ayesheh: I believe there is a great deal of solidarity among women. I don't see as much backbiting as in the old days. Women share a common goal, namely standing up to government pressure in their daily life. Women tend to care more for each other. They have an understanding for your problems as a woman. Every time I have been to an office, it was much easier to deal with women employees. They try to show their friendship to you by helping to get your work done.

Of course I am a feminist when it comes to total equality between men and women. I do not accept that women are inferior. Perhaps because I never let anybody "put me down" just because I am a woman, I feel we women can do anything men do and are as capable as they are, if not more so. But I also don't want to denigrate men. I am against such an attitude. It does not fit into my way of thinking.

■ ■ ■ ■ ■

Fatemeh: I believe in solidarity among women, among friends, among people. Take me, all these years I have helped anybody I could. I am always here for my women friends. My experience is that women stand by each other in time of need, and they can count on women more than men. It is easier for women to talk to one another. All these years they shared the same experiences. There is a bond among women. Whether there is such a support among men, you have to ask them. As for feminism, I really don't know what to say, I have never given it a serious thought.

■ ■ ■ ■ ■

Atefeh: I have not seen solidarity among women. What I have seen is one woman, a friend, helping another woman. This is an individual act. You cannot generalize from it. I don't have any personal experience. I have always worked on my own. Maybe I look at this problem differently. I see women as being forced to fend for themselves over the centuries and resorting to any possible means, even cheating, ruses, lying, etc.

I am not a supporter of feminist ideas. My understanding of feminism is that the law should be applied equally to men and women. I definitely don't want women to be treated as second-class citizens. I don't see what women gain in belittling their husbands, why they want the men to suffer the same humiliation they were exposed to.

All I have seen from feminism is aggressive women resorting to extremes. That is my objection. I ask myself why women have to portray themselves like this. I think such an attitude is very harmful to the women's cause.

■ ■ ■ ■ ■

Masoumeh: I believe there is solidarity among Iranian women. They are no threat to one another. On the contrary, they are a support system. It was only after the revolution that Iranian women were able to show how capable they are and how courageous they are. They have proven themselves professionally and socially. So what is there to be scared of from another woman? They think beyond such matters.

Solidarity occurs between people who are homogeneous. In our case, it is women from the same class and background and who felt the enmity of the government toward themselves. They knew they only had each other. I personally know I can rely on each and every single woman friend I have.

I don't believe in the feminist attitude of the 1960s, I mean the movement. I once read somewhere that feminism is not necessarily hating men, but it is hating the woman you don't want to be. I see around me a lot of women I don't want to be. I don't like passive housewives who live to obey their husbands. I have raised my daughter to be a feminist, too, not to feel inferior to any man and not be subservient to men. There is a paradox in that, too. Whenever her father asks her to do an errand for him, she turns to me and says, "Why doesn't he do it himself?" I then have to explain that respecting your father is a different issue and has nothing to do with being independent.

■ ■ ■ ■ ■

Ladan: I am in agreement with the fundamental ideas of feminism: the principles of equality, of access to work, of providing women with the same opportunities, of having total control over one's body, of setting aside the idea that boys should be raised differently from girls—and my list could go on and on. All my friends who are professional are feminists, but most of those who don't work don't concern themselves with problems like solidarity, feminism, and so on.

■ ■ ■ ■ ■

Touran: Solidarity among women depends on your personal experience. Those who are supportive of women see themselves as feminists and show solidarity to other women. But those who are not supportive of women's issues, well, I divide them into two groups.

The first group is the intellectual women who see themselves as head-and-shoulders above other women and men. They make no distinction between men and women and therefore believe that supporting women is backward.

The second group is women who are culturally underdeveloped. They never dealt with women's issues. They take their treatment by men for granted and see it as men's natural right over women. I refer to these women as those who tear each other's hair out.

I am a very independent woman. As a student in the States, my friends referred to me as a die-hard feminist. For me, women's issues were at the forefront of any struggle we waged. There were other women who thought like me. I never pulled back when it came to women's rights. To this day I am very sensitive to women's issues. I believe women should benefit from total equality under the law in the society in which they live.

■ ■ ■ ■ ■

Ramesh: I don't think there is such a thing as solidarity or loyalty among women. In my own life, most of the women I have encountered are jealous of me. They are jealous because I was able to pull myself up in life. Everybody expected me to stay a pretty, ignorant, doll-like woman. To this day, other women—women who consider themselves among my friends—throw derogatory remarks at me. They call me lucky and fortunate and give all the credit to my husband. Little do they know how hard I work. None of my women friends believed I would take my higher education seriously. They are so envious. It is terrible that as a woman you cannot trust another woman.

I consider myself a feminist. Maybe I do not fit into the standard definition of feminism. I don't care. I have set myself a very high standard in my life and certain goals to reach. I studied French and English. I learned how to play the piano and took calligraphy lessons. I arranged fashion shows and antique shows. I was pregnant with my second child when I sat for the university entrance examination. I am at the top of my class in the university. For me, this is feminism—to be able to improve and progress as a woman.

■ ■ ■ ■ ■

Lili: I don't think women care for each other. Every woman is a power in her own right, but women are unable to unite, to become a force in the society. They are too busy sabotaging other women. As we say in Persian, they shoot at the other's shadow. I personally don't trust women. My experience at work with other women has been negative. Let me give you an example. I was offered a job as a computer technician in a private company. My predecessor not only did not give me any assistance, she did all she could to undermine me. You call that solidarity? I only have one close female friend. I discuss all my problems with her, and I respect her opinion and trust her completely, but that's it. I don't have any other women friends.

■ ■ ■ ■ ■

Monir: Solidarity among women? I see it only in matters of the heart. Otherwise, I see it neither in the place of work nor outside the workplace. For example, none of the women lawyers work together. Without a proper organization you cannot look after each other.

In Iran today, because of economic and social conditions, the problem is how to survive. The attitude is, "If I don't swallow them, they will eat me up." You are involved in a constant battle with men, while you also are aware that women do not put much trust in other women. For example, the court assigned me a case of a woman who had committed adultery.

When her family found out that their lawyer was a woman, they went and borrowed money and hired a male lawyer and did not even bother to notify me.

I don't see myself as a feminist as the term is defined in the West. But if you argue that feminism means equality, I accept this idea and I am all for it. To me, my *chadori* mother who wanted me to study and be an independent woman is a feminist. Ms. Shahla Sherkat, the editor of *Zanan*, is a feminist. Neither of these two women fit into the stereotypes of feminism. I believe all of us are by nature feminists, but we express it differently.

■ ■ ■ ■ ■

Nargess: No, there is no such thing as gender solidarity. Our dominant culture does not provide for that. Everyone has to watch out for her own individual interests. Maybe some understanding is possible among women. There are individual friendships. Women support one another—but there is no solidarity. I don't see strong ties between women who are in the same profession or among housewives. Today our lives are such that we just have to look after our own nuclear families. Even among members of an extended family, a lot of bickering goes on. At work it is worse. All this because of economic pressure.

■ ■ ■ ■ ■

Afsar: I definitely don't see myself as a feminist. My friends are mostly men. On the whole I can establish a dialogue with men more easily than with women. I don't bother myself with issues such as solidarity among women or feminism. I don't want women to be treated unjustly, but I also don't feel I have to struggle for women's rights. I see these problems in their totality, not as exclusive to women.

■ ■ ■ ■ ■

Zohreh: Immediately after the revolution there was a solidarity among women. Women would smile at each other in the street. They were helping one another all the time. The Iran-Iraq War reinforced this attitude. It cre-

ated a bond among women. They shared the same experiences. They stood
in line for hours to acquire the basic necessities of daily life. They lost sons
and husbands in the war. The lines were the best place for women to show
their solidarity. But gradually the atmosphere changed. The war ended, and
everyone started to look out for herself. Today opportunities for women are
limited. There is a lot of economic and social pressure on women, and this
stops them from showing any sympathy for one another.

Women who work in the public sector know that their opportunities for
advancement are limited, so they compete with other women and are criticized for it. But this attitude derives from existing social conditions. Some
women compete over men, too. It is distressing, but it is a fact.

I don't object to feminism, but I am against the "pants-wearing women."
I believe that men and women should have the same rights, and they should
be treated equally.

■ ■ ■ ■ ■

Pouran: I am not a feminist. As a woman I am aware of the sufferings of
women. I would like to confront and fight the root and cause of this suffering by understanding and feeling it. I don't want women to be victimized,
nor do I want women to see themselves as victims. To be a victim means to
be blind about what takes place around you. I feel as women we should pay
a price and earn our rights. For example, if we don't want the *hejab*, we
should be ready for all the consequences stemming from fighting it, including going to jail.

I believe women are not the same as men, but they are equally competent. We need equal rights in Iran, and as women we have to fight for
them.

I have not come across the concept of solidarity among women. There is
a difference between friendship and gender solidarity. Solidarity is not part
of our culture. I have seen competitiveness, and I don't mind it. However, I
despise jealousy, meanness, taking refuge in feminine ploys like screaming
or being a woman the way the men want you to be. When we get together
with other women, we just pour our hearts out. We are among friends. Of
course, you show sympathy and you get sympathy in return, but this has
nothing to do with solidarity.

Jila: Of course, I am a feminist. I side with women because there has been such a great deal of injustice done to women. As a working woman, I always feel I did not get the rewards I deserved, and other women are like me. I never had any negative experiences with women, so I will always hire a woman rather than a man. I incline toward women. I have not seen back-biting among the women I have worked with or known. I have witnessed a sense of solidarity among women. It is a matter of class, and the manifestation among classes is different. As a woman you know that women will not abandon you.

All these years, it is women who stood up for other women and tried to influence the men when it came to women's issues.

■ ■ ■ ■ ■

Lida: I am a professional woman and a very successful woman. My biggest problem is dealing with women at work. They are not happy about my achievements. They are jealous. I can see it in their eyes. I don't mind professional competition, but all I get is petty jealousy. I don't see women showing any solidarity with other women. If they can denigrate a colleague, they will do that. Having said that, I must add that women are more responsible than men and they are not thieves.

■ ■ ■ ■ ■

Partow: I am a simple woman. I don't get a chance to read much. I don't know what feminism is all about. I believe in equality between men and women. I think some women like to help other women, and there are those who do everything possible to undermine their female colleagues. My own experience shows that women who are related to me stand by me and those who work with me are always trying to denigrate my work.

■ ■ ■ ■ ■

Nayyer: I am a feminist. I believe in feminism. I think as a feminist, but I lead a traditional life. As a feminist, my values are clear, but I have to ignore them in my daily life. For the sake of preserving the peace in the family, you basically accept a futile and senseless behavior on your part. In short, I think one way and act a different way. The gap between my way of thinking and my environment widens all the time. I picked up the seeds of feminism before the revolution while working for women. My ideas became accentuated after the revolution.

The revolution turned us women of the middle class into loners. We have to look after our own interests, so there can be no solidarity among women. I always raised my voice against discrimination toward women, but nobody ever supported me.

■ ■ ■ ■ ■

Sousan: I never look at myself as a feminist. For me, men and women have the same problems, professionally they face the same obstacles and difficulties. Our problem is cultural, and we have to deal with the cause and origin of this problem. After that we have to work more for women. I want full equal rights between men and women, but I don't tilt toward women. For me, there is a difference between the problems women have in our society and the concept of Western feminism.

As far as solidarity among women goes, I don't see a general trend. There is a difference between liking someone and helping her, and an attitude that can be defined as gender solidarity. A lot of it is just talk. In my own experience, among women who do not work and lead an affluent life, there is a lot of backbiting against other women.

■ ■ ■ ■ ■

Nasrin: I see myself as a feminist but not in the Western sense of feminism. I believe in equality between men and women, but I don't want a change in their roles. I believe men and women should complement each other. I have two daughters, and I have raised them to see themselves as feminists.

There is a cultural unawareness that results in ignoring the well-being of another woman. For example, the woman who accepts becoming a temporary second wife is not conscious of the pain and humiliation she is causing the other woman. This is all due to economic necessity and lack of social independence for women. In the absence of cultural development, proper education, economic and social freedom, one reverts to traditional behavior and customs. Unless we take major steps toward achieving these goals, there is no way we can expect that the average Iranian woman will become emancipated.

■ ■ ■ ■ ■

Zahra: I don't see any solidarity among women, but I don't see any enmity or backbiting either. I am a very positive person. I see the best in everybody. I have a lot of women friends, and I like to be in the company of women. In my work I always discuss the problems of women and their dilemma in life.

If feminism means equality between men and women, then I am a feminist. I don't have any enmity with men. I tell them it is to their advantage if men and women are equal.

■ ■ ■ ■ ■

Neda: I am not a feminist, but I favor equality under the law and I am against discrimination. In Iranian society you cannot speak of feminism. We are a traditional society. The concept of Western feminism is incomprehensible in this society. Of course, women want to be treated equally. They seek the same opportunities. They don't want to be second-class citizens. For women, the last fifteen years have been nothing but an uphill battle.

As far as solidarity goes, in my experience women act singly. There is no networking among women. We do not look at our problems from an intellectual point of view. As women, we deal with our problems subjectively. Professional women compete with each other. Why shouldn't they? I don't see any problem with that—just as they have to compete with men. On an individual basis you always have women friends you can rely on, whose support you can count on. But you can't say this is the general rule in this society.

Seven

Men

As the Islamic Republic strengthened its hold on the country during the first year of the revolution, it seemed obvious to many women that this was to be a government for men, run by men and built on the presumption of male dominance in both the private and the public spheres. To many women, the victory of the revolution meant a resurgence of male superiority and arrogance, an assertion by men of a claim to control women's lives and their bodies.

Among the women I interviewed, the revolution has resulted in a deep and as yet little appreciated transformation in the attitude of women toward men. In general, if the comments of these women are any guide, respect for men—their competence, good sense, fairness—has sharply declined. The idea of men as "natural" leaders in politics, business, and public affairs has been discredited. Women are much more likely to see men as full of swagger and bravado, but empty shells when it comes to displaying real courage and backbone in crises. Women feel far more independent than before the revolution, and married women far less dependent on their husbands.

Many women continue to resent the rapidity with which men of all classes assumed and took advantage of the male privileges made possible under the new dispensation. Men, Nayyer, an administrator told me, had been given "carte blanche" under the new order; and in taking advantage of the prerogatives now allowed under law and the prevailing social environment, men of "my class" did not differ from the Islamists. "You would be surprised," Nargess, a lawyer, told me, "how many educated young men beat their wives." Another woman felt the revolution had given men a green light to vent against women their long-felt resentments "for all we had achieved." Pouran, a university professor, remarked that since the revolution men no longer have to maintain appearances. "Nobody calls them to account. All the masks are down."

The suspension of the Family Protection Law, many women felt, gave men a sword of Damocles to hang over women's heads. A wife could be unilaterally divorced, thrown out of the house, her children taken from her. I heard story after story of men taking second wives or entering into temporary marriages. Such behavior, to the great resentment of women, has become both legally and socially permissible under the new dispensation. I met a woman who for years had refused to agree to a divorce requested by her husband. After the revolution, he married a second wife; "Taking his revenge on her," he refused her a divorce and would not give her permission to visit their children abroad.

Women lost their respect for their men for other reasons. In the aftermath of the revolution, many men in prominent positions were purged, dismissed, arrested, denied their pensions, and accused of being collaborators with the now much-denigrated former regime. Women saw their men's self-esteem crumble. The men seemed unable to rouse themselves or act. It was left to women to gather up the pieces and put shattered lives together again. "While men have become moaners and groaners, women are the doers," Nargess remarked. Early in the revolution, Ladan told me, "our men were emasculated."

Women also came to feel men lacked backbone when it came to standing up to the authorities. Jila, a businesswoman, pointedly remarked that while nobody required men to stop wearing neckties (the Islamic authorities treated the necktie as a corrupt Western form of dress) all men (except doctors) quickly abandoned ties and, in keeping with the new "Islamic revolutionary" convention, sported two-day-old beards and adopted a generally disheveled appearance. Nargess noted that none of the men she knows understood why wearing the hejab *was such an important issue for women. On the contrary, she said, men scolded women for resisting the Islamic dress code and urged them to conform.*

The revolution also appears to have generated greater sexual awareness among women, who now feel freer to talk about their bodies. Before the revolution, I was told, women never talked about their sexual needs. But since the revolution, women get together and discuss all sorts of things, including sex. We knew, Pouran said, that men get together and discuss women and sex. Now women discuss men and sex. According to a number of women I talked to, a wife who discovers her husband is having an extramarital affair is perfectly capable of reciprocating.

Many women feel that a reversal of male-female roles has occurred. "The Islamic Republic," Sousan, a businesswoman, said, "has created a dependency in reverse," with men dependent on their wives. Women feel they cannot abandon their husbands, another said, because the men are helpless fending for themselves. Some women assert men have become irrelevant to their lives. Others feel that, in the Islamic Republic, to have a man at your side is a necessity. "In short," said Lili, a secretary, "a woman needs her husband to change a flat tire."

■ ■ ■ ■ ■

Amineh: Let me put how women feel toward men in a nutshell: we no longer have men around us, but just people who wear trousers. Since the revolution men's standing has shrunk in the eyes of women. Men were taken by surprise as the revolution unfolded, so they started pushing their wives to deal with the situation. As the women became more involved and had to deal with the day-to-day needs of living under a revolutionary government and surviving the war, and got no help from their men, they naturally lost all respect for them.

The older generation of men went back to the way they were raised. I mean, they took second wives or a temporary wife. The society has also become more permissive, a clandestine kind of permissiveness. I believe morality has disappeared from Iranian society. Secular ideas had barely found some roots in our society when we got a government that dismantled all the existing norms. Men take advantage of this situation. But basically they have regressed while women have progressed.

■ ■ ■ ■ ■

Mari: I don't have much respect for men. I find them quite contemptible. They did not show any sympathy for the difficulties women faced. They basically washed their hands of the problem by blaming women. Deep down they are happy that women must observe the *hejab*. They hid behind their women's skirts. With the first sign of turmoil, they gave up. When their positions and their desks were taken away from them, it did not occur to them to make use of their expertise and their know-how. They just went home and complained, while women immediately found a way to bounce back. Women proved that their instinct for survival is unsurpassable.

After the revolution we opened our eyes and saw that there is not much even to our educated men—a lot of talk and no substance. Women found out how little men know, how trivial they are, and how totally irrelevant their analysis is. Basically, as far as women were concerned, men did not matter any more and women were able to deal with their problems without the help of men.

■ ■ ■ ■ ■

Shokouh: I don't have much esteem for Iranian men. They are selfish and do not have any respect for Iranian women. They belittle their wives both in public and in private. They prefer the company of other men. The Islamic Republic encourages such an attitude. Have you seen how many men take second wives? As soon as their first wife grows old, they go looking for a younger wife. On the other hand, men have weak character. If they had strong personalities and did not feel so vulnerable, they would not make their wives miserable.

Of course, there are women, even in our class, who believe that men are superior. These women are submissive and obedient to men. Again I blame it on our society, which makes women, especially those who don't work, dependent on a man, on a husband. There is no affection between men and women. They just accommodate each other. If men take mistresses, I don't see why women should not take male friends. Today among a lot of people in our social class, both husbands and wives work. In some cases the women earn more than the men. They shoulder all the expenses. Nevertheless, the husbands still expect them to act as traditional, submissive wives. Why should they? What men don't want to understand is that because of the way our society is structured, a lot of women accommodate their husbands only because married women have an easier social life. It is a price women have to pay.

■ ■ ■ ■ ■

Elaheh: I find the behavior of men despicable. It does not matter whether the man is educated or not, married or single. In my experience as soon as men find out I am a single woman, their attitude changes and they start hinting that they would be willing to meet with me privately. They expect any woman to be available to them. I am always shocked by their remarks, am unprepared, and cannot bring myself to accept such behavior. I have come to the conclusion that Iranian men habitually cast lascivious looks on women. It is uncomfortable to be in their presence. On the other hand, we live in a society where it does make a difference if you have a man at your side, just for the sake of appearances. For some women, men have become a passport to freedom, to do what they like, to go where they want to go.

■ ■ ■ ■ ■

Darya: Male chauvinism and male dominance have increased in society. This is the reality. Male chauvinism is not only the law of the land; it also reflects the true historical consciousness of the people that was awakened by the revolution. Women put up a resistance to such attitudes, especially in those families where women carry all the responsibilities. They work outside their homes, they run the household, and they deal with all day-to-day problems. They don't have tolerance for male chauvinist attitudes. There is a lot of arguing and quarreling among spouses. Oddly enough, this is reflected in television programs, too. People don't discuss their differences, they shout each other down. I mean the woman shouts back and answers back.

■ ■ ■ ■ ■

Gowhar: Patriarchal culture has deep roots in our society. Unfortunately, the Islamic revolution was fertile soil for all the greater growth of this culture. For example, when the law permits a man to have four wives, how can you expect that, even if he makes do with one wife, a man should not every day remind his wife that he is doing her a favor in not taking advantage of the law by taking multiple wives.

■ ■ ■ ■ ■

Soudabeh: If women complain about the behavior of men, I blame it on them. It is women who provoke men to act in a condescending fashion toward women. I can give you many examples of how unprofessional, provocative, and frivolous women are, both at work and in the streets. I remember an incident during the war. We were standing in line to buy something, I can't remember what. Women and men were queuing separately. A woman started complaining about the long hours she had to wait in line. A man tried to explain that these were unusual times. The woman lost her temper, and they started shouting at each other and throwing insults. It was a pitiful scene. The man told her she screams because she is a woman and therefore irrational. The woman told him if they were not living in such a patriarchal society, he would never dare throw insults at her. I blame the woman for this incident.

Unlike others, I feel the revolution made it possible for men to evaluate women differently. They do not treat women like made-up dolls. They see how competent and capable women are. I think the revolution created a positive reaction in men toward women. I think the revolution had a maturing effect on women as well as men.

■ ■ ■ ■ ■

Manijeh: The social upheaval that took place necessitated the participation of women. The social, economic, and political participation of women had consequences such that, even in the most traditional strata of the society, basic fundamental changes occurred among women. Willy-nilly, women moved on while men remained fixed in their former attitudes. In this upheaval no attempt was made to peacefully resolve the conflicts arising between men and women. Rather, with an absolute belief in a male-dominated social order, men were given a free hand to make use recklessly of laws underwriting male domination. What was the result? A deep division in this crisis-ridden society—a deep division between women who have acquired a different consciousness of their role and men who have not altered their view of "manliness," women, and the family.

■ ■ ■ ■ ■

Nazanin: How do I see men? The revolution proved to us that men are more vulnerable than women. The pride and ego of men are unbelievably fragile.

Ayesheh: After the revolution, we had to deal with our men who were terribly depressed. It was left to us to pretend that this was a passing state of mind, that they would bounce back. We had to make sure that the family was not going to fall apart. I think among our class the attitude of men toward their wives changed dramatically. Their respect for their wives grew. Women proved to have the necessary credentials, something men did not have.

Of course women don't think much of the men in general, but again it depends on your personal experience with your spouse. I live with a very civilized man who is full of understanding and appreciation for what I have done, but I cannot generalize from our relationship. I have seen how women around me lost all their respect and affection for their men because of their ineptitude and lack of judgment.

■ ■ ■ ■ ■

Fatemeh: What do you want me to say? The less I talk about men the better. Looking around me, I find that immediately after the revolution men abdicated their responsibilities to women. Men withdrew into a cocoon of depression and asked their wives to deal with the pressure and changes the revolution inflicted on them. What I found striking was how easily men lost their bearing and women stepped into the shoes of men.

One did not detect any backbone in men. The funny aspect of it all is that once the situation normalized a bit, men became their old arrogant selves, but women were not buying it any more. Women had lost all their respect for men.

■ ■ ■ ■ ■

Atefeh: I speak of course of men of wealthier classes. I think men have proven more forgiving and more prone to suffer in silence than the women. By the same token, they are more fragile and stand up less well to adversity. This difference became evident after the revolution. The women shrank from nothing, while the men seemed lost. It appears that women have greater endurance.

Masoumeh: I have an overall view on this matter. I believe even an educated woman raises her son differently from her daughter. She implants in him the same self-centeredness his father and grandfather had. The revolution, on the one hand, encouraged all the male chauvinist impulses in men. On the other hand, it created an awareness in women not to put up with a lot of nonsense. The women proved to have more courage and more guts than men. The men became depressed, nagging, resentful, incapacitated, and impotent. Women were able to pull themselves out of this quagmire, while men sank deeper into depression. It is so funny to see that sixteen years after the revolution these men still consider themselves as the victims.

Women not only have adapted themselves to the new situation, they are aware of their needs, both sexually and intellectually. They have their affairs and don't feel bad about it. They don't have any complexes. Had it not been for the revolution, women would not have discovered their capabilities as well as their courage.

■ ■ ■ ■ ■

Ladan: The general attitude of men toward women has been condescending. On the other hand, women barely manage to tolerate men. Women feel if they did not have to live with a man they would make more progress. They feel men are in their way. I personally think I would have been able to achieve much more if there were no men around me. I could do my research, go abroad. I stayed here because of my husband. He could not survive without me. He leaves all the financial decisions to me. He thinks men have less wisdom than women. He does what he wants in public, but if I disagree with him in front of other people, he gets upset. He thinks I am humiliating him. This is not my intention because in my eyes he is not a little man. I sometimes ask myself, "What good does the pity I feel for him do me?"

Many years ago, when I found out about his escapades, I became very upset. I was traumatized. I still find it revolting, but I am used to it now. At some stage I asked myself, "Why not me?" But if I ever reciprocate and have affairs of my own, he will break down. It would kill him. The power of our traditional culture still looms over our heads. They raised us women to be totally submissive and our men expect obedience from us. As it is, men are having trouble dealing with our social and economic independence. Our sexual freedom would destroy them.

The revolution showed us how vulnerable the men are. The revolution accentuated the weaknesses and incapacities of men. I saw it in my own family. Very early in the revolution, our men were emasculated.

■ ■ ■ ■ ■

Touran: Men have become more backward, they are less interesting. All they do these days is get together and reminisce about the past. They don't work. They even don't make an effort to work. They still are stuck in their traditional rut and try to impose their will on women, both at work and in the home.

Women of our generation and the previous generation do not put up with such nonsense. They answer back. On the other hand, you see some working women putting up with the humiliating treatment they get at work. They don't answer back because they don't even respect the men enough to start an argument with them. This attitude makes men more angry and more irrational and insulting toward women.

■ ■ ■ ■ ■

Ramesh: Iranian men are selfish, patronizing, and domineering. They have watched the behavior of their fathers and imitated them. Even the European-educated men behave no differently. The revolution reinforced all these characteristics. If you see women not respecting men and a permissiveness pervading our society, it is because men always did what they wanted. Since the revolution women are following suit. Married women take lovers and their husbands accept it because they have their female "friends." If they reproach their wives, their own affairs are thrown back in their face. It is a two-way affair. The revolution gave self-confidence to women, basically because the men lost their self-esteem. As women became economically more independent, they became socially freer, and today they are no longer intimidated by their men. I look around me among our friends. Most of the women don't get along with their spouses. The rift between them has widened. Men expect respect from their wives. However, their behavior is so selfish, so inattentive, that women don't see any reason to respect their husbands.

Lili: Men are really awful; they are rotten. They are selfish and unappreciative. They don't understand what women want. As for me, I can see through any man. The society and system here are such that men are always on the lookout for women to pick them up. It is disgusting. You see that at work, in the streets, and at gatherings of friends.

On the other hand, men are a necessity in the Islamic Republic. As a woman you need the shadow of a man over your head, I mean in the abstract sense. The man gives you protection from other men. But in real life, men are not an essential part of a woman's life. They are not indispensable. In short, a woman needs her husband to change a flat tire. Men are no longer the decision makers, whether at work or at home. If you are a competent woman, men are more than happy to abdicate all their responsibilities to you. But they also expect you to respect them. How can a woman respect a spineless man?

Let me put it to you this way: if I were single today, I would take a lover rather than a husband. If today in Iran women seek sexual freedom, men are to be blamed. Men don't understand that women not only need love and affection but also sexual satisfaction and pleasure.

■ ■ ■ ■ ■

Monir: The revolution affected a certain class of men in a negative way. It destroyed their sense of self-worth, thus creating a severe depression and, as a result, a noticeable impotence. Women did not have the time or the luxury to become depressed. They had to deal with the problems of daily life. Even women who went to jail came out more stubborn and aggressive. They passed on this attitude to other women. Women were not intimidated by the revolution. Men gave up, maybe because women were willing to take over both roles. Women entered the spheres and domains that had been reserved for men. As women started to make money, they became more open about expressing their feelings and their sexual desires.

I see three reasons for this attitude. First is the growing economic independence of women and the fact that they do not have to rely on their husbands as the breadwinner. Second is the explicit language used by official clerics regarding sexual relationships. Programs such as Ayatollah Gilani's show on television, which expounded on the sexual vocabulary of Islamic

law, or remarks by clerics regarding the acceptability of a temporary marriage that might last only ten minutes made the discussion of sex not only
permissible but acceptable, too. Finally, there is the access to videocassettes,
foreign television programs broadcast via satellite, and foreign television
stations, which can be easily picked up in border towns.

These three reasons, as well as the constant struggle of women and the
weakness and incapacity of men when it came to dealing with the revolutionary organizations and events, destroyed any respect women might feel
for men.

■ ■ ■ ■ ■

Nargess: Men turned out to be just plain bad. They are cowards and incompetent. They turned out to be really conservative. They started treating
women like dirt. Inside the family men took out their frustrations on
women by oppressing them. They encouraged women to observe the *hejab*.
Some even threatened their wives and daughters that they would not put up
bail if the women were arrested or had to appear before a revolutionary
court.

I have heard educated men saying they don't understand all the fuss
about wearing the *chador*—not because they worry about women being
accosted by the authorities. No. Out of sheer selfishness, since they did not
want to come face-to-face with officials.

I think deep down all our men, regardless of their upbringing and education, approve of the Islamic dress code for women and all the measures
the government has taken to limit women in their activities. This attitude
has influenced young men, too. They mistreat their wives as if they still live
in the nineteenth century. They want total submissiveness. You would be
surprised how many educated young men beat their wives. I think basically
our men are suffering from mental illness and depression. As a result they
have developed sexual problems and blame it all on their wives and constantly threaten them either with divorce or a second wife. While men have
become moaners and groaners, women are the doers. Men were too scared
to wage a protest, while it was women who at every stage stood up to the
authorities. This is difficult for men to swallow. Thus their insulting behavior toward women.

Afsar: On the whole, women remained strong all these years, while men crumbled and were unable to cope. Let me be very brief by quoting a friend of mine, who said, "If there is ever a change, we should take a hose and wash the men down."

■ ■ ■ ■ ■

Zohreh: Men are bewildered and don't know how to deal with women. They are faced with the fact that women are doing men's jobs. Since the revolution, women are running businesses that were exclusive to men. They deal in imports and exports, they have become merchants. Revolutionary conditions and the war toughened women, and men started resenting women's competence. They keep on asking women whether they plan to take over. They try to humiliate women publicly by constantly reminding them to observe the *hejab* properly. Privately, the only way men assert themselves is by mistreating their wives.

Men have lost their spirit. They suffer depression and a loss of heart, a condition universal to the whole country. This depression has rendered our men impotent, and since the problem of sex is discussed twenty-four hours a day, and men are aware of it, their impotence is even more accentuated.

■ ■ ■ ■ ■

Pouran: Men's attitude toward women has changed. You can even see it among our intellectuals. They appear to sympathize with the suffering of women. In reality, they don't. In the old days men at least bothered to behave. Since the revolution they don't have to maintain appearances. Nobody calls them to account. All the masks are down.

Let me tell you a story. I had invited a well-known intellectual to talk to a group of students. The next day I went to his house to drop off the tapes of the meeting. He tried to make a pass at me, using all these clichéd expressions. I was in a state of shock. I pushed him away. I left him in a rage. Later I found out that this is a pattern of behavior with him.

The revolution turned Iranian men impotent. Have you noticed how men tell many more dirty, sexist jokes? I find it repulsive, maybe because I find men so unclean. When they pay me a compliment I find it nauseating.

A lot of women complain about their sexual unhappiness and dissatisfaction. They talk about it with other women. I feel that very few women have a satisfying sexual relationship with their husbands. The revolution awakened all these feelings in women. One should not be surprised that, as a change, it is women who look for fulfillment. For a lot of Iranian women their first sexual encounter, which usually was with their husbands, was nothing more than a rape. It left a scar, at least for some of us, forever.

■ ■ ■ ■ ■

Jila: The revolution proved how weak and vulnerable men are. Suddenly all the men we dealt with grew beards, removed their ties, and even developed a new way of talking. Then the laws pertaining to women's rights changed and men started venting their frustrations by abusing their wives.

Let me give you the example of someone I know. This man married a woman younger than himself. At first they were in love. Then he started mistreating her, even beating her. She took her case to court. All the neighbors testified in her favor. To this day she has not been able to get her divorce, but she had enough courage to leave him. He thought she could not survive without him, but it is he whose life fell apart once she left him.

■ ■ ■ ■ ■

Partow: I believe the revolution on the one hand emphasized the arrogance of Iranian men and, on the other hand, proved how insignificant they are. Suddenly men felt they gained the upper hand over women. But I think this was an aberration because soon women saw through this facade and realized how depressed and frustrated they were. Of course men let their frustrations out on women. It bothers them to see that they have lost control over women. They need the income of their wife, but they still want to order her around. Working women and even housewives don't put up with this anymore. So men take refuge in the arms of other women. However, what has come as a shock to them is that it is women who are terminating the relationship. Isn't this humiliating for Iranian men?

■ ■ ■ ■ ■

Nayyer: The revolution "froze" the men. They remained static, the men remained at ground zero, while we women developed, progressed, and became dynamic. The men were like books in the display window of a bookstore.

The revolution dramatically affected the men of our generation. Most of them lost their jobs, and with their jobs went their self-esteem. They hit a depression that some men have not been able to shake after sixteen years. They mistreat their wives because this is the only way they can deal with their frustrations. They expect women to serve them constantly, and, since they do not have permanent jobs, they start interfering in the affairs of the house. The role reversal is destroying them, and they don't want to admit it.

The depression the men suffer is hurting women. People who are losers cannot love anybody or show affection, so women start looking for appreciation, love, and affection elsewhere. Iranian women are raised to be passive in their sexual encounters. Their pride and upbringing did not allow them to discuss their sexual needs with their spouses. Since the revolution women have started talking about sex among themselves. They talk about their frustrations and desires. Men cannot accept this change in women, and this creates a great deal of tension between spouses.

Our generation came to know men when studying at the university. Men and women felt close to each other, probably because of their political activities. This was the foundation of their relationship. A mutual respect existed between the two sexes. However, while the generation that came after us, I mean the men and women who joined the job market in the last years of the Pahlavi era, were able to socialize freely with each other, this generation of men, even if modern, looked at women as instruments for pleasure. The notion of women being "dolls" stems from this period.

I don't think there is much difference in the attitude of these men and that of the Islamists in regard to women. Their appearance is different, but this is a difference between pretending to be modern and being traditional. Both groups prefer to repress women. Neither of these two groups believes in women. Those with the financial means shower their wives with money, gold, and luxury—anything to keep these women busy to prevent them from getting involved in serious matters.

■ ■ ■ ■ ■

Sousan: As I don't view men from a feminist perspective, I think men and women are human beings first and both have their weaknesses. After the revolution many men showed fragility but about the same number showed strength. The fact that women look so strong is because they have the opportunity to prove this strength and not because men are especially weak or fragile.

The attitude of men has not changed toward me. No man has ever insulted me. I won't let it happen. On the surface the men I know did not change their behavior toward their wives. But on the whole Iranian men turned out to be the weaker of the two sexes. I remember during the war it was men who wanted to leave the country and used their wives and children as an excuse. Men who lost their jobs also lost their self-esteem. There were quite a few of them around us. They still try to preserve a dignity, but it is all a facade.

These days women talk much more openly about the irrelevance of their husbands in their lives. They put up with these men because they pity them. Oddly enough, it is men who are dependent on women and not the other way round. In short, the Islamic Republic has created a dependency in reverse.

■ ■ ■ ■ ■

Nasrin: I divide Iranian men in two groups. There are those who believe they own their women like they own a toothbrush or an electric shaver. They require from their women total obedience and submissiveness. They are selfish and arrogant. Then there are men who love their families and try not to be oppressive and cruel toward their women. But even in those men you can detect the seeds of dominance.

As a woman who constantly deals with women's issues, I am aware of the suffering men inflict on women, especially on their wives. You should see the complaints I receive daily: battered women, women who are discriminated against in the courts, women whose husbands threaten to take on second wives. How can women respect men if they are constantly threatened by them? Women start looking to their own well-being. They look for jobs, they try to save and buy gold. The lack of respect is mutual in our society today.

I am more aware of the plight of working-class women. Their men take advantage of them and of the laws that give men the right to marry, remarry, and divorce. This is changing. As women of that class find the courts more amenable to listening to their grievances, their dependence on men lessens. Economic dependency is one of the main reasons why women put up with bullying and repression by their husbands.

The revolution had a liberating effect on women in several respects, one of which was the need for women to start working. In a number of cases, since men lost their jobs and opted to stay home, women had to go out and find jobs. While earning a living, they discovered the benefits of economic independence; there was no need to rely on the men who were so inept. Once you find out that the government does not provide you with welfare services and your husband is incapable in doing so, you learn to rely on yourself and on your capabilities as a working woman.

■ ■ ■ ■ ■

Zahra: The attitude of men toward women has changed. Men are angrier, harsher, more nervous and depressed. The reason is economics. Men know they should be the providers, but they cannot provide. They have become economically dependent on their women. They cannot accept that. Some of our men work long hours and thus neglect the family. It affects their marital relationship. They start abusing women. Women no longer put up with this treatment. There is a lot of separation and divorce. How can women respect men who abuse them and who are incapable of providing for them?

■ ■ ■ ■ ■

Neda: The men just shrank, they regressed, and they fell in our esteem. Women all found a way to deal with their new situation, while men took refuge in the home and started finding fault with their wives' cooking.

Men proved how incompetent they are. They even did not put up the semblance of a resistance. They became disheveled in their appearance and did not care if their wives wore baggy clothes and looked unattractive.

My daughter, who returned to Iran after living for many years in Europe, said, "I feel women have grown big, really big, while men have become small, truly small."

Eight

Taking Stock

I ASKED THE WOMEN I INTERVIEWED, finally, to take stock, to tell me how well they feel they have coped, how the revolution has changed them, how they assess their lives and accomplishments today, more than a decade and a half after the revolution. Their responses were varied and complex.

I sensed a residue of bitterness and anger—at careers interrupted, family life dislocated, unpleasant and sometimes frightening encounters with discourteous revolutionary authorities and, even, a sense of years and lives wasted in a unending struggle to rebuild shattered careers, make ends meet, retrieve honor and reputation, and adjust to an unfamiliar and hostile new order. As one woman said, it was like seeing everything you had worked for, loved, and took pride in trampled on and yet feeling helpless to do anything about it.

The feeling of having lived and struggled in an almost alien environment, among new rulers who were themselves unfamiliar, was widespread. "Our walking and talking was different from theirs," was a sentence I heard over and over. "Swimming against the tide," was how Masoumeh described the experience of the last fifteen years. For some women, life since the revolution has often seemed a question not of long-term planning but of coping from one day to the next; or, as Nahid put it, a question of learning to do everything all over again by trial and error: "I had to start everything from scratch."

On the other hand, many also took satisfaction at having been able, against all odds, to continue their careers or start new ones, or merely at having endured, despite what sometimes seemed unsurmountable difficulties.

Work has been for many an important source of fulfillment. Shokouh, a physician, said she and her husband could have made a good living abroad. But Iran needed her more than she was needed abroad, and serving the

*Iranian people was important to her. Sousan, a former university professor,
now in private business, felt staying in Iran and providing a model for
younger girls to follow was satisfaction enough. And, as the previous pages
show, many women feel vindicated for having stood their ground and
carved out a space for themselves in the new order, as women.*

*While some women can never quite reconcile themselves to the Islamic
Republic, others feel a kind of modus vivendi with the authorities has been
reached. Moreover, from a feminist perspective, these women feel that, on
women's issues, the struggle with the authorities has resulted in a decided
victory for the women. Islamic dress aside (and even here the regime has
been compromised), on issues critical to women the regime is in retreat.*

■ ■ ■ ■ ■

Amineh: I don't know how I coped with the revolution. All I know is that if
it had not been for my work, I could have not lived, especially after my husband died. If I did not have my work, I probably would have committed sui-
cide. I could have gone abroad, but I know I could have not written abroad.
It would have been just surviving, breathing the air. Here, I live. I have a
mission in life. I have a message. When my reader gets that message, I feel it
was worth all the effort I have put into the last sixteen years.

Did I have to reconstruct my life? Of course I did. I had to readjust my
way of thinking, overcome my disappointment. I still live in the house I've
lived all my married life. I have been trying to sell it. It is impossible, so
much paperwork. But I am calm about it. You develop an attitude that
somehow things will work themselves out. You just have to be patient and
wait.

Most of the people around me had to start new careers. Some of us were
luckier than others. We found a profession not very different from what we
did before the revolution. Others had to go into a field completely new for
them. To live, to make money, to survive became our goal. When my husband died I either could have given up on life or continued. I opted for the
latter. He was a university professor. I try to keep his ideas alive by being in
touch with his students. Just seeing the young makes my life more exciting.

Looking back, I am glad I stayed in Iran, and the adjustment, although
difficult, was worthwhile.

Mari: I went along with what happened out of sheer necessity. I looked at it as a historian. For me this was real history. It was bound to endure. A revolution at the end of the twentieth century was not going to disappear. I told myself, "We have to accept the consequences of such an upheaval."

You learned to accept the sharp contrasts between your public life and private life. Of course, the life inside homes is affected by what goes on outside the house—the shortages, the war, and, in the beginning, the shock of my husband being purged from the university after a lifetime of serving his country. And, finally the fear of the *komitehs* coming to search your house. Like other people, we too had relatives whose properties were confiscated. Some were even taken to prison. They made us move from our ancestral home because it was in a "security zone." We had our encounters with the *komitehs*, too.

Having said that, I believe that my life is more comfortable here than anywhere else. I am happy we did not leave the country. Nothing in the world would have made my husband leave Iran. The last sixteen years have been productive years for me. I have taught, I have published, I have done a lot of research. If you are satisfied with your work, it makes it easier to cope with the external problems.

I have had my share of problems with the university, with the authorities, with the students. But I have dealt with them in my own way. Today my husband has his private business and is very successful. It is their loss for having purged him. I can't say that we reconstructed our life. No, we readjusted ourselves to the new situation.

■ ■ ■ ■ ■

Shokouh: I coped with the revolution by disregarding some of my principles. I had to ignore them. It broke my pride. In short, I adapted myself to this new way of life. I am very happy with my work, but is satisfaction at work enough? I am not sure. Over the last few years I have gained an inner strength, I have reached an equilibrium in my life. Maybe that is why these days I can better cope with the situation than before. I feel women on the whole are in better shape than what one expected. After all the hardship inflicted on them, they managed to cope better than the men.

No, I did not reconstruct my life, but I had to conform to a way of life that was alien to me. I did not have to change my profession. I am a physician, and they needed us badly. But this, for example, did not prevent the fellow at the gate of the hospital from stopping me and scolding me for not observing the proper *hejab* or from filing a complaint that I was not dressed properly at work. There is a big difference between the life we lead inside our homes and outside. At home nothing has changed. Outside I feel I move in strange surroundings, totally unfamiliar to me. Over the years you even learn to accept this. It is the humiliation that they inflict on you as a woman that is so unacceptable.

■ ■ ■ ■ ■

Farideh: As for me, I have learned to live with the revolution, I have learned to cope with it. It was not at all easy. Horrible things happened. My family left; I lost my best friend. I took early retirement. This alone meant living more modestly. I learned to scale down my life, to adjust myself to the new environment. It was not easy. I saw the standard of living deteriorating in front of my eyes. There were social pressures, too. Whenever you got together with friends you worried that the *komiteh* would barge in. It happened to us one evening. We were at a friend's house. We were told that the *komiteh* people were outside. We decided to leave in order not to create problems for the host. We were at least forty people. They ordered us to get into our cars. We went in a convoy to the local *komiteh*. We spent the whole night there, protesting our detention and arguing with the head of the *komiteh*. Finally they let us go in the morning. It might sound trivial now, but it was both frightening and humiliating.

The positive aspect of the revolution is the closeness of the people to another, a sense of solidarity, a sense of belonging to this land for those of us who remained here. My heart goes out to the ordinary citizens of our country. They are so vulnerable. You know, it is as if you have a handicapped child among all your healthy children and you have to take more care of him. I feel ordinary people have lost their way, and they need us, and we have to stay close to them and help them to get back on their feet. This aspect of our life makes it possible to accept that everything is far from being perfect, and it makes it easier for us to put up with our daily lives and these difficult conditions.

Elaheh: Coping has been very difficult for me. I have coped with this situation by isolating myself socially. I have solved all my social problems by staying at home and only going out to work. I am a recluse, a hermit. I don't even have a television set. I don't want to know what goes on outside my work. I am not happy with my work. I wish I had not returned to Iran. I feel trapped in this place. I made a down payment on an apartment and moved into it. In doing so I have committed myself even more to this place. I feel I am going round and round in a circle. I see no future for myself. Everything looks black.

I probably sound bitter and disappointed. But I would like to add that I sincerely believe that we have a religious doctrine that is good and a culture that is equally good. But in reality we neither adhere to Hosein and Hasan, nor do we revere Dariush and Kourosh.* That is, we adhere neither to our true religious heritage nor to our cultural heritage. As for me, I don't find myself at home in either of these two cultures.

My family thinks the solution to my problem is getting married. I am a practical person. I have accepted my fate, and I don't think for a minute that my problems and the problems of other women who think like me will disappear once they get married. All I ask is to be treated decently as a human being. That is not much, is it?

■ ■ ■ ■ ■

Darya: The material aspects of our life did not change that much. We live in the same house, we shop in the same stores, we read a lot, we travel, and we socialize. But now let me tell you what changed. Being a woman changed. It is no longer the same. Everything collapsed for me as a woman.

Before the revolution I was a woman lawyer working for a government organization. After the revolution I gave up my job. I never went back to practice law. I just could not face the humiliation of being trampled under their feet because of who I was. I felt as if all I had worked for all my life came to a halt, I mean in the domain of women's rights. For a brief moment

---

*Hosein and Hasan, grandsons of the Prophet, are revered religious leaders in Shi-ite Islam. Dariush and Kourosh (Darius and Cyrus in English usage) are famed kings of the Achaemenian dynasty which ruled over a great empire based in Iran in the 4th–6th centuries B.C.

I thought my world had come to a standstill. The law was always very important to me.

Let me tell you an incident in order for you to make sense of how I felt as a woman. I remember, we were going abroad with my husband. At the airport the body search to which we women were subjected created such a revulsion in me that I could not stop crying for six hours. It was as if I had been raped; by touching my body it was as if they took all my dignity, all my privacy from me. I told you this story to explain that the most ordinary encounter would turn into a humiliating experience.

If I stayed alive, it was because of my husband. His respect and love for me and for what I represented gave me energy to survive the daily ordeals that each of us has had to face.

■ ■ ■ ■ ■

Soudabeh: I had no problem accepting the revolution. I therefore did not have any difficulty with either readjusting or coping with it. I was a professional person and not at all political. So was my husband. There was a logic in what the revolution stood for, and being an objective person I accepted this logic and the arguments that came with it.

The revolution did not change our private life. We live in the same house, and we both work at the same hospitals we worked in before the revolution. We were able to send our older daughter to study in the States, and next year we will send our second daughter. Our standard of living has not changed. We used to socialize with doctors. We still see them. We go to conferences, both inside the country and abroad. So basically it is the same.

Of course, like everybody else, I had encounters with the authorities, but I was always able to solve them. I did not let it become an issue. Maybe being a physician in a country where there is shortage of doctors, maybe being a person with a lot of common sense, maybe being so apolitical, made it possible for me to continue with my life as it was before the revolution. Maybe I was luckier than a lot of other people. How do I know? All I know is that for me there was a continuity and not a disruption.

■ ■ ■ ■ ■

Manijeh: How did I cope? I don't know. Looking back, I must admit those were sad years. But, on the other hand, I am not sad to be a woman. I see myself as a courageous woman. I am very hopeful for the future. I can't give up hope. As an unmarried woman I can't accept an arranged marriage. With my traditional upbringing, I can't accept sex before marriage either. That has been a sensitive issue between me and some of the men I have gone out with. For some men, I am too traditional; for others I am too independent and liberated. I feel I have to shape my life the way I believe is right for me and not pay attention to what others say.

I had my share of problems with the authorities. I will never forget when my sixteen-year-old brother became injured in a street brawl in which he was an innocent bystander. Someone had knifed him. We went to several hospitals. Nobody wanted to take him in. We could not persuade the hospitals that he was a bystander and not a participant. They were scared of taking a Mojahed in. How could you convince them that not every young wounded boy was a Mojahed? Finally the emergency room of a hospital admitted him. He had eighty stitches. For several weeks my mother kept him at home. Then one day I was driving the car and he was sitting next to me. He was still wearing a bandage on his arm. I saw through the mirror that we were being followed by a motorcyclist. At the red light he stopped us and insisted that we go to the *komiteh*. We had no choice but to do as we were told. They called my mother in. I will never forget how rude they were to my mother and how composed she was. The only thing she said was that there was no way she would let her son stay there overnight. We produced a deed of a land and got my brother out on bail. Three days later my brother, accompanied by my mother, appeared in front of the judge. My mother spent the whole day explaining to the judge that my brother was an innocent bystandeer and not a participant. Finally they let my brother go.

The truth of the matter is that our lives depended on the whim, frustration, and inferiority complexes of the individual who dealt with our case.

■ ■ ■ ■ ■

Nazanin: For me there was an element of pride in not talking about my problems. To let oneself go is the easiest way out. I know of a lot of people who went to pieces. A university professor, a friend of mine who lost his job, stayed home, and as a result his body and soul collapsed. I always remembered my father telling us that one should stand firm when faced with difficulties in life. He used to say life is a struggle and one should not bend one's head

You know how I coped with the revolution? By not letting myself fall apart, by not feeling wretched, by not complaining. I hate moaning, it is so tiresome. Over the years I have developed a depth and an understanding for other people. The last fifteen years did not harden me. I don't look back at those years as wasted years. For me they were the ups and downs of life. For better or for worse, this was my choice. Of course I did not have a great time. Like everybody else, I, too, had to compromise; I, too, was frustrated. I tried to keep my morale up. Even during the war, I tried to stay cool and accept all the consequences of the war. I did not want to leave the country. I had seen how the Iranians lived in exile. This was not what I wanted for the rest of my life.

There are very few people who did not have to readjust their way of life during the revolution. We used to live in a large house. We moved into an apartment. I used to be a social secretary. I started giving private lessons at home. I had my encounters with the authorities, too, and they were not pleasant. But I stuck it out, and unlike a lot of my friends I am quite hopeful about the future.

■ ■ ■ ■ ■

Ayesheh: How did I cope? It was so very difficult. I gave all I had. I struggled, I pretended that all is well. My husband was depressed. I would tell him all the time that our future is still ahead of us, but for many years deep inside me I was in mourning. I bore this sadness. I did not show my feelings. I did not let it affect my work or my duties as a wife and a mother. I was not a selfish person. Not for a moment did I think that the country owed me anything.

Of course, it was a big readjustment. For a woman who had worked all her life as a civil servant to become, first, jobless and then start working in the private sector demanded a lot of flexibility. Basically, we had to start from the beginning in our forties and hope that we will make it back to where we were when the revolution occurred. Women like me not only did not have the moral support of their husbands, they had to help their husbands to stand on their feet once more. It was a rough and tough time.

Fatemeh: I coped with the revolution by continuing to work. I had a lot of responsibilities, both family and professionally. I also felt responsible for the well-being of my workers. I had to look after them and the family business. I had to deal with the revolutionary organs. They were all over the place. Our child was born in the first year of the revolution. I had neither the time nor the luxury to sit back and moan over the past or over daily incidents. I was on my feet eighteen hours a day, seven days a week. It hurt a lot to see close friends and relatives leaving the country, going to jail, their properties confiscated and not being able to make ends meet, and finally the war. Very early on I decided this is the way life is in Iran and that I had better make the best of it. I must confess that we were luckier than others. My husband never lost his job, and I was able to continue and even expand the business.

■ ■ ■ ■ ■

Atefeh: I don't know whether I coped or not. All I know is that one gets by, and I did what one had to do. It was a very difficult time. I felt very lonely. I missed my family. I spent time in jail. I was separated from my children.

Of course one had to start over again. But for a person like me it was easier to reconstruct my life here than go and live abroad. I am so happy I did not leave Iran. It is my country despite all the problems and difficulties I have had since the revolution. I faced all the challenges and all the obstacles alone. For a while I had even lost my self-confidence. I constantly worried about how to deal with the authorities. In the first few years of the revolution I was harassed by the *komiteh* people over a property I owned. I remember one day, when they had once again poured into the garden and surrounded me, one of the guys said, "We are going to execute you on the spot." There were a lot of kids watching us. I thought to myself, "If they execute me in front of these children, what sort of an impression will it leave on them?" The people of the village interfered and saved me. I was interrogated for many days and nights. I was put in jail. But finally I was able to prove that the property was mine, and I got it back. These are harrowing experiences. What I saw in one lifetime is what others experience over several generations.

Today I am back where I was. My life is full, and I find it rewarding. Once more my work has picked up, and I have learned to live according to this way of life.

Masoumeh: I did not cope at all. If you cope, it means you are totally at peace with what is around you. We are swimming against the tide. At first our muscles were aching but not today. Looking back at the last fifteen years, I can easily say that my work is my therapy. I recall there were mornings when I got up and all I wanted was to die. I could not take another day. I felt a constant lump in my throat. But once I got to work I pulled myself together, became jovial, and socialized with people. Then I had a hysterectomy, and that rejuvenated me. These days I get a lot of work done and consider myself luckier than a lot of other women. As far as I am concerned, the revolution made it possible for us to distinguish between genuine persons and the phony ones. I mean solid characters stayed solid and the weak ones did not change. The real gain from the revolution was the reassessment of one's values and criteria in life, and that meant a lot to me.

My husband made it possible for me to cope with the revolution. He never complained. He kept on repeating, "We had our turn; now it is their turn." He helped me to look at the situation quite rationally. But I ask myself, "How could one be rational?" One feared the *komitehs*, the white patrol cars, the revolutionary guards, the *hezbollahis*.

Do you know what it means to have a teenage daughter? The number of times I was summoned to the *komiteh* to sign a paper and get her out? She was hauled in on trivial matters, such as having ice cream in a cafe where other boys were present. Of course they were sitting at different tables. Another time I was driving with our daughter. I got out of the car to get a magazine. When I came back from the store I saw my daughter surrounded by several of the *kharara*. They were accusing her of showing some hair under her scarf and insisted on taking her in. It took me two hours of talking and persuasion for them to let us go. By then my daughter was in a state of hysteria, crying, sobbing, and screaming.

Of course we reconstructed our lives. My husband and I both lost our jobs. At first we did odd jobs that had nothing to do with our field of expertise. We went into a business that did not make money. We sold our house to provide for our daughters' education. Our children live abroad. We hardly see them. It was a major readjustment, but we survived it. Today we have come to terms with our present life, and we both would like to accomplish as much as we can in whatever time there is left to us.

Ladan: If I look back at the last sixteen years, I can tell you that I was very hurt. We lived in fear of death, of our house being confiscated, of arrests. This was a high price to pay both physically and mentally. There is hardly anyone I know who escaped an encounter with the *komiteh*. Some got off lightly, others suffered more. I remember we were at a friend's house. It was late in the evening. We were sitting and talking. In the beginning that is all we did—talk, talk, talk. A few *komiteh* people jumped over the wall and burst into the room. They wanted to know who we were and what we were doing there. A doctor among the guests, who had just returned from the front, took them aside and talked to them until four in the morning. He persuaded them to leave and not to arrest us. It is encounters like this that leave a bitter taste in your mouth.

I, personally, cannot forgive cruelty and injustice. I saw a lot of it around me. At some stage I took refuge in mysticism, maybe because of the religious atmosphere around us. It has been very comforting to me. I know of other people among our friends who have developed the same inclination. They, like me, find mysticism soothing. Even among the younger generation you see people who have such inclinations. Each of us found a way to cope with this strange society.

Recently, I have seen a new development in the country. It is people like me who are being vindicated. Once more, people are addressed by their titles—doctor, engineer, Mr., Mrs. No longer this business of being called "sister" and "brother." The authorities know something has gone wrong, and they are calling on experts to help them out, but their hands are tied. They are the victims of their own rhetoric.

■ ■ ■ ■ ■

Nahid: You want to know how I coped with the revolution? Let me be brief. We became like them, and they like us. We have reached a tacit understanding to live alongside each other but not together. After sixteen years we have fallen into place, while they are still trying to figure out what we accomplished that they don't know and must learn.

It is obvious that I and many people like me had to reconstruct our lives, both psychologically and physically. Most of us had to change our careers. For example, in my case, after the revolution I started my own business. Easily said, but it is a nightmare to go from office to office, to learn where to find the right people, and how to make payments to get your work done in government offices. I spent months and months trying to untie the knots that stood in my way, but I was finally issued the relevant permit to start my business. In the old days we knew people who would put in a good word for us. Today "their" friends and relatives take precedence over us.

Let me tell you it is not easy to run your own establishment, especially if you have women employees. For example, I have to constantly make sure that they observe the *hejab*, that they don't wear makeup. At any moment a customer can file a complaint, and an inspector or a member of the *komiteh* will show up. You then have to spend hours arguing and explaining. It drains you of all your energy.

Something else happened to me, too, nothing to do with the revolution, but you can't separate it from the revolution. There was a fire and our house burned down, with all our belongings. Isn't it ironic that I had to start everything from scratch. I physically had to reconstruct our home. It was quite a traumatic experience at my age to start once again to look for the minimum and bare necessities of daily life. It all adds to the pressure and tension. Having said that, let me add that what gives me satisfaction is that not a single one of us women broke down, not even those who went to jail. Our women are made of steel.

■ ■ ■ ■ ■

Touran: I was not able to cope. I could not adjust myself to the revolution and to the changes. As a woman and as a feminist, I suffer. If I were more flexible, my life would have been much easier.

We not only had to reconstruct our lives, my husband and I had to catch up with our lives and the outside world for the years we lost being in prison. We had to make it up to our child, to our families and ourselves.

I am interested in social issues, issues relating to women and young people. Today in our society young people have a very tough time. They are exposed to two contrasting cultures, the prevailing culture at home and the dominant religious culture at school and in the streets. Mothers have their hands full making sure that these children don't become schizophrenics. The children are taught not to talk about what goes on inside their homes. Therefore, they learn to lie constantly and to perform all the time. I think the parents have to create a lot of self-confidence in their children. This is a full-time occupation.

Looking back, I think had we as a family stayed abroad, we would have been more successful. There would have been a continuity in our lives, no disruptions and no upheavals.

■ ■ ■ ■ ■

Ramesh: In a way I had to reconstruct my life. Maybe I should say I had to start all over again. I went through a difficult divorce and married a man who came from a different social class. I had two children. I decided to get a university degree. All this required a lot of effort and adjustment. Then, of course, you could not stay oblivious to what was going on around you.

There was the war and all the problems it created. I was scared during the war. If there is another war I don't know what I will do. As for dealing with the pressure the government brings on women, whenever we go through rough times, I avoid going out. I don't want to have any unpleasant encounter with these people. At the university, I wear the *maghnae* and the rest of the time the scarf.

I also avoid any encounter with the *komitehs*. A number of times when we had guests and they came to the door, my husband managed to send them away by paying them off. I myself only once came face-to-face with the *komiteh* people. We were in the north of Iran. I was walking in the street with my niece and my father-in-law. My husband was parking the car. My niece was wearing a purple scarf and of course leggings under her *roupoush*, which was short. A revolutionary guard stopped us and started shouting at us. My niece apologized and said that she would dress appropriately, but the guy insisted on taking us in. In the meantime my husband arrived and both he and his father tried to reason with the guard. He started asking my husband whether he was not ashamed of accompanying women dressed like we were. I remember him shouting in a rage, "Where do you think you are, in America?" They took us to the *komiteh* and they wanted a written guarantee from us that we would not show our hair any more. I remember distinctly the fellow explaining that women's hair emits "rays that turn into demons." By then I could no longer control my laughter. Maybe because I have an easier life than a lot of other women I learn to look at the lighter side of events.

Lili: For me the crucial question was not whether to cope with the revolution. I and people like me did not have much of a choice. This is our country, and we were staying. We did not have anywhere else to go.

I told you earlier that I am a practical person. After the initial shock of the revolution, I decided to take matters into my own hands. I decided that I had to make the major decisions in the family. The future of the family depended on how realistically I could act. One way of coping was to improve our economic situation. I got a job and started saving. We bought some property. I looked after the children's education and their well-being. It was hard, but I succeeded.

I like many other men and women had my encounters with the *komitehs*. Today I don't care about them. Nobody cares any more. Looking back I feel a sense of satisfaction at having coped with the pressure of the last sixteen years better than I anticipated.

■ ■ ■ ■ ■

Monir: I must have mentioned this earlier to you. I wish I had been twenty years old when the revolution took place. I would have been able to cope with it. When the revolution occurred I was at the peak of my career. I had achieved all I could have wished for. I saw the future stretching its unlimited resources in front of me. Then everything fell apart. It was as if I killed my inner self, I destroyed myself. But the everyday realities of life pulled me out of my despondent condition. I had to look after the family.

My husband had no job. My kind of knowledge and profession as a lawyer was no longer in demand. I had to start studying Islamic law in depth. I started as a legal assistant. I accepted all the humiliating treatment, not only because I was a woman but because I was a woman lawyer.

Today I feel all the effort I have put into the last sixteen years is worth it. It is rewarding to reduce a death sentence for a woman who is accused of committing adultery to a prison sentence. I feel I am an authority on women's rights. I write books and articles. I give speeches. I feel that once more I am climbing up the ladder.

Nargess: We coped with the revolution one step at a time. If on the first day of the revolution we knew how it would end, we would all have left. We took in everything gradually, a sip at a time, a mouthful at a time. We complain, we grumble, we fret, and we live.

We have become more outspoken and aggressive in our dealings with the authorities. They no longer intimidate us. I remember the first time I was taken in by the revolutionary guards. It was very soon after the revolution. I was walking with a friend of mine on the beach in the north of Iran. There was not a soul for miles and miles. Suddenly a car appeared and these men jumped out and started screaming at us—why our scarves were not wrapped properly around our heads. We explained that we were alone and as soon as we had seen a car approaching us we had covered our hair. We got into a heated argument and finally they pushed us into the car and took us to the *komiteh*. They kept us for two days. Our husbands finally negotiated our release. Today such an incident is neither frightening nor scary.

■ ■ ■ ■ ■

Zohreh: For the last sixteen years I have faced nothing but challenges twenty-four hours a day. At first we were all scared. We did not know how to cope with the new system. People were burning books, papers, pictures. The authorities divided books into good books and bad books. You never knew which was which. What was good one day became bad the next day, depending who was setting the standard.

We had hardly begun to rearrange our lives when the Iran-Iraq War broke out and we were cut off from the outside world, even from the people who lived abroad, our own compatriots. We felt isolated, but we did not want their sympathy. There was no connection between us. We had great difficulties in coming to terms with our own problems, let alone trying to understand those Iranians who lived in exile.

Some people gave up very early in the revolution. The daily pressure we faced affected us both physically and mentally. Even now I feel tired. On the one hand, I want to give up. On the other hand, I want to continue to make my presence felt. There is such a duality within ourselves and in our lives.

Because my husband was unwell for a long time, I took over the family responsibilities. And I started my own business. Within that limited range of possibilities, I tried to make the most of it. You learn to become hard and quarrelsome and push yourself to the brink.

Pouran: You want to know how I coped with the revolution? I ask myself, "Did I cope with it?" It is a hate-hate relationship. I constantly ask myself, "Where is my self-respect?" I constantly feel as if I am seeking revenge. I am angry and want to write about this anger. I feel alienated in my own country. I look at the revolution and see that as a woman it does not belong to me. I sense that somehow reform-minded women who lived here before the revolution adapted themselves more easily to their new environment and the *hejab* than a person like me. I still have problems with the *hejab,* the language, and the values in the society. I feel I am back where my grandmother was, helpless and vulnerable.

Having said that, I must add that life here is a challenge for me. It is as if I am constantly in a laboratory studying myself and the revolution. Sometimes I have a sense that my feet are not on the ground, that I am moving in a world that is unreal to me.

I did not have to reconstruct my life, I had to construct it, and not the way I wanted it. I never thought that I would feel like an exile in my own country. This is by far more difficult to cope than being in exile abroad. Our encounters with the authorities, with the *komitehs,* are so surrealistic, verging on the absurd.

I remember, we were hiking in the mountains with my husband and the children. A revolutionary guard stopped me and told me to pull my scarf down. I told him to get lost: "Who the hell do you think you are?" The guard insisted on taking me to the *komiteh.* I started screaming and became hysterical. The children were crying. People gathered around us and tried to persuade the fellow to let me go. At the *komiteh,* I got into a long argument with the man in charge and quarreled with him for the way they were treating women. He finally let me go. The incident left a terrible, scary impression on the children. It did not make any difference to these people that we were there as a family. Don't believe for a moment what they say about respecting women or family values.

These days I socialize much less. I have so little time. I teach, I write, and I spend time with my children. They are growing up and resent my not being there. My husband, sensing my despair, built a house in the mountains. I take refuge there and do my writing. My life is a constant struggle and hassle; I feel tense and exhausted all the time. My only escape is when I am asked to go abroad to participate in a conference.

Jila: Sixteen years have passed, and I still have not come to terms with the situation. I look at it as a passing phase in my life. When will it end? I don't know. Have I reconstructed my life? On the surface the answer is no. I run the same private company I had before the revolution. Some of my partners left. I have hired a few new people who know their way around these days. They know how to deal with the relevant government agencies. Our company is slowly getting some business. This has nothing to do with me; it is the economic situation in the country.

But if you scratch the surface you see that all of us, I mean our class of people, had to start at the beginning. The mental adjustment is taking its toll more than the physical change, much more. Just being on your guard all the time is nerve-racking. The fear of the *komiteh,* of the "morals police," of the revolutionary guards, turns any sane person into a basket case. Let me give you an example. One day I received a call from the *komiteh,* which wanted to send someone to look at our files in the office. I told the fellow to come at nine. I wanted my colleagues to be present in the office. After he went through all our papers, he asked me why I had insisted that he should come at nine? I told him as a woman I did not feel safe alone with him. He was shocked and said, "I am sorry to hear that is what you think of us."

■ ■ ■ ■ ■

Lida: I did not have any problem coping with the revolution. The last sixteen years were the years of my success, the years I developed into what I am today. A successful doctor, I have a prosperous private practice. I am the head of a government hospital. I do research in my field and go regularly to conferences.

In my private life, I have a loving and supportive family. My husband is a businessman, our son studies well. What else could I have hoped for?

What is rewarding for me is that I made it all on my own, with no connections at all. My promotion came through my merits. I think I probably would not have been able to progress this fast if it were not for the revolution.

Partow: It was one thing to cope with the revolution and another thing to survive during the war. We were all affected by the war. My brother was a prisoner of war. For three years we did not know whether he was dead or alive. Then one day they brought us a picture showing him in the camp. We knew he was alive. When he came home, he had changed so much. He was emaciated. He looked like a skeleton and had developed kidney and heart disease. We nursed him, and today he is studying dentistry.

In my case, I really had to reconstruct my life. Once my husband stopped working and we sold everything we had, our standard of living dropped dramatically. Then he left us and went to Europe. With the help of my parents, the children and I moved into a smaller place. I got a job, and for the first time in my life I felt responsible for myself and three children. Until that time, somebody else had always taken care of me, first my parents and then my husband. I had never had any monetary problems. I had to learn to budget the little income we had. As the boys grew up they started working, too. My daughter is also very responsible. If I stay late at work, she prepares dinner. I want my children to stay in Iran and to go to university here.

My children will not forgive their father for abandoning his family, for exposing us to all the hardship we faced the last sixteen years. It is not easy to be a young, working, single mother. I think I was able to cope with my situation because I had a supportive family, parents, brothers, and sisters, who helped us rebuild our life. I must confess that without a job, I would be at a total loss. My job gave my self-esteem back to me.

■ ■ ■ ■ ■

Nayyer: You want to know how I coped with the revolution? I am very happy with all I have achieved since the revolution. I did not have one idle moment. Of course, there were times when I was a wreck. I did not know how to come to terms with all the problems around me, but I never lost my self-confidence. I feel the revolution had a maturing effect on me. I am a more seasoned and experienced woman. I am not dissatisfied, but I am tired. I feel I have been running for sixteen years.

At first I was not ready to shoulder all the responsibilities that up to that time I was sharing with my husband. When he lost his job and stayed home, I did not have much choice. Somebody had to be the provider, somebody had to make sure that the boys would make it through university. The reversal of roles automatically leads to a change in one's life-style. New ways replaced the old habits. I tried very hard to keep our standard of living at a decent, acceptable level.

It was important to make sure that the boys didn't go astray. The contrast between the atmosphere inside the house and the schools, the universities, the streets needed a lot of adjustment. Our young people are exposed to foreign films on videos, to programs broadcast via satellite dishes. You constantly have to explain the contradictions to them. All this became my duty. My husband not only did not help, but there was also a constant clash between him and the boys. Whether I admit it or not, all this has affected my life, my outlook, and my actions. As I said, I am a more mature person, but it has also hardened me.

■ ■ ■ ■ ■

Sousan: Over the years you learn to cope with the revolution and the changes. It was not a question of adjusting gradually. Your reflexes become faster. You react more quickly to events as they unfold before you. I could have stayed home, but I did not. I started working. They wanted women like me to give up their public careers. I did not play up to them. You learn to cope with different revolutionary organs interfering in your daily life, whether it is the *komitehs* searching your home or the revolutionary guards controlling your appearance. Let me tell you a story. I remember I was having lunch at home when the gardener told me that three men wanted to see me. I knew it meant the *komiteh* people were after somebody or something. Three *hezbollahis* walked into our living room, asking to see my brother. They also explained that they were looking for gold and foreign currency. They started searching the house, looking in drawers, emptying closets, and taking out books. When they got to my room, there was a box where I kept memorabilia. They found my university diploma. They took it out and said, "This is your 'Freemason membership certificate.'" I was quite amused and explained to them that this was my diploma and that women cannot become Freemasons. That is how naive they were.

Although the revolution changed the course of my life, and although I had to change professions, I am quite happy with what I have achieved in the last sixteen years. As a woman, I feel I have proven my abilities, and as a woman of a certain class I feel I am setting a very positive example for

ordinary girls who come into contact with me. This, to me, is very rewarding and compensates for all the other shortcomings.

■ ■ ■ ■ ■

Nasrin: My case is different from other women you have talked to. I am who
I am because of the revolution. I was involved in the revolutionary movement. I am a supporter of the idealism of the revolution.

The revolution made it possible for me to grow professionally. I started
working after the revolution. I got married and had my two children in the
last ten years. Of course, I have my problems. These problems have nothing
to do with the revolution. These are the everyday problems that a working
woman faces both at work and at home.

Because I run a progressive women's magazine, we constantly run into
difficulty with the authorities. For example, they don't give us subsidized
paper for the magazine; they cut us off from government advertising. So far,
we have managed to survive on a shoestring budget.

I think I have explained to you that I finished my studies after the revolution. I started my career by teaching in villages, then worked for an established women's magazine. After a short time I became the editor of that
magazine. Had it not been for the revolution, I probably would have not
been employed in that magazine, let alone become its editor. Today, I am the
founder and editor of my own women's magazine. My dream has come
true. I wish I did not have financial problems. If I worried less, I could have
done a much better job. I get much support from women who work and
write for free for us. It is so rewarding to get recognition for all the effort
you put in.

Unlike me, it took my husband a long time to find a permanent job. For
a while we lived on my modest income and his occasional earnings. Even
today, in the back of my mind there is the constant worry of how to manage the next month. I cannot give up hope. We are the children of the revolution and the symbol of its success.

■ ■ ■ ■ ■

Zahra: It was not easy to overcome the feeling that the years of your youth
were totally wasted. The war also left its mark on all of us. For a long time

any noise would make me jump. I could not tolerate the color red; it reminded me of blood.

I grew up during the revolution. My adult life started after the revolution, so I basically started my life with a bitter taste in my mouth. In the beginning it was a game for young people like me to defy the *komitehs,* to outwit them. But not any more. You prefer to stay away from them. Maybe they are keeping their distance from us, too. They have stopped bothering people for unimportant and trivial matters.

Let me give you an example. It was shortly after the revolution. It was evening and I was carrying some books in a bag. I was stopped by a patrol car. Before they could search my bag, I asked them to please rush me to the hospital since my sister was giving birth and she needed clothing. I got into their car and they dropped me in front of that hospital. Today they no longer stop you for carrying a bag, nor can they force you to go with them because we will refuse and create such a commotion that the people won't let them pick you up.

Having said that, I want you to know that I consider myself a very successful professional woman. I think the revolution made it possible for women like me to achieve the goals they had set for themselves. Do you sense the duality in what I have been telling you? I am fascinated by it myself.

CONCLUSION

THE PARLIAMENTARY ELECTIONS in Iran in the spring of 1996 and an incident in a Tehran park a month after the voting graphically illustrate the conflicting currents that characterize the Islamic Republic's policies toward women and the contrasting, often incompatible, roles demanded of women in Iran today.

In the elections, the incumbent Speaker of the Majlis, or parliament, Ali-Akbar Nateq-Nuri, secured the highest number of votes in the capital, Tehran. But hot on his heels and elected as Tehran's second deputy was Faezeh Hashemi, the daughter of President Ali-Akbar Hashemi-Rafsanjani and head of the National Council of Women's Sports Organizations. Popular rumor had it that Ms. Hashemi had secured the highest number of votes but that the authorities were embarrassed to admit that a woman had beaten a senior cleric in Iran's most prestigious constituency. Faezeh Hashemi, moreover, contested the elections as a member of a group of technocrats and senior government officials calling themselves the Servants of Construction, who campaigned on a platform emphasizing economic development, technical know-how, and more moderate policies. The Construction group was the main rival to the conservative clerics associated with Majlis Speaker Nateq-Nuri.

Altogether, some two hundred women ran in the elections, many of them from small rural constituencies. Several of these women were independent candidates. But all the major political groups contesting the elections, including the conservative clerics, felt they had to include women on their candidate slates. Ms. Hashemi was one of ten women to win election to the 270-seat Majlis. More women might have been elected but for the interference of the authorities. In Esfahan and Malayer, for example, women came in first, but election officials, citing "irregularities," declared the elections in these constituencies void. Many of the women candidates, especially in urban constituencies, ran on women's issues and presented themselves as spokespersons for women's interests.

A striking example was Sohaila Jelowdarzadeh, an engineer by training and a high-ranking civil servant. She was elected as a deputy from Tehran on the Servants of Construction ticket. Interviews Jelowdarzadeh gave during the election illustrate how thoroughly "regime women" have absorbed the language of women's rights and the agenda of their feminist predecessors and how routine a part of the political debate women's issues have become. Jelowdarzadeh, a special assistant for women's affairs to the minister of labor, said she felt impelled to run for parliament because of the women who came to her office with their economic, legal, and workplace problems. She argued for promotion of women to upper-level jobs, equal benefits for equal work, legal reform in the interests of women, and a larger voice for women in economic policy. She was dismissive of men who laud women as the rearers of children—"the men of the future"—but who consider women unqualified to do a "man's" job. She was also dismissive of men prepared to pay lip service to women's equality and, to please international opinion, prepared to make superficial, but not substantive, concessions on women's issues. She argued that a large bloc of female deputies in parliament would be good for women since "there is not a single woman in Majlis who would vote against the interests of women."

Just one month after the parliamentary elections, club-wielding bully-boys, calling themselves Ansar-e Hezbollah, or the "Partisans of the Party of God," attacked girl cyclists on a bicycle path especially set aside for women in a Tehran park. The attack outraged many women and gave rise to much adverse comment in the press. Nevertheless, Ayatollah Ali Khamenei, Khomeini's successor as Iran's spiritual guide, issued an opinion that cycling by women in public places "involves corruption" and was therefore forbidden. The Partisans of the Party of God had previously distinguished themselves by vandalizing the offices of a publisher, torching a bookstore, and attacking a cinema house for showing a film presumably offensive to religious sensibilities.

The prominent role given women in the parliamentary elections and the attack on female cyclists are the two faces of feminist policy in Iran. On the one hand, the regime and its clerical leaders are exercised to display to Iranians and the world their "enlightened" policy toward women in the areas of education, employment, women's legal and marital rights, and the presence of women in the public arena—in parliament or the government. Thus a young woman, modest but chic of dress, carried the Iranian flag and marched at the head of team of Iranian athletes sent to the 1996 Olympics at Atlanta. The message at Atlanta was that, in the Islamic Republic, women and men are equal participants in athletics as in other spheres.

On the other hand, the Islamic Republic feels impelled to enforce the dictates of its own traditional ideal of the Islamic woman—pious, modest of dress, wife, mother, and housewife, and, even if educated and employed, still occupying a sphere distinctly separate and different from that of men. Deep down, many of the clerics continue to fear that equality and the involvement of women in the public sphere will spell moral corruption and the collapse of society; others feel they must cater to traditional and conservative elements in their constituency—like the otherwise unemployable young men recruited into the Partisans of the Party of God. The attack on women cyclists in a Tehran park in the name of Islam was by no means an isolated incident. Periodically, the government lets loose its "morals police" on the streets of Tehran, and their targets are primarily women—how they dress, what they wear, the makeup they use, how they interact with men. The flag-carrying female athlete at Atlanta was a member of Iran's sharp-shooting team—a "safe" sport. There were no women athletes competing in track and field events that required wearing shorts and exposing female legs. In fact, there were no women athletes on the Iranian team except for the one flag-carrying sharpshooter. At Atlanta, Iran sought to substitute the symbol for the substance of women's participation. Elsewhere, as we have seen, symbol and substance exist side-by-side, in unequal portion and in uneasy symbiosis.

Given the role women have managed to carve out for themselves in Iran today, seventeen years after the revolution, it is easy to forget the original women's agenda of the Islamic Republic. The new regime suspended the Family Protection Law and closed down the Family Protection Courts. It reinstated marriage at puberty and also a man's right to take multiple wives and to secure divorce on demand. In the civil service and the universities, it purged women employees or encouraged and harassed women to leave work and take early retirement. The constitution enshrined the centrality of the family as the foundation of society, with this ideal implied for the freedom of women to pursue education, careers, and employment. The new regime imposed Islamic dress and the segregation of the sexes. At the university, it excluded women from a range of disciplines and fields of study. Even today, partly as a result of these policies, the percentage of women in higher education as compared to men is lower than prerevolutionary levels. Preachers and quasi-official government spokespersons expounded on the ideal of woman as mother, wife, and homemaker.

As we have seen, however, several factors worked to undermine the agenda of the conservative clerics. Even before the Islamic revolution, women were in the workplace and in the schools and universities in large numbers. In a period of expanding opportunities, the aspiration to education, employment, careers, and advancement had spread to lower-middle-class and working-class women. This process, once under way, proved difficult to reverse. In imagining women first and foremost as mothers, wives and daughters, the Islamic Republic was swimming against the tide. Islamic reformers like Ali Shariati and Morteza Mottahari, though fundamentally conservative in their attitude toward women, nevertheless planted the seeds for an intepretration of Islam that, after the revolution, allowed women to be differently imagined and for women themselves to demand expanded rights and opportunities.

The Islamic revolution, as noted, injected women into the public arena and politicized them. In the campaign against the former regime, the clerical leaders mobilized women as well as men, and women continued to be mobilized by the clerics, as well as by other political groups, in the postrevolutionary struggle for supremacy among the factions that had made the revolution. In this struggle, the clerics were forced to compete for the allegiance of the younger generation with left-wing groups, such as the Islamic-Marxist Majahedin-e Khalq and the Marxist Fadayan-e Khalq; and this competition, too, encouraged a revision of the Islamic Republic's policies toward women. Economic need, engendered by revolution, war, and inflation, made two-income households a necessity and pushed many more women into the work force.

Moreover, the obsession of the clerical community with women as repositories of family honor and sources of sin and temptation, and with issues of women's dress and public behavior, served to keep the women's issue at the forefront of public discussion and to heighten the consciousness of women, and especially the young, of their own condition. Segregation of the sexes also cut both ways. It denied women many opportunities. But, ironically, segregation also increased the demand for professional women—physicians, schoolteachers, physical education instructors, adminstrators—to deal with women and manage female activities.

The Islamic Republic proved sensitive to international opinion. It did not wish to project itself, or the Islam it professed, as backward on women's issues. The regime also wished to differentiate itself from conservative Islamic regimes in the Middle East. It denigrated Saudi Arabia and the Gulf sheikhdoms as reactionary, elitist, lackeys of America, and purveyors of an outdated version of Islam. By contrast, the Islamic Republic allegedly stood for a revolutionary, popular, fiercely independent, and "authentic" Islam, different not only in its politics and foreign policy but on the women's issue as well.

The attempt of the Islamic Republic to reverse the advances women had achieved before the revolution under the Family Protection Law and other legislation in matters of marriage age, divorce, child custody, and spousal financial support; or in matters of employment, maternity leave, and daycare provision for children; or, more broadly, in opportunities for education, employment, and careers caused women from all classes to rise to the defense of rights that women had taken for granted. In seeking to define the proper place of women in society in a manner implicitly hostile to the role women had begun to play under the monarchy, the Islamic Republic, as we have seen, faced the opposition not only of supposedly Westernized, upper-class women but also the women of its own lower-middle-class and working-class constituencies.

For all these reasons, the agenda of the conservative clerics was frustrated in Iran. When the veil was imposed in March 1979, mostly educated, professional upper-middle-class women came out in the streets to protest, and the regime mobilized working-class, *chador*-clad women to taunt the protesters as tarts and prostitutes. Seventeen years later, when young club-wielders attacked women cyclists, they were attacking young, working, and lower-middle-class women from traditional families who were trying out a new form of exercise and enjoyment. It was these girls from traditional families, and their parents, who seethed with resentment against the enforcers of supposed Islamic orthodoxy. Today it is mothers—and fathers—from traditional families who avidly desire for their daughters one of the limited and keenly sought after places at the university or the opportunity for employment and a career.

My rental car driver in Tehran worries when his eight-year old daughter, riding in the taxi with us, suddenly pulls a fringe of hair from under her scarf over her forehead, in imitation of the smart young girls she sees on the street, with their saucy *kakols* showing beneath their headress. But he tells me that though his wife wears a *chador*, he won't insist on his daughter wearing one. He doesn't want his daughter to get married at fourteen, he says; and while he does not care if his son goes to university—"he is a man, he can take care of himself"—he will insist his daughter go to college because she needs a profession and the means to earn a living. My friend Homa's maid tells me she works long hours so her daughter can attend university. Sharbanou, who also earns a living as a maid, was overawed when her bright, eager daughter passed the difficult university entrance examinations.

"Regime women," the daughters and wives of prominent clerics and officials, owe public office, places in parliament, and heavy executive responsibilities to family connections and proximity to the men in power. But their prominent role is also due to personal ability, the desire of the regime to give prominence to women in public roles, and the rapid proliferation of organizations dealing with women's activities. "Regime women" provide an example to younger girls, in schools and universities, of possibilities. Faezeh Hashemi and Sohaila Jelowdarzadeh may wear the *chador* and adhere on many issues to the politically correct line. For example, asked about foreign policy, Jelowdarzadeh echoes the hard-liners by saying the Islamic Republic does not need and should not establish diplomatic relations with the United States. But she is articulating an agenda that subverts the conservative religious view when she says Islamic law must be implemented *in order that* women can secure their rights and when in the same breath she lays out a women's rights program that echoes her counterparts in the West or Iranian women activists before the revolution.

The changes that have already taken place are striking. But they did not come easily. Middle-class and professional women bore the brunt of the early attack on "modern," "Westernized" women and the attempt to exclude women from university teaching staffs and the workplace. The jailings and executions in the first year of the revolution were frightening and intimidating. For adult, professional women, to be called to account for their dress or demeanor by boys and girls young enough to be their children was humiliating. Many will never forget their searing, demeaning encounters with the enforcers of "public morality." For all women, it was unsettling suddenly to be regarded as "sin-provoking" or, as one woman put it, "to be scrutinized twenty-four hours a day."

Working and professional women gritted their teeth and endured, some out of economic necessity, some because they valued their careers, most because they simply refused to be intimidated. Today many of these women feel vindicated. In area after area on the subject of women, the authorities are in retreat. Laws on women's rights, once suspended, have been reintroduced. Women are at work in large numbers. Professional women have won a grudging respect from the authorities. Young girls routinely challenge the official dress code. The government, zigzagging on women's policy, wants to cast women in a traditional mode but also feels compelled to create a clutch of women's organizations and to create space for women in parliament and in high government offices. Wives and daughters of high officials and the ruling clerics seek a public role, have appropriated the vocabulary of women's rights, and feel it incumbent on themselves to appear as champions of women's causes. Most important, a younger generation of women in secondary schools, universities, and the job market, in the arts and in women's magazines, promote and aspire to roles that make it difficult for the clock to be turned back once again.

Nevertheless, the toll on women in these last seventeen years has been heavy. Women take satisfaction from simply having endured, continued to work, and refused to acquiesce in the role the state tried to carve out for them. They are proud they faced down the "morals police," officious bureaucrats, unsympathetic judges, and rude male supervisors. But many also speak of these as wasted years. Careers were interrupted or stunted. Family life was disrupted. Years and energy that might have been used creatively were squandered in the struggle to work and maintain self-respect, in a daily enervating and unending tug-of-war with bureaucrats, revolutionary committees, and guardians of morality over petty rules about dress, or lipstick, or bicycling.

Ramesh simpy doesn't leave the house during crackdowns when women are being treated roughly in the streets. Touran, speaking fifteen years after the revolution, feels she has never adjusted: "As a woman and a feminist, I suffer," she says. Jila shares this view. Despite the passage of time, she says, she has not come to terms with being a woman in the Islamic Republic. Pouran feels like "an exile in my own country," that the revolution "does not belong to me." Elaheh feels "trapped," her life and career "going round and round in a circle." Darya gave up practicing law rather than face the humiliation visited on women in the courts in the early years of the revolution. For Monir, "everything fell apart," "as if I killed my inner self." Zohreh feels the daily tangle with the authorities has made her "hard and quarrelsome."

These feelings are not confined to the older generation. The young feel restricted and confined. Young women fear an unpleasant encounter with the "morals police" everytime they go out, visit an ice cream parlor, or attend a party. Such encounters, says the young Zahra, "left a bitter taste in my mouth." My own discussions with university students confirm what the teacher, Ladan, and the university professor, Pouran, told me: every single one of their young, female students waits impatiently for the day she can go abroad. The young find confusing the contrast between the private and the public, the standards and life-style they observe at home and that they must adhere to in school, university, and on the street. In school the young are compelled to pretend—to piousness, to forms of dress, to segregation between the sexes, to disinterest in popular music—to attitudes they do not practice at home. Touran, like Nayyer, worries about the effect on the children of this "cultural schizophrenia," the fact that children are learning to pretend, to act, when in public.

For some women, of course, the revolution has meant expanded opportunity. Lida, a doctor who now runs a government hospital, regards the years since the revolution as a period of professional success. The revolution, she says, made her professional advancement possible. Nasrin, a journalist, thinks the revolution gave her the chance to fulfill a lifetime ambition to run a women's magazine. Zahra, who came to adulthood during the revolution and feels her youth as a woman was "totally wasted," nevertheless, in the same breath, tells me that, for her, these have been years of professional success. She smiles to herself as she reflects on the "duality" of her feelings.

Nevertheless, "equality" in work is far from being achieved, and women from all classes are still treated as second-class citizens. The corridors of the Ministry of Justice, where the Special Civil Courts dealing with family disputes are located, are crowded with working- and middle-class women seeking or attempting to prevent a divorce, fighting child custody cases, pleading for unpaid alimony, and filing complaints against wife-beating and harassment by husbands. Working women with small children sorely feel the absence of day-care centers. Nasrin told me that in summers and on holidays, she drives an hour each day to leave her children with her mother before going to work. She drives back to pick them up at the end of the day. Private day-care centers are flourishing but expensive. A woman in her thirties pays half the salary she earns as a consultant to a government department for day-care. But she wants a career, she and her husband need the money, and she wants the security of a pension after retirement.

The government has expanded employment opportunities for women. But these opportunities remain limited, and competition is fierce. Men, considered the basic family providers, are still accorded first priority in jobs. But it is not always the case that women are merely "second" wage earners or that their income is unessential to the family. Lili holds two jobs because the family could not manage otherwise. Partow, a technician and a single mother, took a second job to see her three children through university. Nahid's husband still does not have a steady job, and the income from the business she established feeds the family. Nargess, a lawyer, is weary of arguing women's cases before unfriendly judges but cannot give up her practice because she and her husband need two incomes to see their children through school and college.

Many of the professional women I interviewed persist out of a sense of patriotism, because they feel attached to Iran. As Atefeh put it, "It is my country despite all the problems and difficulties." Although not involved in politics, they are concerned about what they see as a decline in civility, about the problem of individual rights, and about the economic and political future of the country. So they soldier on. Several, particularly the teachers and university instructors, feel a responsibility to the younger generation of women. Pouran thirsts to return to the vigorous intellectual environment of the American universities where she studied, but she feels she cannot abandon her women students. These young girls, she says, are confused and need nurturing and guidance; often they are on the edge of despair. She encourages them to remain intellectually engaged, to think, to acquire skills, to hope for a brighter future. Even Elaheh, who responds with dismissive irony when I ask her about "job satisfaction," is motivated to continue teaching by the needs of her women students. They do not lead normal lives compared to young women in the West, she tells me. They feel confined and hedged in. She encourages them to take their work seriously, to put off marriage, to pursue a profession.

After seventeen years, women have obviously also learned to put up with existing conditions. "We complain, we grumble, we fret, and we live," says Nargess. Others, like Zohreh, grapple with their own mixed feelings. "I want to give up . . . I want to continue," she says. As Nargess and Zahra remark, the encounters with the "morals police" are no longer so traumatic; they have learned to take them in stride or to shout back and cow the authorities. A certain modus vivendi has been reached. Nahid describes it as "a tacit understanding to live alongside each other but not together." The women put up with what continue to be restricted lives; but on a large number of fronts, the authorities have also beaten a wide retreat.

If a modus vivendi has been achieved, however, it is unlikely to last. The situation of women in Iran today is still evolving, and neither professional women nor a younger generation are content with things as they are. The signs are everywhere. The weekly sermons in which the ruling clerics struggle to formulate and reformulate a policy on women; the lone young female athlete marching at the head of Iran's Olympic team at Atlanta; the Partisans of the Party of God attacking women cyclists in a Tehran park; the women who continue to cycle despite the attacks; Sohaila Jelowdarzadeh, the parliamentary deputy, demanding more rights for women from behind her *chador;* the young girl with her saucy *kakol* evading the the "morals police"; and the dozens of women on these pages who simply will not give up—all are striking evidence that the women's issue remains center stage in the Islamic Republic today.

GLOSSARY

baradar, baradara: brother, brothers. A form of address that, like "comrade" in the Russian revolution, gained currency after the Islamic revolution and is widely used for men and boys. In popular parlance, it is also a term used to refer to members of the revolutionary guards, revolutionary committees, and "morals police."

chador: a form of Islamic dress; a loose cloak cut from lightweight cloth in a manner to cover a woman from head to ankle. The ends of the *chador* are pulled together also to cover much of the face, leaving only the eyes showing.

hejab: a generic term for proper Islamic dress for a woman.

hezbollahi: member of "the party of God." The term is used in Iran today to refer to bearded men who consider themselves adherents of a fundamentalist form of Islam and the revolution and are regarded as enforcers of the strict Islamic codes prevalent in the Islamic Republic.

kakol: a fringe or bob of hair showing from under a scarf and falling across a girl's or woman's forehead. The *kakol* has become particularly fashionable among young girls and younger women.

khahar, khahara: sister, sisters. A form of address that, like "comrade" in the Russian revolution, gained currency after the Islamic revolution and is widely used for women and girls. In popular parlance, it is also a term used to refer to female members of the revolutionary guards, revolutionary committees, and "morals police."

komiteh: revolutionary committee.

maghnae: scarf that fits tightly under the chin and covers a woman's head and hair, making an oval around her face. The *maghnae* is usually large enough to fall across the shoulders as well.

roupoush: a long robe resembling a housecoat, buttoned across the front and running from shoulders to ankles, usually worn by women over regular clothes when out in public and as an alternative to the *chador.*

sigheh: temporary marriage; the wife in such a temporary marriage.

taghuti: a Koranic term meaning "idolator"; after the Islamic revolution it gained currency as a term denoting the old regime and the wealthy classes in generally.

toman: monetary unit equivalent to ten rails. The toman was worth about eight cents in 1980 and, due to inflation, substantially less in subsequent years.

SELECT BIBLIOGRAPHY

Books

Abu-Lughod, Lila. *Writing Women's Worlds: Bedouin Stories*. Berkeley: University of California Press, 1991.

Adelkhah, Fariba. *La Revolution sous le Voile: Femmes Islamiques d'Iran*. Paris: Edition Karthala, 1991.

Afkhami, Mahnaz, and Erika Friedl, eds. *In the Eye of the Storm: Women in Post-Revolutionary Iran*. Syracuse, N.Y.: Syracuse University Press, 1994.

Afkhami, Mahnaz: *Women in Exile*. Charlottesville: University Press of Virginia, 1994.

———, ed. *Faith and Freedom: Women's Human Rights in the Muslim World*. London: I. B. Tauris, 1995.

Afshar, Haleh, ed. *Women, State and Ideology: Studies from Africa and Asia*. Albany: State University of New York Press, 1987.

Ahmed, Leila. *Women and Gender in Islam*. New Haven: Yale University Press, 1992.

Azari, Farah. *Woman in Iran: The Conflict with Fundamentalist Islam*. London: Ithaca Press, 1983.

Badran, Margot, and Miriam Cooke, *Opening the Gates: A Century of Arab Feminist Writing*. Bloomington: Indiana University Press, 1990.

Bamdad, Badr al-Moluk. *From Darkness into Light: Women's Emancipation in Iran*. Edited and translated by F. R. C. Bagley. New York: Exposition Press, 1977.

Beck, Lois, and Nikki Keddie, eds. *Women in the Muslim World*. Cambridge: Harvard University Press, 1978.

Belsey, Catherine, and Jane Moore, eds. *The Feminist Reader: Essays in Gender and the Politics of Literary Criticism*. New York: Basil Blackwell, 1989.

Bonine, Michael, and Nikki Keddie, eds. *Continuity and Change in Modern Iran*. Albany: State University of New York Press, 1981.

Bowles, Gloria, and Renate Duelli Klein, eds. *Theories of Women's Studies*. London and New York: Routledge and Kegan Paul, 1983.

Esposito, John L. *Women in Muslim Family Law*. Syracuse, N.Y.: Syracuse University Press, 1982.

Farman Farmaian, Sattareh. *Daughter of Persia*. New York: Crown Publishers, 1992.

Fathi, Asghar, ed. *Women and the Family in Iran*. Leiden: J. Brill, 1985.

Fernea, Elizabeth Warnock. *Women and the Family in the Middle East: New Voices of Change*. Austin: University of Texas Press, 1985.

Fernea, Elizabeth W., and Basima Bazirgan, eds. *Middle East Muslim Women Speak*. Austin: University of Texas Press, 1977.

Friedl, Erika. *Women of Deh Koh: Lives in an Iranian Village.* Washington, D.C., and London: Smithsonian Institution Press, 1989.

Haeri, Shahla. *Law of Desire: Temporary Marriage in Shi'i Iran.* Syracuse, N.Y.: Syracuse University Press, 1989.

Kandiyoti, Deniz, ed. *Women, Islam and the State.* Philadelphia: Temple University Press, 1991.

Keddie, Nikki, and Beth Baron, eds.. *Women in Middle Eastern History: Shifting Boundaries in Sex and Gender.* New Haven: Yale University Press, 1991.

Mayer, Ann Elizabeth. *Islam and Human Rights: Tradition and Politics.* Boulder, Colo.: Westview Press, 1991.

Mernissi, Fatima. *Beyond the Veil: Male-Female Dynamics in a Modern Muslim Society.* Cambridge, Mass.: Schenkman, 1975.

———. *The Veil and the Male Elite: A Feminist Interpretation of Women's Rights in Islam.* Translated by Mary Jo Lakeland. Reading, Mass.: Addison-Wesley, 1991.

Milani, Farzaneh. *Veils and Words: The Emerging Voices of Iranian Women Writers.* Syracuse, N.Y.: Syracuse University Press, 1992.

Millet, Kate. *Going to Iran.* New York: Coward, McCann and Geoghegan, 1982.

Moghadam, Valentine M., ed. *Modernising Women: Gender and Social Change in the Middle East.* Boulder, Colo.: Lynne Rienner Publishers, 1993.

Mohanty, Chandra T., Ann Russo, and Lourdes Torres, eds. *Third World Women and the Politics of Feminism.* Bloomington: Indiana University Press, 1991.

Mutahhari, Murteza. *The Islamic Modest Dress.* Translated by Laleh Bakhtiar. Albuquerque, N.M.: Abjad, 1988.

Najjar, Oryab Aref, with Kitty Warnock. *Portraits of Palestinian Women.* Salt Lake City: University of Utah Press, 1992.

Najmabadi, Afsaneh, ed. *Women's Autobiographies in Contemporary Iran.* Harvard Middle Eastern Monograph Series, Cambridge: Harvard University Press, 1990.

Nashat, Guity, ed. *Women and Revolution in Iran.* Boulder, Colo.: Westview Press, 1983.

Pahlavi, Ashraf. *Faces in the Mirror.* Englewood Cliffs, N.J.: Prentice Hall, 1980.

Paidar, Parvin. *Women and the Political Process in Twentieth-Century Iran.* Cambridge: Cambridge University Press, 1995.

Sanasarian, Eliz. *The Women's Rights Movement in Iran: Mutiny, Appeasement, and Repression from 1900 to Khomeini.* New York: Praeger, 1981.

Shariati, Ali. *Fatima Is Fatima.* Translated by Laleh Bakhtiar. Tehran: Hamdami Foundation, 1980.

Sullivan, Soraya. *Stories by Iranian Women since the Revolution.* Austin: University of Texas Press, 1991.

Tabari, Azar, and Nahid Yeganeh, eds. *In the Shadow of Islam: The Women's Movement in Iran.* London: Zed Press, 1982

Taj Al- Saltana. *Crowning Anguish: Memoirs of a Persian Princess from the Harem to Modernity, 1884–1914.* Edited by Abbas Amanat, and translated by Anna Vanzan and Amin Neshati. Washington, D.C.: Mage Publishers, 1993.

Vielle, Paul, and Farhad Khosrokhavar, *Le Discours Populaire de la Revolution Iranienne.* 2 vols. Paris: Contemporaneite, 1990.

Articles

Afary, Janet. "On the Origins of Feminism in Early 20th-Century Iran." *Journal of Women's History* 1 (1990): 65–87.

Afkhami, Mahnaz. "A Future in the Past: The Pre-Revolutionary Women's Movement." In *Sisterhood Is Global: An International Women's Movement Anthology*, edited by Robin Morgan, 330–38. Garden City, N.J.: Anchor Books, 1984.

Afshar, Haleh. "Behind the Veil: The Public and Private Faces of Khomeini's Policies on Iranian Women." In *Structures of Patriarchy: State, Community and Household in Modernising Asia*, edited by Bina Agarwal, 228–247. London: Zed Books, 1988.

———. "Women and Reproduction in Iran." In *Woman-Nation-State*, edited by Nira Yuval-Davis and Floyal Anthias, 110–125. New York: St. Martin's Press, 1989.

———. "Women, State and Ideology in Iran." *Third World Quarterly* 7 (April 1985): 256–79.

Bauer, Janet. "Iranian Women: How Many Faces behind the Veil?" *East-West Perspectives* 1, no. 4 (Fall 1980): 21–25.

Benard, Cheryl. "Islam and Women: Some Reflections on the Experience of Iran." *Journal of South Asian and Middle Eastern Studies* 4 (1980): 10–26.

Bettridge, Anne H. "The Controversial Vows of Urban Muslim Women in Iran." In *Unspoken Words: Women's Religious Lives in Non-Western Cultures*, edited by N.A. Falk and Rita Gross, 102–111. Belmont, Calif.: Wadsworth Publishing Co., 1989.

Darrow, William R. "Woman's Place and the Place of Women in the Iranian Revolution." In *Women, Religion, and Social Change*, edited by Yvonne Y. Haddad and Ellison Banks Findly, 307–20. Albany: State University of New York Press, 1985.

Esfandiari, Haleh. "Iran: Women and Parliaments under Monarchy and Islamic Republic." *Princeton Papers in Near Eastern Studies* 2 (1993): 1–24.

Ferdows, Adele K. "Shariati and Khomeini on Women." In *The Iranian Revolution and the Islamic Republic,* edited by Nikki R. Keddie and Eric Hoogland, 127–43. Syracuse, N.Y.: Syracuse University Press, 1982.

———. "Women and the Islamic Revolution." *International Journal of Middle East Studies* 15 (May 1983): 283–98.

Hegland, Mary Elaine. "Traditional Iranian Women: How They Cope." *Middle East Journal* 36 (1982): 483–501.

Higgins, Patricia J. "Women in the Islamic Republic of Iran: Legal, Social and Ideological Changes." *Signs: Journal of Women in Culture and Society* 10 (1985): 477–94.

Mahdavi, Shireen. "Women and the Shi'i Ulema in Iran." *Middle Eastern Studies* 19 (January 1983): 17–27.

Mernissi, Fatima. "Muslim Women and Fundamentalism." *MERIP Report* 18 no.4 (1988): 8–11.

Moghadam, Valentine M. " Islamist Movements and Women's Responses in the Middle East." *Gender and History* 3 (Autumn 1991): 268–84.

———. "The Reproduction of Gender Inequality in Muslim Societies: A Case Study of Iran in the 1980s." *World Development* 19, no. 10 (1991): 1335–49.

———. "Women, Work, and Ideology in the Islamic Republic." *International Journal of Middle East Studies* 20 (1988): 221–43.

Musallam, Basim F. "Why Islam Permitted Birth Control." *Arab Studies Quarterly* 3 (1981): 181–97.

Ramazani, Nesta. "The Veil: Piety or Protest?" *Journal of South Asian and Middle Eastern Studies* 7 (1983): 20–36.

———. "Women in Iran: The Revolutionary Ebb and Flow." *Middle East Journal* 47 (1993): 409–28.

Shahidian, Hammed. "The Iranian Left and the 'Woman Question' in the Revolution of 1978–1979." *International Journal of Middle East Studies* 26 (May 1994): 223–47.

Shoaee, Rokhsareh S. "The Mujahid Women of Iran: Reconciling Culture and Gender." *Middle East Journal* 41 (August 1987): 519–37.

Tabari, Azar. "The Women's Movement in Iran: A Hopeful Prognosis." *Feminist Studies* 12 (1986): 343–60.

INDEX

Abadan, 85; in Iran-Iraq War, 112–13; Rex Cinema fire in, 55n, 62–3, 69
abortions, ban on, 46–7
adultery, 31, 40–1, 202
Afkhami, Mahnaz, 33
Afsar (interviewee), 11, 70–1, 96–7, 123, 148–9, 167, 183
Al-Ahmad, Jalal, *Westoxication,* 95, 95n
Algiers Agreement, 129, 129n
Amineh (interviewee), 11, 54–5, 79, 106–7, 134–5, 158, 174, 190
Ansar-e Hezbollah, 211
arrests, 148; experience of, 72, 108, 116, 120, 191, 197, 200, 203; fear of, 53–4
Atefeh (interviewee), 11, 64–5, 89, 116, 142–3, 163–4, 178, 197, 218
athletes, women, 211–12
Ayesheh (interviewee), 11, 63–4, 77, 87–8, 114–15, 134, 141–2, 163, 178, 196

Bahai, 27n
Bakhtiar, Shapour, 54n
Bani-Sadr, Abol-Hasan, 146, 146n
"battle of the hairlines," 48–50
Bazargan, Mehdi, 54n; and women's dress code, 19–20
birth control. *See* contraception; family planning
breadwinner, women as: in family business, 115; and increasing self-awareness, 181; as result of

abandonment, 100, 105–6; as result of purges, 7, 44–5, 66, 74, 117–18, 127, 206–7; as result of separation, 121; as violation of tradition, 141
Bureau for Women's Affairs, 153
businesswomen: adjustment to Islamic regime, 105–6, 151, 200, 205; apolitical attitudes of, 64–5; as entrepreneurs, 89, 109, 118, 124, 183, 203; in family business, 115; training of, 88

career change, 105–6, 108, 111–14, 116–20, 122–3, 128–9, 190, 196, 199–200
chauvinism, male. *See* behavior; dominance, male
child custody, 30, 40, 43, 86, 89, 94, 98, 121
child rearing, 200–1
cities, migration to, 29, 36
class. *See* lower class, women of; middle class, women of; upper class, women of; working class, women of
clerics, Islamic: discussion of sex, 181–2; and elections of 1996, 210–1; *marja's,* 30n; and mobilization of women, 5; opposition to European dress, 24; opposition to women's voting rights, 27; role under Mohammad Reza Shah, 26; and women's issues, 49–50. *See also*